Elite-Led Mobilization and Gay Rights

ELITE-LED MOBILIZATION AND GAY RIGHTS

Dispelling the Myth of Mass Opinion Backlash

Benjamin G. Bishin, Thomas J. Hayes,
Matthew B. Incantalupo, and Charles Anthony Smith

University of Michigan Press
Ann Arbor

For questions or permissions, please contact um.press.perms@umich.edu

Published in the United States of America by the University of Michigan Press
Manufactured in the United States of America
Printed on acid-free paper
First published September 2021

A CIP catalog record for this book is available from the British Library.

Library of Congress Cataloging-in-Publication data has been applied for.

ISBN 978-0-472-13270-6 (hardcover: alk. paper)
ISBN 978-0-472-03864-0 (paper: alk. paper)
ISBN 978-0-472-12932-4 (e-book)

Ben:
To Laura, the kindest and most intrepid person I know.
You inspire me every day.
Thank you for helping to make everything possible.

Tom:
To Ruby for her unwavering love and support.

Matt:
To Dayna, who turns bad days into good days, and good days into great days.
Thank you for being by my side through every step of this project.

Tony:
To Julio, who makes everything about my life, including my work, better and who combines brains, beauty, and humor better than anyone I've ever known. And also to all of those members and allies of the LGBT community, past and present, who fought and fight daily for our human rights.
Finally, to David Goetze, my academic godfather.

Contents

Digital materials related to this title can be found on the Fulcrum platform via the following citable URL: https://doi.org/10.3998/mpub.11927173

Figures

Tables

Preface

Jean Bishin was a proud Jew. She and her husband, Arthur, regularly donated money to charitable causes in Israel. At her breakfast table, however, presumptive Democratic presidential nominee Al Gore's announcement that Connecticut senator Joe Lieberman would be his running mate elicited enmity. Asked why she wasn't more excited about the nomination of the first Jew to be named to a major party's ticket, her response was unexpected: "It's better when Jews aren't so visible." She explained that visibility increases anti-Semitism. She opposed Lieberman's selection because she feared increased discrimination and violence against Jews. In short, she was afraid the nomination of Lieberman would elicit backlash against Jews.

Seven years later, during a conversation in the Palmer House book room during the Midwest Political Science Association, a similar question was raised. This time, however, the topic was the recent legalization of gay marriage in California. A political science scholar noted that the inevitable backlash against gay rights that followed such advances could be counterproductive. The nationwide slate of ballot initiatives banning gay marriage in 2004 and 2006 and the prospect of another attempt to ban gay marriage in California in 2008 seemed to be clear evidence of backlash. But when pressed, none of us could think of any studies that convincingly confirmed backlash. The only studies we were aware of seemed reasonable enough but were dated and left some important questions unanswered. And while we, like most everyone else it seemed, assumed that backlash occurred, we thought it would be important to document it, assess its magnitude, and identify who was most likely to lash back and under what conditions.

We quickly decided this was a topic worth pursuing, with the idea that we would employ a multi-method approach to use both existing observational evidence and advances in online experiments to try to answer some of these basic questions about backlash.

Our initial foray into the topic of anti-gay backlash made its broad implications clear. Reports describe backlash against Latinos, Italians, Irish, Jews, Catholics, Protestants, immigrants, and women. Virtually every stigmatized group in American history that has fought for equality has been warned, often by those who would profess to be allies as well as by those who hoped to prevent progress, to be careful to avoid acting too fast or risk public backlash. Perhaps the most famous response to such claims had been written over fifty years earlier by Martin Luther King Jr. in his 1963 "Letter from Birmingham Jail" (also titled "Why We Must Not Wait"). This was King's public response to eight white ministers who counseled Blacks not to march for their civil rights. Despite this persistence of claims of backlash across the spectrum of the pursuit of civil rights, very few studies actually examine backlash against stigmatized groups.

Our goal was to document and explore how, when, why, and who lashed back against attempts to advance gay rights. We hoped to use recent advances in online surveys and experiments to identify and estimate the causal effects of backlash in a way that had not been available to earlier scholars. We began by considering how to design our experiments by examining existing survey data to assess the magnitude of the backlash effects we were likely to see. By doing so, we could better determine how many observations we would need to detect the size of the effects we expected.

A funny thing happened when we set out to estimate how much of an effect backlash had on public attitudes. First, it became clear almost immediately that despite the wide use of the term "backlash," not only was the concept understudied, but its meaning varied somewhat from study to study and certainly across its usage in the press. Instead of a clearly defined concept that was rigorously assessed, "backlash" was used in a variety of ways to loosely refer to some type—or really any type—of reaction.

Second, no matter which data we examined, we could not find evidence of the negative changes in public opinion on gay rights that we expected to see, given the persistent backlash narrative. Despite using a wide range of tools, methods, and tests—we did all we could to identify backlash—we were never able to find the expected result. This posed a challenge since null findings are tricky to document and convincingly demonstrate. What started as a straightforward project became extraordinarily complex. Ultimately, about seven years after we began our project about backlash, our paper documenting its absence was published in the *American Journal of Political Science*.

Our null findings raised another puzzle in the form of a question that we were asked almost everywhere we presented the paper: If there is no public opinion backlash, how do we explain the widespread opposition to gay rights that emerged and has accelerated across the country over the last roughly three decades? Answering this question, and explaining the rise of opposition to gay rights, became the basis for this book.

We first laid out the answer to this question in a paper that would be published in *Law and Society Review*. Our central argument is that rather than a bottom-up movement driven by the public, anti-gay elites, primarily those from conservative Christian religious organizations, use gay rights to mobilize like-minded supporters in order to enhance their organization and political power. These elites choose to emphasize gay rights for the political benefits they might confer to their struggling movement. Developing and testing this theory, the details of which are presented in chapters 1 and 2, became the focus of this book.

This theory met a somewhat different response than did our initial work on backlash. While scholars of LGBTQ politics were interested in better understanding the nature of backlash even if they were skeptical of the finding, the reception to the argument that opposition to gay rights was elite-led was much more mixed. This argument directly claims that (mostly) white conservative Christian religious leaders choose to emphasize gay rights not because of their threat, or importance to their ideology, but rather to increase their social relevance and political power. In part the argument has been controversial because it challenges key findings of the scholarship on religion and politics that emphasize the apolitical nature of the clergy. In particular, we document the politicization of conservative Christian clergy on the issue of gay rights through reference to historical analysis, seen in chapter 6 and, for example, extensive newspaper documentation of the hundreds of local Iowa clergy who publicly committed to opposing the retention of three Iowa judges following their legalization of gay marriage (which we present in chapter 7).

Some readers may view the language we use to describe the opposition to gay rights—in particular our use of the term "anti-gay elites"—as pejorative or excessively antagonistic. Therefore, we think it is useful to explain why we employ this term. Our main reason is because advocates of these anti-gay and anti-trans policies prioritize these policies not because of their philosophical opposition but because of the political utility of the issue. Their decision to emphasize opposition to various pro-gay policies was driven not by the threat such policies pose to Christian theology—indeed though led by white evangelical Christians, conservative religious leaders from a variety of faith traditions worked together to oppose gay rights and place the anti-marriage amendments on state ballots—or the mission of the church as much as their desire to find an issue to rally their supporters around after experiencing a string of defeats and a fear of declining political relevance (e.g., Fitzgerald 2017). After all, gays and lesbians are a tiny portion of the population, and their actions and empowerment pose little threat to the church and its theological teachings. Moreover, they could have chosen to emphasize other issues on which they held shared views consistent with their theology (such as immigration reform or poverty abatement). Issues of gay rights, however, were unpopular with both the American public and their adherents and served as an issue that conservative religious elites sought to use to revive their organizations and build their political power. We therefore use the term because the political movement was organized around the political act of being anti-gay.

We also faced obstacles in publishing this work that are typical of those shared by many LGBTQ scholars. Reviewers regularly questioned the importance of the work because it was about the LGBT community. A program officer refused to provide reviews for our rejected grant proposal. A major press book editor asked for suggestions of reviewers drawn from a broad collection of American politics scholars who studied other areas of public opinion and different groups rather than those who study LGBT politics. Some reviewers suggested that studying gay rights was insufficiently compelling, generalizable, or interesting, and that instead we should study some other issue to test our theory of opposition to gay rights. We wondered if books and papers on, say, the presidency or Congress were also intentionally sent to reviewers who are not experts in the topic or took seriously reviews suggesting that the history we examine was uninteresting or unimportant. One reviewer even went as far as to claim that gay rights are no longer contested and we should therefore add several other cases to make the topic interesting.

Our obstacles were neither unique nor unusual for scholars of LGBTQ politics or even scholars of underrepresented groups more generally. These obstacles were overcome, however, owing in large part to the support of a research community that can be simultaneously critical and constructive. The research questions that motivated this book emanated from the constructive criticism and skepticism of members of this community. We are extremely grateful both for those who initially supported the project and those who questioned it, because both made the research better and the findings stronger. We were given an extraordinary amount of support to help publicize and improve our research from a remarkably broad number of scholars. Andrew Flores at UCLA, Matthew Lebo at Stony Brook, and Gary Segura at Stanford each generously invited us to give talks to broad audiences of scholars with expertise in LGBTQ politics and history. We also benefited immensely from the feedback at a number of university workshops, including the Identity Politics Research Group (IPRG), the Political Economy Workshop at UConn, UC Irvine's Law & Latte Workshop, UC Riverside's Mass Behavior Workshop, and the UIUC Faculty Speaker Series. We also received similarly helpful and constructive feedback from a large number of discussants and conference attendees from this community, including Tom Keck, Steve Sanders, Melissa Michelson, Pat Egan, Erin Mayo Adam, Chris Hare, Sam Best, and Lyle Scruggs. We are particularly indebted to David Karol for his extensive and careful feedback on chapter drafts as well as advice throughout the project. We are also grateful for extraordinary access provided by the National Institute for Money in State Politics (FollowtheMoney.org), whose data provided the basis for much of the analysis in chapter 7.

Moreover, we have received incredible support and advice from friends and colleagues throughout the academic community, including Mike Abrams, Lee Badgett, Jason Barabas, Scott Barclay, Dan Biggers, Sarah Brayne, Tyler Buller, Cindy Burack, Alyson Brysk, Royce Carroll, Stephen Chaudoin, Loren Collingwood, Lauren Davenport, Kim Yi Dionne, Justin Freebourn, Jeremiah Garretson, Martin Gilens, David Glick, Allison Harris, Sarah Hummel, Jennifer Jerit, Rebecca Kreitzer, Amy Lerman, Dean Lombardi, Joseph Luders, Tali Mendelberg, Jennifer Merolla, Mike Miller, Scott Peters, Shawn Schulenberg, Kenneth Sherrill, Heather Smith-Cannoy, Jeff Staton, Jami Taylor, Sandy Todd Webster, Tiffany Willoughby, and Angie Wilson.

Of course the most important support we have received is personal. Ben would like to thank his wife, Laura Bishin. Tom would like to thank his wife, Ruby Diaz, for her patience and support. Matt would like to thank his wife, Dayna Judge, a political scientist married to a political scientist, and thus counted on not only for emotional support and patience but also substantive feedback. Tony would like to thank his husband, Julio Rodriguez, for his insights and unwaivering support.

The recent political conflicts over the rights of the trans community as well as the recent activism of the Black Lives Matter movement demonstrate that the contest over civil and political rights is far from over. Today we see the same cautions of "too much change too fast" being offered to members of both communities as they publicly stand up and speak out for equal treatment. In addition to prejudice and discrimination, members of these groups must deal with being told to keep quiet and to wait for a reluctant majority to recognize their rights. Irrespective of the lessons of this volume about whether and when backlash occurs, King's admonition from his "Letter from a Birmingham Jail" reminds us that the demand for rights should never be compromised or postponed for fear of offending the oppressor. While we find no evidence of backlash on gay rights, it may occur against other stigmatized groups under different circumstances. In a majoritarian system that can often be slow to embrace change, however, minority groups seeking equal treatment should feel emboldened to push for progress.

One of the often overlooked implications of research about historically marginalized and stigmatized groups is that the challenges they face speak to broader questions of democracy. So the politics that surround such groups directly affect all who are interested in better understanding the extent to which fundamental democratic values are extended broadly across the polity. It is therefore extraordinarily important to discover and present evidence using rigorous scientific methods in order to identify the conditions they face, both to advance and document knowledge and to allow policy makers to develop effective strategies to address these conditions. With the support of this academic community, our friends, and our families, we were able to complete a project that we think is important, timely, and relevant to continuing challenges to gay rights. We hope that our scholarship helps illuminate the opposition to gay rights and provides ideas and suggestions for strategies about how equal rights might be advanced. We leave it to the reader to determine the extent to which our efforts are successful.

ONE

Iowa's Irony

In November 2010 three Iowa State Supreme Court justices were voted out of office—the first removal of supreme court judges in Iowa's almost fifty-year history of retention elections. By Election Day the defeat of Marsha Ternus, Michael Streit, and David Baker was unsurprising. The only three members of the unanimous court's 2009 ruling legalizing gay marriage who were up for reelection had faced a blizzard of opposition advertising and refused to campaign for their own retention. Their collective loss was widely reported as a case of opinion backlash, as their unpopular marriage equality ruling galvanized an angry public to punish the justices (Associated Press 2010; Jackson 2014; A. Harris 2019).

The election results reinforced the views of pundits, activists, and academics who argued that pursuing marriage equality through the courts both endangered the long-run fight for marriage equality and had the potential to derail the broader gay rights movement. Pundits excoriated the chilling effect that voter backlash would have on other judges' willingness to make rulings that advance minority rights (e.g., Queerty Staff 2009; Sulzberger 2010). Gay rights activists worried that judges who were fearful of a vindictive public might create a negative precedent that would impede their ability to achieve change through the courts in future cases (Fuchs 2013). Perhaps most importantly, the ruling held the possibility of galvanizing widespread opposition to policies benefiting gays and lesbians and thereby fostering antipathy toward gays and lesbians as a group.

The events that culminated in the removal of Ternus, Streit, and Baker began twelve years earlier with the 1998 passage of House File 382, a bill defining "marriage" exclusively as a relationship between a man and a woman. The bill was nominally designed to protect Iowa from having to recognize same-sex marriages performed in other states. A series of judicial rulings in Hawaii had found that laws banning gay marriage were likely unconstitutional under the state's equal protection provision of their constitution (e.g., Jaffe 1996; Oshiro 1996). While Hawaii quickly acted to change their constitution to prevent gay marriages, the rulings raised the salience of the issue among conservatives who feared that an Iowa court might rule to legalize gay marriage. More broadly, opponents of same-sex marriage feared that if another state legalized gay marriage, the equal protection clause of the U.S. Constitution might force Iowa to recognize those unions and, in so doing, legalize same-sex marriage in Iowa.

Despite these arguments, Iowa's law was unnecessary. In 1996 President Bill Clinton signed the Defense of Marriage Act (DOMA), a law that in addition to preventing same-sex partners from receiving numerous government benefits, limited federal recognition of marriage to one man and one woman and made clear that states could not be forced to recognize same-sex marriages legalized by other states. Moreover, if a ban on gay marriage were held by the U.S. Supreme Court to be unconstitutional by violating the Constitution's equal protection clause, the passage of a state law would do little to delay its implementation. The passage of DOMA by the U.S. Congress in combination with the fact that no jurisdiction in the United States had ever allowed same-sex marriage led some to criticize the passage of House File 382 as unnecessary (Witosky and Hansen 2015). By passing the bill, however, the legislature and governor unwittingly expedited the legalization of gay marriage in Iowa.

In 2005 gay marriage supporters in Iowa filed suit against the law after six gay couples were denied marriage licenses. Same-sex marriage advocates argued that by preventing some people from marrying the person of their choice, the bill violated their constitutional rights to equal protection under the law (Davey 2009). In 2007 a district court judge agreed. Judge Robert Hanson ruled that same-sex couples could marry but quickly stayed the ruling pending appeal to the state supreme court. On April 3, 2009, the state supreme court unanimously held the ban unconstitutional, which made Iowa the third state to legalize same-sex marriage. Ironically, the state's attempt to outlaw marriage equality legalized it in Iowa a little more than six years before the Supreme Court ruling in *Obergefell v. Hodges* legalized it nationwide. The unnecessary effort to thwart marriage had instead delivered it to Iowans.

Having lost the fight to ban gay marriage, opponents of marriage equality looked to the judicial retention election as their avenue for roll-back and retribution. Aging, disproportionately rural, overwhelmingly white, Iowa is home to a relatively large and politically active evangelical Christian community. It is not a surprise that surveys taken just a few months before the ruling showed that only about 28 percent of Iowans supported gay marriage (Redlawsk and Tolbert 2008). Together, these conditions created an inviting climate for national conservative religious groups that sought to use the judicial retention elections to make a statement about their clout, their antipathy toward marriage equality, and their ability to mobilize their voters.

In mid-September 2010, anti–marriage equality ads targeting the judges began flooding the airwaves (Belin 2010a). By Election Day the groups opposing the judges had spent just under $1 million to defeat them. The justices and their supporters were largely taken by surprise by the furor over the unanimous court ruling, as competitive retention elections were unprecedented (Stern 2014). The justices refused to raise money or campaign, arguing that accepting money from donors who might come before the court would pose a conflict of interest. After initially being caught off guard by the onslaught and getting a late start, a national independent group seeking the judges' retention spent $417,267 in their defense (Casey 2016). It was not enough. In a vote that was closely tied to the judges' support for gay marriage, each of the three judges was narrowly defeated (Clopton and Peters 2013; A. Harris 2019). The judges' defeat was national news, reported by outlets including CNN, the *New York Times*, and National Public Radio as an example of public opinion backlash against gay rights (Simon 2010; Sulzberger 2010a and 2010b; Coleman 2010). The defeat also set the stage for future challenges to the other justices who voted to overturn the marriage ban. In 2012, the same groups mounted a similar but ultimately unsuccessful campaign to defeat Judge David Wiggins, who had also voted to overturn the ban.[1]

Backlash across Issues and Groups

The anti-gay mobilization that targeted Iowa's justices is not unique.[2] Reactions against those advocating gay rights are widespread and go back decades. A search of just one newspaper data base shows that between February 1992 and August 2016, journalists published 2,242 articles that include both the terms "gay" and "backlash" in the same article.[3] Important examples of claims of anti-gay backlash date at least to 1977, when religious conservatives in Miami–Dade County used a special election referendum to repeal a nondiscrimination ordinance that had been passed by the county commission. This anti-gay effort is credited with galvanizing the political arm of the modern conservative movement referred to as the "religious right" (Fejes 2008; Fitzgerald 2017). By 1978 strategies developed by Save Our Children in Miami-Dade County were employed to fight nondiscrimination ordinances in St. Paul, Minnesota; Wichita, Kansas; Eugene, Oregon; and Seattle, Washington—losing only in Seattle—and allies advocated further restrictions on gays and lesbians, like the Briggs Initiative, a California ballot measure designed to ban gays and lesbians from working in public schools (Biggers 2014).

Claims of backlash against gay rights are similar to the challenges faced by other stigmatized groups (Shapiro and Higham 1986). The idea that mass opinion backlash might inhibit the advancement of rights is not a challenge unique to the LGBT community. Scholars and journalists describe backlash on a variety of issues ranging from religious freedom laws (e.g., Margolin 2016) to immigration (e.g., Abrajano 2010; Abrajano and Hajnal 2017). Following the January 2017 Trump administration ban on travel from seven "Muslim" countries, journalists and academics described a widespread public backlash by activists and against the discriminatory policy (e.g., Collingwood, Lajevardi, and Oskooii 2018). The administration's efforts to limit travel were both salient and controversial as more than twenty Republican legislators joined Democrats to publicly oppose the president's policy (Makarechi 2017). Similarly, scholars describe an anti-green backlash developed in response to environmental protections, especially anti-pollution provisions, among others (Beder 2001; Burke 1993).

Perhaps the most widely referenced and best documented examples of backlash, however, are on issues of racial and ethnic civil rights. Throughout American history claims of backlash are documented against virtually all traditionally marginalized racial, ethnic, gender, and sexuality minority groups. Perhaps most pronounced throughout American history is extensive reference to white backlash against African Americans (e.g., Weaver 2007). A substantial academic literature blames backlash on opposition to racial justice—including the Black civil rights movement and busing—and, more recently, to acceptance of multiculturalism (e.g., Rogin 1966; Rubin 1973; Hughey 2014). The 2020 protests of the murder of George Floyd and increased support for Black Lives Matter were met by renewed claims that "all lives matter" and "blue lives matter" (Asmelash 2020). Similarly, recent immigration debates highlight examples of anti-Latino backlash that extends back decades (e.g., Preuhs 2007; Abrajano and Hajnal 2017).

As just one example, the 2006 nationwide immigrant rights marches are reported to have increased membership in the anti-immigrant vigilante Minuteman Project (Associated Press 2006). Moreover, mounting evidence suggests that backlash itself can provoke a counter-reaction by the marginalized group, often in the form of public protest, as seen by the 2010 immigration marches that arose nationwide in response to Arizona's passage of SB 1070 (e.g., Preuhs 2007).

While African Americans and Latinos are perhaps the most visible targets, backlash against other groups is widely reported. Claims of backlash against Asians, especially Chinese immigrants, led to the Chinese Exclusion Acts of the late nineteenth century and the Alien Land Laws in the early twentieth century (e.g., Gaines and Tam Cho 2004; Andreas 2014). Scholars describe and explain anti-Irish (Catholic) backlash by Protestant nativists (e.g., Dunne 2002; Golway 2014), anti-Italian backlash (e.g., Lizzi 2008), and anti-Semitic backlash (e.g., Shapiro 1986). Claims of backlash against women and feminism are also common (e.g., Faludi 1991; Mansbridge and Shames 2008; Sanbonmatsu 2008). Studies of women professionals, for instance, suggest that across a variety of settings (e.g., policewomen, West Point cadets, etc.), as the number of women in roles traditionally perceived as "gender inappropriate" increases, backlash in the form of "harassment, blocked mobility, and lower wages" occurs (Yoder 1991, 188).

The reaction described as backlash can be seen as part of a recurring social process. Albert O. Hirschman (1991) illustrates how conservatives throughout history have argued that negative reactions are sure to follow progressive movements. Examining the French Revolution, the fight for universal suffrage, and social welfare policy, a common theme emerges: attempts to advance the social condition lead to a reaction in which opponents argue that the benefits of the policy are at best illusory. These arguments take three forms. The first holds that progressive policy advances lead to a perverse outcome that will make conditions worse for the group intended to benefit. The second holds that attempts at change are futile and will have no effect. The third holds that attempts at change, while desirable, are so costly that they jeopardize some previous gain made by the group.

With respect to gay rights, opponents and even some allies most commonly argue that attempts to make policy will lead to perverse outcomes or will jeopardize some existing benefit, policy, or advantageous social condition. Despite little more than anecdotal evidence to support the notion of mass opinion backlash, judges and social movement leaders carefully weigh the fear of possible backlash as they craft opinions and strategies.

The preoccupation with backlash spans political ideologies and modes of jurisprudential interpretation. In *The Hollow Hope*, Gerald N. Rosenberg (2008; 2018) claims that the Supreme Court has generally been unhelpful in promoting social change because of the backlash its progressive opinions have sparked. Cass Sunstein, the most cited contemporary legal scholar, argues that jurists should, at least in some respects, actively consider potential public opinion backlash as they craft their opinions. The historian and gay rights leader John D'Emilio (2006), who was cited in Justice Anthony Kennedy's majority opinion in *Lawrence v. Texas*, once argued that the gay rights gained through the courts have largely been thwarted by state legislative responses to public opinion backlash at both the state and federal levels. Gay rights advocacy groups have taken a similar position. As just one prominent example, the Human Rights Campaign, the largest and most powerful gay rights advocacy organization in the country, initially opposed the ultimately successful marriage equality litigation for fear of backlash (Fuchs 2013).

Why Opinion Backlash Matters

The idea behind backlash is that marginalized groups' challenges to the status quo, whether by advocating particular policies or by increasing their visibility, activate an otherwise disinterested or unaware public and galvanize opposition to the group and its cause. By rallying the public against the group, the act of pursuing policy, acceptance, or legitimacy makes it even more difficult for the group to make policy gains. In short, backlash implies that advocating one's interests is counterproductive. By causing policy loss and inciting public opposition, backlash leaves the group worse off than if they had done nothing at all. Moreover, if scholars, judges, and activists take the threat of public opinion backlash seriously and adjust their strategies and behaviors to try to avoid such backlash, they may delay the advancement of rights, despite an absence of compelling evidence to support the backlash thesis.

While the costs of backlash are often accepted as a given, the specific conditions that underlie backlash as a social process across groups, issues, venues, and outcomes are less well considered. The dominant explanation for the reaction known as backlash lies in mass opinion change. Events challenging or threatening the status quo lead people to take notice and change their attitudes. With respect to the politics of race, for instance, Vesla Weaver defines "backlash" as "the politically and electorally expressed public resentment that arises from perceived racial advance, intervention, or excess" (2007, 237). More generally, backlash is characterized politically by two important traits: (1) the notion that some event is causing a reaction in the form of a change in opinion and (2) the concern that such a reaction is likely to have lasting and adverse consequences for the group that promotes the policy. Consequently, we employ backlash to describe "*a large, negative, organic, and enduring shift in opinion against a policy or group that occurs in response to some event that threatens the status quo*" (Bishin et al. 2016, 2).

The scholarly and popular understanding of opinion backlash is straightforward: Groups challenge the status quo in ways that range from increasing their public visibility to pressing for a specific policy change. The reaction to these challenges typically takes the form of a sharp change in public opinion against either a policy or against the group. Opinion change occurs when challenges to the status quo trigger a sense of threat among the public. Perceived threat increases the emphasis people place on extrinsic goals, such as defeating a policy or group (e.g., Sheldon and Kasser 2008). The perception of threat can be induced in a variety of ways, ranging from threatening one's physical well-being, as when one fears crime or job loss, to a symbolic threat that results from violations of one's values or norms about what behavior is acceptable. This perception of threat leads to opinion change, which incites opposition to the policy or group. We refer to this process as Mass Opinion Backlash.

Driven by individuals' reactions and behavior, Mass Opinion Backlash describes a "bottom-up" process in which citizens share a common reaction to some challenge to the status quo. Backlash may be evidenced by changes in any of several aspects of opinion, including a change in policy preferences, an increase in one's intensity of feeling about an issue, or in the attitudes expressed toward members of the group more broadly. Importantly, increased intensity, either in the degree to which one cares about an issue or in the changes in attitudes toward members of the group, may increase one's likelihood of participating in politics.

In one sense, Mass Opinion Backlash reflects "politics as usual," a battle between factions with opposing preferences common to pluralist democracy. While the system may disadvantage traditionally marginalized groups like gays and lesbians, owing to their relative lack of resources, small size, unpopularity, and need to navigate institutions that often structurally disadvantage them, this process of interest group competition does not directly prevent them from obtaining policy. Instead it requires building support coalitions that are sufficiently large and powerful to defeat their opponents.[4]

Mass opinion backlash raises significant challenges to those concerned with expanding democratic rights. While critiques of pluralism frequently recognize its class bias, mass opinion backlash is even more problematic than pluralist accounts suggest, because the act of working to obtain policy or recognition changes the incentives political actors have for advocating their cause over the longer term. By igniting changes in public support, mass opinion backlash alters the incentives political actors have to either vocally advocate for or oppose the group and its preferences. Specifically, they impede the group's ability to achieve policy gains over the longer term using democratic institutions that are influenced by public opinion and through which policy change typically occurs.

Indeed, research suggests that the shift in public support that mass opinion backlash describes is particularly problematic because it is especially likely to endure (Converse 1964; Snow 2000; Burstein 2014). One of the hallmark studies of public opinion research holds that because attitude change is often incited by a sense of threat, an individual is more likely to more deeply consider the issue, and as a consequence, the opinions that result are more likely to last (e.g., Zaller 1992). Once people's attitudes are well developed, they are very difficult to change (e.g., Zaller 1990; Zaller 1992). The significant and lasting opinion change that mass opinion backlash describes presents marginalized groups like gays and lesbians with a troublesome paradox: by mobilizing opinion against themselves, pushing to obtain rights may make those rights increasingly difficult, or even impossible, to obtain in both the short and long term.

These opinion changes also have potentially significant downstream effects both on policy and on who is selected to serve in political institutions. First, and most immediately, the status quo is that existing institutions are more likely to oppose policy supported by the marginalized group and pass legislation contrary to these groups' preferences. This might occur, for example, either through direct votes on legislation or when legislative leaders keep bills, especially those that are unpopular among their party, off the chamber floor in order to prevent consideration using a process called *negative agenda control* (e.g., Gailmard and Jenkins 2007). Backlash may embolden executives to issue orders that punish the group, like President Donald Trump's 2018 executive order banning transgender Americans from serving in the armed forces. Second, enduring opinion shifts can alter the makeup of institutions in the future. Lasting opinion change incentivizes candidates to take positions opposing the group and, once elected, to push for additional policy supported by the group's opponents.

The implication of opinion change and institutional responsiveness is that mass opinion backlash decreases a group's chance of obtaining their desired policy from the institutions most directly influenced by public opinion. The result is that the group must then pursue policy through institutions that are better insulated from the public. Consequently, groups like gays and lesbians may become increasingly reliant on courts or administrative bodies. Moreover, those opposing gay rights also recognize the importance of the courts and work to elect and have appointed justices who reify their views. Indeed, many of the initial advances in gay rights, such as the legalization of gay marriage in Iowa and Massachusetts, and impediments, like the Trump administration's attempt to ban those who are transgender from serving in the military, were achieved through the courts after institutions more directly influenced by the public worked to circumscribe gay rights.

While insulated, the courts are not immune to the negative repercussions of opinion backlash, as public opinion influences at least some Supreme Court decisions (e.g., Hall 2015). Scholars and jurists recognize and debate the possibility and extent of judicial backlash in which groups pursuing rights through the courts face opposition there as well (e.g., Eskridge 2013; Fontana and Braman 2012; Krieger 2010). The main concern is that judicial backlash can be especially pernicious, because the rulings against the group may serve as negative precedents that bind future courts to anti-gay positions. While Thomas Keck (2009) shows that significant anti-gay judicial backlash is less common than widely believed, the concept is nonetheless taken as somewhat conventional wisdom among many scholars and activists (e.g., Klarman 2005). For example, the initial reluctance of the Human Rights Campaign, the nation's largest gay rights advocacy organization, to support judicial strategies for advancing marriage equality was based on the fear that losses in the courts would set the movement back (Fuchs 2013).[5]

Backlash can also highlight conflicts among democratic values. Democratic governance is characterized by attempts to extend popular sovereignty, liberty, and equality to all citizens in order to create a society that is more inclusive (Dahl 1956). Among these, popular sovereignty is perhaps most closely associated with democracy by the public and politicians alike, and it incentivizes politicians to follow the public's preference. To the extent that the group's challenge to a majority-supported status quo impedes the group's ability to obtain rights fundamental to democratic citizenship, like liberty or equality, backlash is also significantly more problematic than "politics as usual."[6]

Such a case reflects a classic example of majority tyranny by allowing a majority to prevent members of a minority from achieving full equality as citizens (e.g., Madison 1787).

To summarize, the premise of Mass Opinion Backlash is that it creates conditions that are hostile to stigmatized or marginalized groups like gays and lesbians. To the extent that attempts to advance pro-gay policies the public to oppose a policy, it becomes more difficult for LGBT groups to achieve their goals. As opinion becomes more supportive of anti-gay measures, election-seeking politicians are incentivized to oppose the policy demands of gays and lesbians, and those who oppose such policies are incentivized to run for office. Opinion change may also make politicians who are personally supportive of such policies or groups but are electorally vulnerable or ambitious less likely to voice their support. When these politicians win, the political institutions in which they serve become more difficult for gay rights advocates to navigate. Finally, adverse opinion change also makes obtaining policy through the referendum process substantially more difficult. Moreover, since attitudes tend to endure, and politicians' behavior often responds to it, the ancillary effects that backlash produces are also likely to endure.

The Puzzle of Gay Rights

The possibility of mass opinion backlash threatens the ability of gays and lesbians to make policy advances and gain public acceptance over both the short term and the long term. Indeed, a central implication of the theory of backlash is that strong negative reactions result from challenges to the status quo. This fundamental tenet of backlash raises an important puzzle. The last two decades have been characterized by a dramatic increase in the visibility of gays and lesbians in society, in the media, and in acceptance of gays and lesbians and policies they support. If challenges to the status quo lead to short- and long-term opposition to gay rights and to increased antipathy toward gays and lesbians, then the increased number of challenges to the status quo made by gay rights activists over the past two decades should have been met by a strong public opinion backlash in the form of shifting attitudes against gays and lesbians and an inability to make policy advances. The exact opposite, however, has occurred. The seismic advances both in policy supporting gay rights and in public opinion toward gays and lesbians are astonishing (Lax and Phillips 2009a; Lax and Phillips 2009b; Baunach 2012).

The last two decades have been characterized by a dramatic increase in the visibility and acceptance of gays and lesbians in American society (e.g., Garretson 2018). These changes are partly the product of a concerted effort by gay rights groups to normalize the public's perception of gays and lesbians, that date back at least to the 1978 Briggs Initiative campaign in California and the recognition that people were much more likely to support gay rights if they knew gays and lesbians personally (Milk 1978). One strategy of this campaign was to encourage gays and lesbians to "come out" (e.g., Khalil 2012). Perhaps one legacy of this campaign can be seen in the dramatic increase in the proportion of Americans who report knowing someone who is gay or lesbian. In 2004 about 58 percent of Americans reported knowing someone who was gay or lesbian (Morales 2009). By the fall of 2016, the number reached 87 percent (Pew Research Center 2016). Similarly dramatic increases in the public visibility of gays and lesbians occurred in the media. While precise data are not available, popular television shows like *Will and Grace* and personalities like Ellen DeGeneres publicized positive portrayals of gay characters to massive audiences (e.g., Garretson 2018). The increased visibility of gays and lesbians in society and in the media is precisely the type of challenge to the status quo that one might expect to trigger backlash.

Contrary to the expectations of mass opinion backlash, even a cursory glance at policy made over the last two decades depicts dramatic advances in gay rights in the United States. The Supreme Court issued rulings striking down sodomy laws (i.e., *Lawrence v. Texas* 2003), policies banning same-sex couples from receiving federal benefits (*United States v. Windsor* 2013), and gay marriage bans (*Obergefell v. Hodges* 2015). In 2010 President Barack Obama negotiated with the U.S. Congress to end the ban on gays and lesbians serving in the military known as "Don't Ask, Don't Tell." In 2012 the first openly gay U.S. senator, Tammy Baldwin (D-WI), was elected. In 2015 the Pentagon lifted the ban on transgender people serving in the U.S. military. And, in an act symbolizing how much some of society's most conservative institutions had changed on the issue, in 2015 the Boy Scouts of America lifted their ban preventing gays and lesbians from serving in or working for their organization. Perhaps most surprisingly, in 2020 a conservative majority Supreme Court ruled in *Bostock v. Clayton County* that employers could not fire people simply for being gay or transgender.

Just as policy backlash did not occur, neither did the widespread negative shift in opinion the advocates of backlash predicted. On virtually every issue for which data exists, large increases in public support for gay rights are apparent (e.g., Flores 2015; Garretson 2018). And while significant opposition to gay rights still exists—Gallup reported that in May 2017, 34 percent of Americans believed that gay marriages should not be valid—the increased acceptance of gays and lesbians as a group is especially remarkable (Gallup 2017). "Thermometer scores" for gays and lesbians, which assess on a scale of zero to one hundred how warmly the public feels toward an issue or group, have increased from thirty in 1984 to almost sixty in 2016.

Despite numerous highly visible challenges to the status quo on a wide range of issues, remarkably little evidence of anti-gay opinion backlash exists. Predictions that a massive increase in pro-gay policy proposals and increased public opposition to discrimination would drive politicians to increasingly oppose gay rights and lead elected and appointed bodies to further restrict gay rights have fallen short. To the contrary, the nation has seen extensive acceptance of gays and lesbians and advances in rights. Taken together these events raise significant questions about the extent to which Mass Opinion Backlash occurs. Indeed, even a close examination of arguably the most celebrated recent example of mass backlash—the defeat of Iowa's three supreme court justices who ruled to legalize gay marriage described at the beginning of this chapter—suggests that the story of backlash is not what it seems. A closer look at public opinion polls shows that while just 28 percent of Iowans supported gay marriage a week before the ruling, by the time of the Iowa election almost eighteen months later, that support for gay marriage had dramatically increased to 38 percent.[7] That is, to the extent that the court ruling changed opinion, it seems likely to have *increased* rather than decreased support for gay marriage in Iowa. And as for the policy of gay marriage being said to initiate backlash? While the justices were removed, gay marriage remained legal in Iowa.

Toward a Theory of Elite-Led Mobilization

Claims of anti-gay backlash are widespread. Policies opposing the acceptance of gays and lesbians as full and equal citizens are continually introduced at various levels of government. Despite the increased visibility of gays and lesbians in society, the past two decades are characterized by the unprecedented acceptance of gays and lesbians by the public and dramatic advances in policies benefiting gays and lesbians. How can we explain this apparent contradiction?

We argue that the roots of this contradiction lie in the ambiguity that surrounds the term "backlash" and the imprecision with which the term is used (e.g., Weaver 2007). Those who employ the concept of backlash take for granted a shared but almost always implicit understanding of what backlash is, yet the term is seldom defined. It is typically unclear what constitutes backlash, when it occurs, what the response precisely entails, who is reacting and how, and, to the extent that the reactions are described, whether they have the negative effects ascribed to them or lead to the defeat of the policy in question (e.g., Keck 2009). In short, backlash is poorly theorized and uncritically applied (e.g., Weaver 2007). One result of this ambiguity is that alternative explanations to backlash are seldom considered. The central task of this book is to describe, define, and rigorously test Mass Opinion Backlash and to develop and evaluate an alternative theory that explains opposition to gay rights. We call this alternative explanation the theory of Elite-Led Mobilization.[8]

While a closer look at the tenets of Mass Opinion Backlash raises substantial questions about the extent to which it occurs, and while the last two decades have seen extraordinary and unprecedented policy successes for gays and lesbians, opposition to gay rights has hardly disappeared. Opposition to the acceptance of gays and lesbians and attempts to restrict gay rights increasingly employ varied and sophisticated tactics across a wide range of political venues. Often, these actions appear to be responses to the activities of gay rights advocates. In short, the same period that saw unprecedented expansion of gay rights also saw persistent and significant opposition to gay rights. In 2004, for example, President George W. Bush announced support for the Federal Marriage Amendment, which would amend the Constitution to ban gay marriage. Later that year eleven states passed gay marriage bans via referendum, a strategy replicated in eight additional states in 2006. Building on their success with the issue of abortion, white evangelical groups have increasingly used the courts to oppose gay rights by making legal arguments based on First Amendment protections of an individual's religious freedom (A. Lewis 2017). Similarly, states with Republican legislatures regularly pursue policies of preemption to limit the ability of local governments to extend protections to gay, lesbian, and transgender Americans (Taylor et al. 2018). Moreover, anti-gay groups have been richly rewarded for their political support of former President Trump. In addition to issuing executive orders repealing benefits and protections to the LGBT community, the president has made conservative judicial appointments that are expected to support the positions of anti-gay organizations at a record pace (e.g., Diamond 2018; Paul 2018). In short, while the principal expectations backlash describes are not met, gays and lesbians continue to face significant opposition in their attempts to be recognized as full and equal members of American society in diverse venues by opponents that employ increasingly creative strategies.

Though the advances made over the last two decades seem to contradict the theory of backlash, gays and lesbians face continued opposition.[9] We argue that the ongoing opposition to gay rights that is often attributed to Mass Opinion Backlash is instead a product of a well-organized campaign by elites who oppose the acceptance of gays and lesbians as full and equal members of society. Specifically, anti-gay elites oppose public acceptance of gays and lesbians, the policy changes advocated by the LGBT community and its allies, and these elites work to initiate new anti-gay policies. These elites employ a wide range of legal, electoral, legislative, and public relations strategies to help achieve organizational and policy goals.

Elite-Led Mobilization Theory holds that the organizations and elites—religious conservatives, especially white evangelical Christians—typically play key roles in strategizing organizing, and mobilizing their supporters to politicize their opposition to gay rights and object to gays, lesbians, bisexuals, and transgender people as amoral. The fight against gay rights helped to unify their movement and facilitate development of the Moral Majority (Fitzgerald 2017). It also provides a political rationale for their organizations and motivates their adherents to provide resources in the form of money, electoral and popular support, organizational manpower, and expertise (e.g., Bull and Gallagher 1996; Fitzgerald 2017).

The theory of Elite-Led Mobilization argues that what appears to be a bottom-up mass-driven response to challenges to the status quo is just one aspect of the anti-gay elites' broader strategy to oppose the acceptance of gays and lesbians as legitimate members of the polity and enhance the relevance and legitimacy of their own organizations to their supporters and funders. That is, the opposition to gay rights described as backlash is instead a "top-down" reaction instigated by representatives and leaders of organizations seeking to prevent advances in gay rights and to oppose public acceptance of gays and lesbians. These organizations act both proactively, when they see an opportunity to advance their agenda, and reactively, in response to attempted policy advances by gays and lesbians. In either case, their strategy often entails mobilizing those who already share their views and activating those with uncrystallized but sympathetic attitudes.

Elite-Led Mobilization is mistaken for backlash partly because of the lack of specificity surrounding exactly what backlash is and partly because anti-gay elites use tactics consistent with backlash to mobilize existing and potential supporters. They are led, after all, primarily by white *evangelical* Christians. Often these mobilization efforts occur following some prominent policy challenge or advance by gay rights advocates, which makes differentiating elite-led mobilization from the process of mass backlash difficult. But where backlash requires the challenge to the status quo to catalyze the opinion change, elite mobilization requires people to be told that expanding gay rights is bad for them.

Importantly, however, mobilization of the like-minded and of potential supporters is just one tactic in a broader campaign that anti-gay elites use to achieve their goals. Moreover, mobilizing someone who already agrees with you and opposes a policy is not actually backlash—rather, it is mobilization. Alternative tactics include cultivating and recruiting candidates, lobbying politicians, pursuing legislative and legal strategies, and working to influence the platforms of candidates and the Republican Party (e.g., Haider-Markel 2001). Indeed, a case could be made that opposition to gays and lesbians is itself just one of many tactics employed by religious conservatives in order to help build their own organizations, obtain resources, remain visible, and garner institutional legitimacy as powerful political actors.

Plan for the Book

This book seeks to answer the question, What best explains the politics of opposition to gay rights? Have attempts to advance gay rights led to opinion backlash? Or does some other elite-driven phenomenon better describe the reaction we observe? The question is crucially important because opinion backlash implies a system that makes attaining equality for gays and lesbians increasingly difficult as even small steps toward equality are taken. Simply put, backlash impedes the ability of LGBT people, or any minorities, from obtaining basic freedoms or equality before their government.

Our central argument is that elite-led mobilization rather than mass opinion backlash best explains the politics of opposition to gay rights. The book proceeds in three sections, each examining a claim central to our argument. Section I continues in chapter 2 by documenting the ambiguity that characterizes backlash claims and by more clearly articulating and defining the theories and implications of Mass Opinion Backlash and Elite-Led Mobilization Theory.

As opinion backlash is the conventional wisdom explaining reactions to demands for gay rights, section II focuses on evaluating the theory of Mass Opinion Backlash. If the theory of elite-led mobilization is correct, evidence of mass opinion backlash should be scarce. In chapter 3 we present results from a series of online survey experiments designed to elicit backlash, and from natural experiments conducted around the Supreme Court ruling in *Obergefell v. Hodges*, to examine the extent to which Mass Opinion Backlash explains opinion change on gay marriage following salient events. One limitation of these experimental findings is that they are time-bound, as recent changes in opinion may eliminate the possibility of backlash. We address this possibility in chapter 4 by examining attitudes on gay marriage from a large nationally representative survey from 2004, well before national attitudes on gay marriage changed to become favorable. The results show little evidence of backlash. Chapter 5 investigates the extent to which attitudes toward gay rights are influenced by different actors or institutions. Specifically, we examine whether our findings might result from the focus on the courts, as the extent to which backlash occurs may be a function of the institution or actor making the policy. In some states, gay rights have been advanced by legislatures, and in such cases one might expect mass opinion backlash to be strongest where elected officials contravened the public will. To examine this question, we conduct experiments in which we vary the institution that makes the law (e.g., court, legislature, referendum, etc.). We find that the institution that makes the law seems to have little influence on people's reaction to the policy, as there is little evidence of opinion backlash irrespective of the institution making the law.

Having found very little evidence for Mass Opinion Backlash, section III turns to examine the theory of Elite-Led Mobilization and whether it or Mass Opinion Backlash better explains the salient challenges to gay rights. In chapter 6 we examine the history of gay rights with attention to how salient historical events speak to theories of opinion backlash and elite-led mobilization. While some of the history is well documented, past treatments largely overlook how these events affect attitudes toward gays and lesbians, which allows us to gain historical purchase in assessing these competing explanations. In chapter 7, using financial contribution and voting data, we examine the politics behind arguably the most salient example of anti-gay backlash in modern times—the 2010 Iowa judicial retention election—a case that provides a difficult test for elite-led mobilization. Chapter 8, the conclusion, summarizes the arguments and evidence from the book, considers the evidence presented, and examines the implications of elite-led mobilization for the future of gay rights, especially on issues of religious freedom.

TWO

Toward a Theory of Elite-Led Mobilization

The gay rights movement is characterized by a curious puzzle: widespread claims of backlash coincide with rapidly growing public support for gay rights. Recall that backlash is an enduring negative change in public opinion in response to a challenge to the status quo. Cases of what appears to be public backlash, such as the removal of justices in Iowa or the widespread passage of state referenda banning gay marriage, occur just as academic research increasingly documents the absence of the anti-gay opinion change thought to be at its heart. Despite unprecedented policy advances on gay rights issues ranging from military service to the right to marry, claims of backlash persist. And yet, despite these successes, persistent and significant opposition to gay rights that cannot be explained by the theory of backlash remains. These contradictions raise the fundamental questions addressed in this book: What best explains the politics of opposition to gay rights? To what extent does anti-gay public opinion backlash occur? Have attempts to advance gay rights led to public opinion backlash or does some other phenomenon better explain the opposition to gay rights that we see?

In this book we argue that the conventional wisdom of anti-gay public opinion backlash among the American public is misguided and inaccurate. Instead, the backlash described in journalistic and academic accounts reflects the actions of elites and interest groups who work to oppose acceptance of gays and lesbians as full and equal members of society. We refer to the opposition to acceptance of gays and lesbians in society as "Elite-Led Mobilization." In essence, anti-gay interest groups, particularly white evangelical Christians, work with their allies not only to oppose advances in gay rights and to pass laws that limit gay rights where possible but also to oppose the acceptance of LGBT people as equal and legitimate members of society. Their most prominent strategy is to use events surrounding gay rights to take public positions designed to mobilize their followers, enhance their status, maintain the legitimacy and esteem with which their organizations are held, increase or maintain fund-raising, and oppose public acceptance of gays and lesbians.

The phenomenon so often referred to as "backlash" is a misnomer that stems from the imprecise use and an ambiguous understanding of the term. While references to anti-gay backlash are common among academics, activists, and journalists, and are often used to describe salient events in the public conflict over gay rights, these references seldom reflect the widespread public opinion change that is thought to be at the heart of mass public opinion backlash. Instead, "backlash" is typically used as a catch-all to describe any reaction to challenges to the status quo, especially to advances in gay rights by those elites and interest groups who already strongly oppose gay rights. In other words, the attitudes of individuals who oppose gay rights are often attributed to backlash after any advancement of gay rights, even if the hostility was present before the rights advanced.

This chapter describes how Elite-Led Mobilization Theory explains the puzzles we describe above and begins to explain why it, rather than the conventional wisdom of Mass Opinion Backlash, better explains reactions to advances in gay rights. We begin by documenting and defining the term "backlash" and show that its use is often characterized by a lack of specificity and empirical scrutiny. Perhaps owing to the wide range of uses and lack of precision about what does and does not constitute backlash, scholars seldom consider alternative explanations for the reactions and processes usually attributed to backlash. Building on research on opinion formation and attitude change to clarify its meaning, we describe the theory of Mass Opinion Backlash in order to better understand how the antipathy at the heart of backlash claims is triggered and to specify its implications. While the academic literature provides insight into the factors that drive attitude formation and change, it also raises questions about the extent to which it should occur. We then summarize survey and experimental evidence for Mass Opinion Backlash. The conflicting evidence for backlash invites an alternative explanation—Elite-Led Mobilization Theory—which explains the paradoxical findings of claims of backlash coincident with increases in public support for gay rights. The final section develops implications of the two theories that are tested throughout the remainder of the book.

The Importance and Definition of Backlash

Activists and scholars have long been concerned that attempts by marginalized minorities to address inequalities might lead to backlash. Perhaps the most prominent recent example has emerged over gay rights and the quest for marriage equality. Gay rights proponents feared that attempts to legalize gay marriage through a litigation strategy might result in the paradoxical situation where not only would marriage equality be denied, but the effort to achieve it would lead the public to recoil against other policy objectives and gays and lesbians in general. If the marriage equality effort failed and it caused mass public opinion backlash, it could leave the gay community in worse shape than if no effort toward marriage equality had been made.

"Backlash" is broadly used to describe almost any negative reaction to a marginalized group's challenge to a dominant group's status, power, or values (e.g., Lipsett and Raub 1970). This broad description introduces challenges to understanding backlash. Vesla M. Weaver (2007) shows that backlash is remarkably ambiguous, seldom defined and theorized, and its conditions and expectations are poorly articulated. Indeed, the simplicity of the term lends itself to describe any sort of reaction, irrespective of how vaguely defined it is, rather than a precise type of response. Few studies carefully examine what causes the reaction, who reacts, how they react in terms of the form the backlash takes, whether and the extent to which mass backlash differs from other types of reactions, and whether the reactions have the intended effect in defeating the policy (e.g., Weaver 2007; Keck 2009). It is unclear whether backlash requires attitude change among a group's supporters, among the indifferent, or increased activism among those who already dislike the group or disagree with a policy. With only a handful of exceptions, seldom is any distinction made between reactions by the masses or by political elites, or whether the reaction takes the form of media visibility, opinion change, lobbying activity, campaign contributions, voter turnout, vote choice, party registration, or something else (e.g., Weaver 2007, 237).

The term "backlash" is used to describe a variety of concepts. What some call backlash others refer to as "resentment," "countermobilization," or "reaction." At times these different terms seem to be used interchangeably even within subfields (e.g., Hirschman 1991; Rosenberg 2008; Keck 2009). Doing so, however, conceals important nuances among a wide variety of social reactions. While some law and society scholars emphasize that backlash is typically the immediate and adverse reaction by the public as a consequence of losing in court (e.g., Rosenberg 2008; Klarman 2013), others describe a more complex and nuanced countermobilization in which elites play a significant role (e.g., McCann 1994; Adam 2017). As one example, Legal Mobilization Theory holds that the law helps shape society by influencing social meaning, creating norms, and shifting the perception of rights and group legitimacy in ways that may not be immediately evident in the days following a ruling (e.g., McCann 1994; Goldberg-Hiller 2002). In short, the law can have complex mobilizing and constraining effects, the latter of which may include opinion backlash, countermobilization, or even the inability of intersectional minorities to influence the agenda of their own allies (McCann 1994; Adam 2017).

These complex and indirect effects illustrate the difficulty of assessing imprecise accounts of backlash. In Hawaii, for example, journalists describe how a state supreme court ruling supporting marriage equality provoked backlash in the form of a 1998 constitutional amendment banning gay marriage (Eckholm 2013). Despite this, Jonathan Goldberg-Hiller (2002) describes how some gay rights activists saw the constitutional amendment's passage as an important *advance* by providing a lexicon for discussing gay rights that would positively frame the marriage equality debate going forward. This came about despite the politics surrounding the court case and amendment inciting a campaign advocating the passage of marriage bans in dozens of states by a coalition of religious conservatives (e.g., Haider-Markel 2001; Goldberg-Hiller 2002).

In at least some cases, the ambiguity surrounding the term "backlash" may impede our ability to distinguish between important but subtly distinct social phenomena. Ambiguity about the conditions under which backlash occurs and precisely what constitutes backlash makes it difficult to identify who reacts and in what ways. Some accounts of backlash emphasize a broad opinion change among the mass public about an issue or group, while others describe any reaction, including narrow ones by individuals or interest groups, even when made by those who already oppose the group or policy. Identifying who lashes back is especially important because backlash as mass opinion change indicates broad-based opposition to a group's attempt at redress. Mass opinion change makes it more difficult for a marginalized group to obtain not just policy but fundamental rights and legitimacy as well, thereby subjecting it to a paradox: the act of pressing for policy makes that policy more difficult to obtain.

Over time the concept of backlash has become something of a conventional wisdom in understanding opposition to gay rights in the United

States (e.g., Ball 2006; Klarman 2013; Rosenberg 2008). A central focus is on public opinion backlash against court rulings establishing gay rights (e.g., Stoutenborough, Haider-Markel, and Allen 2006). The development of the backlash narrative to explain opposition to gay rights, however, shares many of the limitations of the backlash described in other contexts (Weaver 2007, 237; Ball 2006). While research has just begun to define and theorize anti-gay backlash, questions about what sorts of events are most likely to elicit backlash and what form it takes are still largely overlooked. Historians, journalists, and scholars of social movements documenting the history of gay rights and the religious right commonly recognize the different and important roles that elites and masses play but seldom examine how they interact or clearly define what constitutes backlash (e.g., Bull and Gallagher 1996; Fetner 2008; Fejes 2008; Burack 2008). Vesla M. Weaver's assessment is that the term "backlash has been volleyed around as a term for describing any negative reaction to a whole host of racial threats, perceived and real. This lack of uncritical propositions for what constitutes a backlash has enabled an unspecified . . . and an uncritical application of the term to a wide variety of groups and contexts" (2007, 237). This applies equally well to the study of gay rights.

A consensus holds that backlash reflects a phenomenon of mass behavior among the few studies that carefully examine backlash. Despite the ambiguity surrounding use of the term, backlash is framed as "a fundamentally populist reaction" (Weaver 2007, 238). Even those studies less interested in the causes than the effects of backlash tend to see mass behavior as central to (undesirable) downstream policy effects. The only detailed theoretical examination of anti-gay backlash, however, focuses primarily on whether and among which groups it occurs (e.g., Bishin et al. 2016; Bishin et al. 2020). Synthesizing research on mass attitudes and psychological threat, Bishin and his colleagues (2016) identify the circumstances likely to trigger backlash, the groups that should be expected to lash back, and the form the backlash should take. In particular, challenges to the status quo that violate an individual's sense of importance, safety, symbolic values, or status are most likely to foster backlash.

Even this articulation of the scope and conditions that might foster backlash does little to clarify the distinction between different types of reaction or their implications. As one example, the 2003 Massachusetts Supreme Court ruling was the first of a series of events that is credited with leading to both the widespread public rejection of gay marriage across society during the 2004 presidential election cycle and mobilizing the most ardent religious conservatives to turn out to vote (e.g., Fitzgerald 2017).

Clearly, the political implications of a backlash that might mobilize millions to vote who otherwise might not show up at the polls differs dramatically from one in which opinion changes but does not lead to any action.

The distinction between mass and elite behavior driving reactions is obscured by the lack of clarity about who is reacting. The term "backlash" is used to describe both opinion change as a reaction among the masses as well as a reaction by elites and their followers who already hold firm opinions. The ambiguity that characterizes the distinction between "bottom-up" mass-driven politics from "top-down" elite-based explanations for opposition to gay rights has important implications for public policy, political activism, and interest group politics. It also impedes advancing our understanding of how marginalized groups might hope to achieve policy in the United States.

Given this overlooked complexity, it seems reasonable to consider that ambiguity in the use of the term "backlash" might camouflage the possibility that an alternative social process better explains reactions to gay rights. We argue that the reactions to attempts by gays and lesbians to advance their interests are instigated by elites and groups who already oppose gay rights rather than by a large broad-based negative opinion shift that lies at the heart of Mass Opinion Backlash. In short, while the term "backlash" is often used in an ambiguous way to describe an unclear reaction, more commonly the reactions we observe are consistent with mobilization of specific groups. These reactions are led by elites who already oppose gay rights and who use the judiciary, the legislative process, referenda, and any other prominent institutions or events to oppose the legitimation and acceptance of gays and lesbians as full members of society. From a distance, backlash and Elite-Led Mobilization are likely to appear most similar in those cases where elites seek to mobilize citizens to support their immediate policy agenda. The mobilization of supporters, however, is just one of many strategies anti-gay elites employ. Simply put, the ambiguity in the use of the term "backlash" impedes our ability to understand the social processes that drive opposition to marginalized groups—in this case, gay rights.

Why Ambiguity Matters

The lack of precision in both the use and the understanding of the term "backlash" inhibits rigorous assessment of its causes and consequences. Mass backlash is particularly likely to have far-reaching consequences for minority groups who seek more comprehensive inclusion in the polity through policy gains. To the extent that mass opinion change describes a negative and broad-based public response to a marginalized group's demand for policy, and that the group's actions change how the public views the group, mass backlash makes it more difficult for the marginalized group to obtain any policy at all or ever obtain equality in civil society.

The fear of setting back their own cause as a result of advocacy has long been used to dissuade marginalized groups from pursuing policy. Opponents use the threat of backlash to deter the group from pursuing policy. Notoriously, during the Civil Rights Movement, for example, white clergy in Alabama warned Martin Luther King Jr. not to march, triggering his seminal response "Why We Can't Wait" (or "Letter from Birmingham Jail"). Concerns about backlash also encourage self-censorship. Fear of opinion backlash led the Human Rights Campaign, the most prominent gay rights advocacy group in the United States, to oppose using litigation to pursue gay marriage for fear of setting the movement back by changing mass opinion and by creating adverse legal precedent that would be difficult for future court rulings to overcome (Fuchs 2013). The threat of backlash also incentivizes group members to settle for suboptimal policies, as when gay rights advocates supported civil unions as "good enough" (Eskridge 2002).

While the policy impediments that mass opinion backlash introduces are important, they also introduce a more general problem. Of particular concern for democratic societies are reactions by the majority that curtail fundamental rights of the minority (e.g., Madison 1787). With respect to gay rights, majorities can use and have used democratic institutions to deny gays and lesbians equal access to a wide range of policies from the ability to obtain a wedding cake celebrating a gay marriage, to fundamental rights like marriage itself. For this reason, understanding whether opposition to gay rights is driven by elites or by mass opinion backlash speaks to one of the most basic questions of democracy.

Perhaps most importantly, the wide variety of meanings ascribed to backlash impedes our understanding of opposition to stigmatized groups like gays and lesbians. It is difficult to assess the extent to which a mass reaction to the status quo even occurs if we are not clear about what should stimulate such a reaction, who should react, and what form that reaction should take. With these key aspects left unspecified, it is extraordinarily difficult to identify and evaluate alternative explanations for these anti-gay reactions or for groups to devise appropriate and effective strategies for the advancement of gay rights. With respect to the politics of gay rights, "we are not sure where backlash begins and ends and what the unique characteristics of backlash are" (Weaver 2007, 238). We begin to articulate and clarify these concepts in the sections that follow.

The Theory of Mass Opinion Backlash

The conventional wisdom relied upon to explain people's negative reactions to gay rights is the theory of Mass Opinion Backlash. Mass Opinion Backlash holds that the public reacts to challenges to the status quo by shifting their attitudes to oppose the policy or group. More specifically, Mass Opinion Backlash is *"a large, negative, organic, and enduring shift in opinion against a policy or group that occurs in response to some event that threatens the status quo"* (Bishin et al. 2016). Mass Opinion Backlash may be evidenced by changes in any of several aspects of opinion, including policy positions, the intensity of feeling about an issue, or differences in the attitudes expressed toward members of the group advocating the policy. These opinion shifts have important short- and long-term policy consequences, both of which undermine the group's goals.

One important aspect of Mass Opinion Backlash lies in the effect the opinion change has on the politics surrounding the issue and group. In the short term, mass backlash may lead to policy defeat as the public rallies to oppose the policy being considered. It may also activate latent attitudes that serve over the longer term to build momentum for opponents that leads to both the creation of a better-organized or intense opposition and increased antipathy toward gays and lesbians as a group.

Most prominently, backlash is characterized by a *negative* change that occurs in a direction opposite the position espoused by the group or policy that disrupts the status quo. Following the Supreme Court ruling in *Lawrence v. Texas*, for instance, which struck down the prohibition on sodomy, opposition to "homosexual relations" being legal increased by about 7.6 points (Flores 2014; Egan and Persily 2009). Activating latent opinions among those who already oppose the group, or publicizing existing opposition, does not induce net attitude change among the public. Mobilizing those who already oppose or are predisposed to oppose the policy may reduce advocates' prospects of victory in a particular election, but it is unlikely to shift the political incentives sufficiently to dissuade policy advocates from speaking out. While it might make those people who are predisposed to oppose gay rights aware of the particular issue, merely activating existing opposition does not create any additional costs of advocacy beyond those already known by politicians on both sides of an issue.

By shifting opinion against the group, backlash differs from other types of dramatic public opinion change, particularly those in which opinion changes in ways that benefit the group. Consider that in some cases salient issues or events raised by marginalized groups might galvanize opinion in the group's favor. The peaceful civil rights marches of the early 1960s saw protesters met with physical violence, events that are widely credited with helping to turn national opinion in favor of the civil rights movement (Lee 2017; Nelson, Clawson, and Oxley 1997; Wasow 2020). More recently, President Trump's ban on immigration from some majority Muslim countries led to increased acceptance of and support for Muslims (Collingwood et al. 2018).

Mass opinion backlash is powerful to the extent that a challenge to the status quo changes attitudes or increases an opponent's likelihood of participating in politics. To the extent that backlash reflects changes in citizens' interests and preferences, it may also alter elites' considerations about an issue. Opinion changes that are small or fleeting often occur, especially on topics to which people have given little thought (Campbell et al. 1960). One important characteristic of Mass Opinion Backlash, then, is that the magnitude of the opinion change must be large enough to alter elites' political calculus surrounding an issue. Both the size of the change and the substantive impact of the shift are important. Backlash occurs when, for instance, opinion shifts are large enough to either encourage politicians who were uncommitted on an issue to oppose it or to dissuade those who might have supported the policy or group by getting them to step back and refrain from weighing in.

Backlash must also reflect an enduring shift in opinion. An opinion change that endures is much more likely to be politically consequential. In the *Lawrence v. Texas* ruling described above, opinion initially shifted against the ruling but very quickly returned to previous levels (Flores 2014). Ephemeral changes in opinion are not uncommon but are unlikely to change the political calculus for politicians seeking to build new support coalitions, because they will be more difficult to capitalize on going forward. Changes that appear unlikely to endure provide fewer incentives and indeed may be quite costly to politicians, who may quickly find themselves on the wrong side of the public's preferences. Politicians who change positions may be seen as unreliable, a trait that can be exploited by challengers. Moreover, new candidates will find it difficult to exploit changes that do not last, and even incumbents who propose and seek to pass legislation need time to allow their policy proposals to manifest.

Mass opinion backlash is also characterized by an "organic" opinion change caused by the visceral reaction of the mass public as opposed to one mobilized by politicians, political parties, or interest groups. Specifically, the change in opinion should primarily result from the public's reaction to the issue and its violation of some important aspect of the status quo that triggers a sense of loss or threat rather than to prompts from elites attempting to instigate them. By reflecting people's reaction, the opinion shift is legitimized as an expression of the public will, as it is less easily dismissed as the product of political calculation or mobilization. The organic nature makes this opinion change harder for elected officials to ignore, as its authenticity makes those whose attitudes change more likely to act on them.

What Causes Backlash?

A variety of triggers can precipitate the threat to the status quo necessary to cause backlash. Research suggests that backlash occurs among those who experience a feeling of threat to or loss of power, importance, or status due to gains by an out-group. Research on group threat describes several ways that the feelings of loss that trigger backlash can occur. Any challenge to one's physical or economic security (real group threat), to one's moral values, sense of self, or way of life (i.e., symbolic threat), or one's desire for hierarchy or social order (e.g., authoritarianism or social dominance orientation) may lead to the feeling of threat to or loss of power sufficient to incite backlash. In some cases, these feelings are stimulated as the result of policy change, while in others merely increasing the visibility of a group's demands might activate a threat or sense of loss sufficient to incite backlash. Even people living outside of a jurisdiction where policy is threatened or changed, and thus who are not directly affected by the policy, may perceive a symbolic challenge triggering a sense of threat or loss due to the changed status quo.

A variety of threats are shown to affect attitudes toward gays, lesbians, and transgender Americans. Increased visibility of the group or proposing policy can trigger a sense of loss or threat that can elicit a strong emotional response—like disgust, to take just one example—that drives attitudes (Cottrell and Neuberg 2005; Sheldon and Kasser 2008; Casey 2016). With respect to gay rights, disgust is caused by "perceived physical or moral contamination" (Cottrell and Neuberg 2005, 772). Feelings of disgust about homosexuality are associated with lower support for a wide range of gay rights policies (Gadarian and van der Vort 2018). Similarly, threats to one's sense of self also drive attitudes. Brian F. Harrison and Melissa R.

Michelson (2017), for instance, find that threats to masculinity elicit negative attitudes toward transgender people. It is worth noting, however, that attempts to elicit disgust can also result in an emotional counter-reaction among some who defend gays and lesbians (Gadarian and van der Vort 2018). Taken together, threats sufficient to induce backlash can be incited by a wide range of governmental and social activity that evokes a variety of feelings (Lipsett and Raub 1970).

Those who see a group's policy preferences as a challenge to social order are also prone to lash back. Psychological triggers for negative attitudes are not activated exclusively by threat or loss but may also occur as a function of an individual's social outlook. The theories of authoritarianism and Social Dominance Orientation hold that that a hierarchy describing one's social position conditions how some individuals perceive groups. Authoritarianism reflects a desire to defend a notion of order and sameness, which leads to intolerant attitudes toward those who challenge this order (e.g., Stenner 2005). Similarly, Social Dominance Orientation (SDO) is rooted in the notion that society is organized by hierarchies, and one's SDO describes the desire that their group be superior to other groups (Pratto et al. 1994). Both authoritarianism and Social Dominance Orientation are highly associated with attitudes toward groups and social and political opinions (e.g., Pratto et al. 1994; Hetherington and Weiler 2009).

What sorts of events incite backlash? Accounts vary but, in general, highly visible events that resonate with at least some segments of the public are most likely to induce backlash. These might include public protests, the election of members of a marginalized group to office, judicial rulings, or the passage of legislation. Regardless of the specific event, it must be sufficiently visible for people to notice and relevant to evince a sense of threat or loss. The Supreme Court ruling in *Bowers v. Hardwick* (1986), for instance, was followed by a drop in support for "homosexual relations" being legal despite the court ruling that states could outlaw them (Egan, Persily, and Wallsten 2008). That is, even in a case where the court protected the status quo, the increased salience of the ruling still led to an increase in opposition to the pro-gay position. Marisa Abrajano and Zoltan Hajnal (2017), for instance, argue that a massive increase in the number of immigrants and the media publicity afforded them, along with ancillary issues the media has tied to immigration, such as crime, job loss, or the dilution of American values (each of which provides a prominent and relevant challenge to the status quo), has led to an anti-immigrant backlash (but see Hui and Sears 2018). Made salient by the media, the rapid increase in the number of immigrants makes a sense of threat or loss apparent to those who live in close proximity to immigrants. Sharp increases in the Latino population, for instance, led to increased support for Donald Trump among whites (Newman, Shah, and Collingwood 2018). In both of these accounts, threat seems to be increased through the physical experience and recognition of societal changes (e.g., Wilcox-Archuleta 2018).

Threats may become relevant in different ways, changing even on the same issue over time as the context surrounding the issue changes. Omar Wasow (2020) finds that in areas with peaceful protests during the Black Civil Rights Movement, the public became more favorably disposed to the cause, supporting pro–civil rights candidates at higher levels, while areas with violent protests saw increased opposition to politicians supporting the movement. In this case, physical violence appears to have enhanced the threat perceived by citizens living in areas where marches occurred.

Research generally suggests that mass opinion backlash is most likely to occur among the public as a whole or among subconstituencies. Both journalistic and academic accounts frequently argue that challenges to the status quo activate the public en masse. Similarly, extensive evidence documents group members' sensitivity to issues that members see as important or that speak to one's social identifications (Bishin 2009). Irrespective of the process, the trigger is the same. Members of these groups, seeing some aspect of the status quo as being challenged or threatened by an out-group, are especially likely to lash back (e.g., Bishin, Kaufmann, and Stevens 2012).

The most prominent example of a group whose members are activated on the subject of gay rights is white evangelical Christians. As we will see, white evangelicals view gays as amoral and view the advancement of gay rights as contrary to their own personal values and posing a threat to their worldview. Anti-gay elites see gay rights, and marriage in particular, as a valuable issue for generating resources for, and maintaining the relevance of, their group (Burack 2008; Claassen and Povtak 2010; Lugg 1998; Bull and Gallagher 1996). Moreover, the activation of white evangelicals into a political movement referred to as the "religious right" began, in part, as a response to the movement to end employment discrimination against gays and lesbians in Miami–Dade County (Fejes 2008). Thus, the group's political activism is partly attributable to opposition to gays' and lesbians' attempts to secure basic protections (Stone 2012).

The Evidence of Anti-Gay Backlash

The past several decades have seen a raft of laws proposed and passed in response to advances in gay rights. In addition to the referenda overturning local nondiscrimination laws in the 1970s, numerous state and federal laws seeking to prevent gays and lesbians from being treated equally (e.g., to work as schoolteachers, to adopt children, or to marry) have been passed in apparent response to the increased visibility and activism of the gay community. Some reactions are triggered by the attempted passage of policy benefiting gays and lesbians; others are spurred by the increased visibility or public acceptance of the LGBT community. The election of gays and lesbians to state legislatures, for instance, has led to an increase in the number of bills limiting gay rights that are proposed in those same legislatures (Haider-Markel 2010). In other cases, the reaction is symbolic and provides no direct policy benefit to anti-gay forces. In the Iowa judicial retention election, for instance, the ruling that led to the ouster of the judges was unaffected by their removal. Most recently, reactions have taken the form of laws seeking to protect religious freedom.

The widespread public opposition to gay rights throughout contemporary American history has required most initial advances in gay rights to occur through the courts. It is therefore unsurprising that the judiciary is the institution most frequently held to trigger the sense of loss or threat necessary for backlash to occur. Judicial backlash invites the possibility that a favorable court ruling will either serve to incite anti-gay opinion or lead to the creation of a legal precedent that not only defeats the policy before the court but also serves as a barrier to the advancement of other rights in future cases (e.g., Ball 2006; D'Emilio 2006; Keck 2009). With respect to mass opinion backlash, the fear is that a court ruling incites a negative reaction among the public that may lead to further attempts to curtail gay rights in the legislature via constitutional amendment, referendum, or through the election of politicians who promise to work to oppose gay rights.

Given these concerns, it is unsurprising that a number of studies find evidence consistent with backlash. Research shows that the U.S. Supreme Court can and does move aggregate public opinion, at least on visible landmark issues (Johnson and Martin 1998). Others find that court rulings may influence different groups differently, causing opinions among groups to diverge from one another (Franklin and Kosaki 1989). On gay rights issues, as we have seen, research suggests that court decisions on both *Bowers v. Hardwick* and *Lawrence v. Texas* caused the public to be less supportive in the short term of the proposition that "homosexual relations" "should be legal" (Stoutenborough, Haider-Markel, and Allen 2006; Egan, Persily, and Wallsten 2008).[1] A similar pattern characterizes the opinion trends following the state supreme court ruling in *Goodridge v. Department of Public*

Health (2003), an opinion that ushered in gay marriage in Massachusetts (Egan, Persily, and Wallsten 2008). The defeat of the three judges in the 2010 Iowa judicial retention elections was driven by their ruling in *Varnum v. Brien* (2009), which legalized gay marriage (Clopton and Peters 2013; A. Harris 2019).

Even the mere threat of judicial action seems to incite backlash. Between 1994 and 1997, for instance, in response to a 1993 Hawaiian judge ruling that the state constitution denying same-sex couples the right to marry constituted sex discrimination, legislators from forty-eight states introduced bills banning gay marriage (Haider-Markel 2001). Twenty-eight states passed the bills into law. This happened despite the judge immediately staying his decision and the ruling never being implemented, as the citizens of Hawaii ultimately passed a referendum banning gay marriage. It also resulted in the federal Defense of Marriage Act passed (in 1996) to prevent marriage legalization in one state from requiring other states to also legalize marriage.

The judiciary is not the only institution reputed to incite backlash. Passage of referenda circumscribing gay rights is often attributed to backlash against state or local governments. The most important example of this was the 1977 special election referendum overturning the Miami–Dade County Commission's nondiscrimination ordinance (Fejes 2008). Public reactions to legislative action have also been common. Colorado's Amendment 2, a ballot initiative preventing sexual minorities from using civil rights laws to protect themselves from discrimination, was passed in 1992 as a response to a series of laws passed by the state as well as local legislatures that protected a range of gay rights (Grauerholz 1995). Similarly, San Francisco mayor Gavin Newsom ordered city clerks to issue marriage licenses in 2004. The ensuing uproar was one of the factors cited by President Bush announcing his support for the Federal Marriage Amendment (Fitzgerald 2017). Similarly, the 2004 and 2006 elections saw constitutional amendments barring gay marriage pass in eleven and seven states, respectively, in apparent response to a series of events that, along with Mayor Newsom's directive, included the 2003 Massachusetts Supreme Court ruling and the state legislature then passing a bill legalizing gay marriage.

When one considers how challenges to the status quo can trigger out-group antipathy, along with the intensity of opposition to gay rights that these symbolic and substantive efforts represent, it is easy to understand why the conventional wisdom about mass opinion backlash seems to explain opposition to gay rights so well (e.g., Riek et al 2006). At the same time, however, there is reason to question the conventional wisdom that mass opinion backlash occurs in response to gay rights advocacy or increased visibility of the LGBT community. There is a certain irony that those who most vociferously warn gay rights advocates about the possibility of backlash are often themselves among the most visible opponents of gay rights.

Perhaps most curiously, the last two decades are characterized by dramatic increases in social acceptance of gays and lesbians and support for gay rights. If challenges to the status quo trigger opinion backlash, then the increased activism and visibility of the gay rights movement seen in recent years should correspond to substantial decreases in support for gay rights. The frequent defeat of gay rights at the ballot box during the early 2000s notwithstanding, surveys of public opinion show just the opposite. Trends in attitudes toward gay rights depict a remarkable shift toward acceptance and thereby highlight a challenge to the backlash narrative. Moreover, academic research on political psychology and public opinion demonstrates that once attitudes are well formed, opinion change is rare.

These findings have three important implications for the theory of Mass Opinion Backlash. First, the rapid opinion change described by backlash is unexpected, as it is extraordinarily unusual for any issue to exhibit dramatic but long-lasting change. Second, the gradual increases in support that have occurred are not likely to be shifted by singular events—that is, the increased support for gay rights seems likely to endure. Finally, owing in part to this apparent contradiction, scholars have just begun carefully exploiting advances in survey and experimental research to study backlash. These results cast further doubt on the backlash thesis. A growing body of research finds that anti-gay opinion backlash in response to salient events is much less common than conventional accounts would suggest. The sections that follow examine each of these challenges to Mass Opinion Backlash.

Increased Support for Gay Rights: Trends in Public Opinion

The arguments raised above supporting backlash seem especially curious when considered in the broader context of trends in American public opinion. Contrary to the expectations from the theory of Mass Opinion Backlash, rather than leading to massive opinion change among the public or among various subconstituencies of those threatened, advances in gay rights appear to have had little if any negative impact on public support for gay rights. Public attitudes toward gays and lesbians and on virtually all issues related to gay rights policy have become strikingly more favorable over the last two decades (Flores 2014; Garretson 2018).

The central logic underpinning Mass Opinion Backlash is that advocacy for gay rights and increased public visibility of gays and lesbians should be met by a large, negative, and enduring shift in public opinion against them. More specifically, if the increased visibility of gays and lesbians and advocacy of gay rights provide salient challenges to the status quo, then Mass Opinion Backlash implies that the public should provide a sharp and sustained rebuke, with opinion becoming increasingly negative as the challenges to the status quo become more prominent. Despite widespread visibility of gay rights issues, however, it is hard to miss the fact that public opinion has become substantially more *supportive* of gay rights over the last decade—a period during which gays and lesbians and gay rights have become visible at an unprecedented rate (Garretson 2018). Indeed, among the most compelling explanations for the increased acceptance of gays and lesbians are the growth in the number of people who report knowing someone who is gay or lesbian and the increased visibility of positive portrayal of gay characters in the media (Garretson 2018).

To illustrate trends in both opinions on gay rights and attitudes toward gays and lesbians, we present data on public attitudes toward three of the historically more contentious gay rights policies: support for gay marriage (as measured by the Gallup organization), support for nondiscrimination in employment, and the right for gays and lesbians to adopt (taken from the American National Election Study). To examine attitudes toward gays and lesbians as a group, we collect thermometer ratings, which encourage people to assess how warmly they view members of a group on a scale from 0 to 100 where higher scores indicate more positive evaluations. These trends are seen in figure 2.1.

The results depict a striking trend. On each measure of policy, support for gay rights and attitudes toward gays and lesbians, attitudes have become increasingly supportive over time. While there is some variation, both in rate of change as well as overall levels of support, the trends are unequivocal. Even policies that were opposed by a majority of the public less than two decades ago, such as legalizing same-sex marriage and adoption, today meet with very strong public support. On every dimension, the American public have become significantly more supportive of gay rights and view gays and lesbians much more warmly than they did just a decade earlier.

Importantly, these trends in opinion run precisely opposite to the predictions of Mass Opinion Backlash. The last decade has seen unprecedented challenges to the status quo on gay rights with regard to a variety

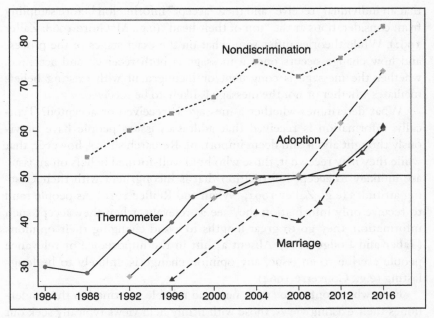

Figure 2.1. Support for workplace nondiscrimination law, gay marriage, adoption by gays and lesbians, and thermometer ratings, 1984–2016

of issues but especially marriage. If such challenges trigger backlash, then the negative response should be most apparent in these opinion trends. Moreover, as the most contested gay rights issue during this period was gay marriage, we should be most likely to see backlash on that issue. Clearly, these trends are inconsistent with such expectations.

Opinion Stability Is Inconsistent with Backlash

The opinion data presented in figure 2.1 are remarkable in that not only do they show no evidence of opinion change against gay rights, but instead they show a steady and large increase in support for gay rights. Extensive research in political science and psychology examining public opinion and attitude formation also raises questions about the prevalence of backlash by suggesting that opinion change of any kind is rare (e.g., Zaller 1992). This scholarship calls the logic of the opinion change that lies at the center of backlash into question. Attitude formation and change, which are central to opinion backlash, are a function of a multistep process that requires that an individual "receive" and then "accept" information before sampling from considerations at the "top of their head" (e.g., McGuire 1968; Zaller 1992). While theories differ somewhat on the exact stages of the process and how change occurs once a message is both received and accepted, whether the message is congruent or incongruent with existing beliefs mediates whether or not the message is likely to be received.

What determines whether a message is received or accepted? Typically, information is received that addresses issues people have previously thought about and deem important. Research shows, however, that while they may receive it, those who hold well-formed beliefs on an issue are unlikely to accept information that is incongruent with their existing attitudes (e.g., Zaller 1992; Nyhan and Reifler 2010). As people tend to receive only information they see as relevant, when they accept such information, they go to great lengths to avoid changing their opinions (Taber and Lodge 2006). Absent a shift in the importance or relevance people ascribe to an issue, any opinion change is unlikely to be long-lasting (e.g., Converse 1964).

Even when confronted with new and reliable information that undermines their existing views, those with firmly held views typically seek out information that reinforces their preexisting views (Redlawsk 2002; Lebo and Casino 2007). Early studies show that contradicting one's views on an issue could elicit increased acceptance of the incorrect position, which scholars have dubbed a "backfire effect" (Nyhan and Reifler 2010; Berinsky 2015). This "backfire effect" is quite consistent with what we might expect were backlash to occur. Examining a wide range of fifty-two different issues, however, Thomas Wood and Ethan Porter (2019) find no evidence of backfire. Specifically, they find that people are willing to accept factual corrections that correct misperceptions, even when they contradict positions held by people or groups with whom they strongly identify. Moreover, on topics that aren't direct questions of fact, such as whether one supports gay marriage, attitudes are primarily cued by elites. One example of this is how attitudes toward transgender individuals changed as elites polarized on the issue (Jones and Brewer 2018). Taken on the whole, this research suggests that mass backlash is much less likely than widely believed but also that individuals who are predisposed to support a position can be mobilized by elites on an issue.[2]

For somewhat different reasons, those who have not developed meaningful attitudes on an issue are also unlikely to change their views. People develop attitudes on issues they see as relevant or important, and they are unlikely to receive or accept information about issues they view as irrelevant or unimportant. When events arise that cause them to receive new information on issues they previously saw as irrelevant, however, they are more likely to accept it and, lacking strong views, are more amenable to change their poorly formed views (McGuire 1968; Zaller 1992). Consequently, among those lacking strong views, only a portion are likely to change their opinions in response to salient events. Rather than shifting from one position to an opposite one, however, opinion research suggests that change from no opinion to a well-formed one is much more likely. Indeed, research on public opinion also speaks to the conditions under which attitude change consistent with backlash is likely to occur. In order for backlash to ensue, social conditions would have to present such a great threat to one's perception of the status quo that the way one viewed the issue would change by both altering the considerations at the top of the head and making them more likely to receive and accept the information. Issues that generate such a great sense of direct threat to individuals arise only rarely.

Does Anti-Gay Opinion Backlash Occur?

Given the contradictions between the claims of backlash and trends in public opinion, and the research on attitude formation, it is perhaps unsurprising that in the area of gay and lesbian politics, studies increasingly disagree about the extent to which gays and lesbians face backlash following favorable judicial rulings (e.g., D'Emilio 2006; Keck 2009), the mobilization of protests (Klarman 2013), or the passage of state laws (Bishin et al. 2016). Because democratic governance allows popular opinion to foster or frustrate policy innovations, actions that foment backlash may stall policy advances that benefit small or unpopular groups. While the existence of opinion backlash has traditionally been taken as given in the literature (see Keck 2009 for a review), the question of whether public opinion backlash actually occurs and the individual-level antecedents that might motivate backlash, as well as the mechanics of how and when it might manifest, remain largely unexplored.

Increased interest in anti-gay backlash has fostered a series of studies seeking to assess the extent to which advances in or challenges to the status quo on gay rights might lead to backlash. Experimental tests designed to stimulate backlash and studies employing observational evidence find no evidence of changes in opinion on gay rights or attitudes toward gays and lesbians (Bishin et al. 2016). Scott Barclay and Andrew Flores (2014) find that not only do salient events not lead to opinion backlash but that the little attitude change observed occurs among opponents who became more *accepting* of gay marriage. Similarly, Rebecca J. Kreitzer and her colleagues (2014) find no evidence of opinion backlash but instead suggest that Iowa Democrats became more supportive of gay marriage following the state supreme court's ruling legalizing it. Further building on these findings, Margaret E. Tankard and Elizabeth Levy Paluck (2017) find that the U.S. Supreme Court ruling in *Obergefell* did not change opinions about gay marriage but did lead to increased acceptance of social norms typically supportive of gay marriage.

Questions about the existence of anti-gay backlash are not limited to research on public opinion. Studies of voting also find little evidence to support the changes implied by backlash. In 2004 and 2006, for instance, a total of eighteen states saw gay marriage bans placed before voters. In 2004 these initiatives were placed on the ballot in strategic coordination with the Bush reelection campaign (Smith et al 2006; Campbell and Monson 2008; Fitzgerald 2017). Despite this, broad increases in voter turnout consistent with Mass Opinion Backlash did not occur (e.g., Hillygus and Shields 2005). Instead, while anti-gay marriage referenda mobilized evangelical Christians in 2004, they also demobilized secular voters (Campbell and Monson 2008). Rather than a clear and singular reaction by the public as a whole, gay marriage bans appear to mobilize people in nuanced ways, a finding consistent with research examining the effect of referenda on voter turnout (Biggers 2014). Jeremiah J. Garretson (2014a), for instance, finds that increased turnout is contingent on how strongly one feels about gay marriage, while Michael P. McDonald (2004) finds that turnout increased among the general public only in non-battleground states. Moreover, examining the electoral aftermath of dozens of judicial rulings, Thomas Keck (2009) finds that while some judicial rulings are followed by negative electoral reactions, they are also sometimes followed by increased support for gay rights or candidates supporting gay rights. Taken together, these results find little evidence consistent with a conclusion that the negative opinion change so central to opinion backlash actually occurs.

Most claims of backlash rely on snapshots of opinion following judicial decisions. Careful study of public reaction to salient gay rights events over time is much more scarce. Indeed, academic studies of public opinion finding evidence consistent with Mass Opinion Backlash on gay rights is limited (Stoutenborough, Haider-Markel, and Allen 2006; Egan, Persily, and Wallsten 2008).[3] The small size of the opinion shifts, the fact that the opinion shifts do not endure, and that the changes were limited to opinion on a question about the legality of homosexual relations raise additional uncertainty about these findings. More recent work finds no evidence of backlash on gay marriage, the most visible gay rights issue of the era. Further, to the extent opinion change occurs at all, policy advances lead those who previously held no opinion to become slightly *more* supportive of the policy (Barclay and Flores 2014).

Similar findings are increasingly seen on issues other than gay rights. Linda Greenhouse and Reva B. Siegel (2011) find that the conventional wisdom that the public lashed back against the court's legalization in *Roe v. Wade* (1973) overlooks the fact that abortion opinion had started to shift before the ruling. Vesla M. Weaver (2007) finds that the racialization of crime policy occurred through an elite-driven process she calls "frontlash." Echoing themes similar to those presented here, Ruth Bloch Rubin and Gregory Elinson (2017) find that in many states, opposition to Black civil rights was driven by organized elite opposition rather than grassroots efforts. Similarly, René D. Flores (2017) finds that negative sentiment in response to Arizona's anti-immigrant bill AB 1070, as expressed through tweets, is driven not by mass opinion change but by the mobilization of those who already hold anti-immigrant attitudes.

Taken together, despite continued opposition to gay rights, these results suggest that while the public became less supportive of gay rights following some court cases, in other circumstances no shift in public attitudes occurred in response to equally salient cues. Moreover, the changes in opinion that did occur seem to have been fleeting or to have occurred in unexpected directions for different groups. Generally, these lack a consistent pattern (e.g., Barclay and Flores 2014). Nor does a consistent effect of backlash seem to emerge in voter turnout. Overall, these results raise questions about not only the extent to which backlash occurs but also whether some other theory might better explain opposition to gay rights.

Backlash as Elite Politics?

The ambiguity that characterizes backlash not only limits our understanding of the concept; it also impedes consideration of alternative explanations for the reactions that seem so common. One possibility is that the opposition to social change that is often attributed to mass backlash might actually be driven by elites, either directly through elite action or through some combination of elite action and cue giving to mobilize the masses (e.g., Weaver 2007; Dorf and Tarrow 2014; Bishin et al 2020). Among the most common explanations for political conflict are pluralist accounts of politics in which organized interests battle one another over policy (Truman 1951; Frymer 1999; Bishin and Smith 2013). While scholars describe important differences between whether majoritarian interest group pluralism or biased pluralism led by economic elites is most influential, they nonetheless share a common theme (e.g., Schattschneider 1960; Bishin and Klofstad 2012; Gilens and Page 2014). According to pluralist theory, those challenging the status quo are opposed by elites and the groups they lead rather than by the masses in a bottom-up reaction in which the public changes their opinions to oppose the policy or group.

Consistent with the notion of biased pluralism, elite behavior seems to play a central role in the conflict over gay rights (Bratton 2002; Bishin et al 2020). Numerous studies of the gay rights movement document the strong role that gay rights advocates play in strategically organizing and mobilizing supporters and in publicizing and advancing key issues (e.g., Fetner 2008; Fejes 2008; Burack 2008). Even more extensive strategic efforts characterize the rise of the Christian Right. Leaders of the Christian Right make strategic decisions about which issues (e.g., abortion) and arguments to emphasize (e.g., individual rights vs. community standards), how to implement sophisticated media-driven efforts to mobilize existing members, and how to grow their membership in pursuit of more effective political activism (Berlet 1998; Frankl 1998; Lesage 1998; Fetner 2008; A. Lewis 2017).

While the specific mechanism in the various theories may differ, pluralist theories share an important (elite-driven) contrast to the bottom-up mass-driven process seen with backlash. More specifically, the countermobilization hypothesis articulated in pluralist theories reflects a "top-down" process in which elites organize and mobilize in favor of policies they support and against those they oppose (e.g., Truman 1951). With respect to gay rights, this process is more consistent with Zein Murib's description of backlash as "resistance and opposition that is mobilized in response to increased visibility for minority groups [and] motivates the formation of interest group coalitions" (2017, 18). While facing organized opposition makes achieving policy more difficult, it does not present the same impediments as does mass opinion change. In fact, to the extent that elite opposition leads to countermobilization, it may help to "develop a shared agenda, and present a strong united front to defend against opponents" (Murib 2017, 19).

Political scientists debate the extent to which politicians should pay attention to public opinion polls. John Geer (1996) argues that the advent of polling created a new kind of politician who was able to operate without uncertainty about what the public wanted, to demonstrate responsiveness to the public's demands, and to offer proof for his or her claims of public support. However, subsequent work identifies that polls have had a decreasing influence on government politics over time, as policy-minded politicians use public opinion not as a guide about what to do but to scan for opportunities for leadership and influence (Jacobs and Shapiro 2000). The strategic elevation of issues by opportunistic politicians is a primary driver of issue evolution or of party position change, the process by which issues change in importance to voters, parties, and coalitions (Carmines and Stimson 1989; Karol 2009).

The emphasis on the ill-defined concept of backlash overlooks the fact that elites are more strategic in their choice and use of issues to achieve their goals than is widely appreciated (e.g., Haider-Markel 2001; Murphy 2005; Eshbaugh-Soha 2006; Dorf and Tarrow 2014). Developed to explain the politics of race and the development of punitive crime policy, Vesla M. Weaver's (2007) incisive theory of frontlash, for example, holds that losers in a conflict "propose new programs of action" and "manipulate the agenda in a way favorable to" their interests on other related issues (236). With frontlash, strategic and proactive "elites aim to control the agenda and resist changes through the development of a new issue" in order to overcome "defeat of [a] longstanding political discourse or elite program" (238).[4]

Irrespective of the precise mechanism by which elites act, the idea that opposition to gay rights is led by elites rather than masses seems especially likely given the dramatic rise in the prevalence of advocacy groups seeking to influence policy concomitant with the decline of voluntary membership organizations in the last few decades (Skocpol 2003). Advocacy groups funded by wealthy individuals and run by policy experts are particularly well positioned to respond to perceived challenges to the status quo. Indeed, evidence documents the rise and influence of a wealthy and well-organized donor activist network opposing gay rights (Capehart 2016). Moreover, it seems likely that in at least some cases elite-led opposition might appear similar to mass backlash to the extent that part of an elite advocacy group's strategy is to mobilize popular support in order to pressure elected officials, enhance their own perceived legitimacy, and raise money (e.g., Fetner 2008). With respect to opposition to gay rights, the idea that elites lead the masses makes sense given that the chief opponents to gay rights are part of the religious right who derive much of their power from the religious organization of white evangelical Christians (e.g., Bull and Gallagher 1996).

Toward a Theory of Elite-Led Mobilization

Our central argument is that campaigns against gay rights are led by well-organized and highly motivated elites, primarily white evangelical Christians, who view gays as amoral, oppose equality for members of the LGBT community, and reject their acceptance as legitimate participants in society (Klemp and Macedo 2011; Egan and Sherrill 2009; Fitzgerald 2017). While others, like Catholics and Mormons, also frequently work to oppose gay rights, white evangelical advocacy groups are the largest and the most unified, focused, and effective on the issue (Bull and Gallagher 1996; Fitzgerald 2017).

Efforts to limit gay rights are the product of these well-organized interests rather than an organic response by the mass public to challenges to the status quo. These elites hold both policy goals and instrumental goals. Their primary policy goal is to prevent gays and lesbians from achieving full inclusion as legitimate members of the polity. They oppose advances in gay rights as issues arise and look to find new areas in which to limit gay rights where possible. These elites also pursue instrumental goals by raising money, building public support, and cultivating relationships with politicians in order to obtain the resources needed to pursue their policy goals (Fetner 2008). Consequently, elites opposing gay rights work to enhance the visibility and legitimacy of anti-gay sentiment in order to obtain resources for their organizations, and in turn enhance their ability to achieve their policy goals.

Elite-Led Mobilization occurs when powerful and well-resourced individuals work to oppose advances in gay rights and the acceptance of gays and lesbians as legitimate members of society. A common strategy in many of these efforts is to advocate by informing, activating, and mobilizing those who already agree with them or who are inclined to do so. The strategy has become central partly because the primary tool anti-gay elites have used to obtain policy has been the referendum process, where pubic support is necessary for success. It is important to note that this is not the only strategy that elites use. As we will see, their efforts extend to writing and lobbying for legislation, encouraging candidates to support their agenda, bringing lawsuits to oppose policies with which they disagree, and recruiting and financing candidates for office who share their views, among others. Mobilizing supporters, however, helps procure resources even when votes and manpower are not immediately needed.

The most forceful opposition to gay rights has emanated from the organization of the religious right (e.g., Burack 2008; Fejes 2008; Fetner 2008).

While the modern movement known as the religious right initially developed out of a general concern about social change—especially increased societal permissiveness and laws banning school segregation—it politically crystallized in the campaign to repeal Miami-Dade's nondiscrimination ordinance in 1978 (Fejes 2008). The political organization created in Miami was nationalized and exported to cities across the country to repeal local nondiscrimination ordinances protecting gay rights and to extend opposition to gay rights to other issues, such as allowing gays and lesbians to work as teachers (Fejes 2008). Building on well-developed evangelical Christian organizations, anti-gay elites fueled an agenda that opposed gay rights and feminism, became staunchly pro-life, and helped bring religious conservatives into the Republican Party (Clendinen and Nagourney 1999; Fetner 2008; A. Lewis 2017). The white evangelical community exploited these issues in order to increase their power and leveraged their well-organized and professional institutions to mobilize supporters through their connections to churches and their media empire, which had television and radio stations reaching millions of followers (Burack 2008; Fetner 2008).

While appeals often go unseen by the broader public, opposition to gay rights is among the most effective issues for mobilizing and raising money from evangelicals (Fetner 2008; Fitzgerald 2017). Beginning in the 1990s, conservative Christians increasingly emphasized opposition to gay rights in order to tap into popular opposition on an issue that was financially lucrative (Fitzgerald 2017). Despite changes in public opinion, they still remain heavily committed to opposing gay rights today. Jonathan Capehart (2016), for instance, demonstrates that financial backing to oppose gay rights disproportionately comes from a relatively small number of wealthy anti-gay elites who donate heavily to religiously affiliated socially conservative political organizations.

The Role Elites Play

Anti-gay elites are those individuals who are sincerely or strategically opposed to the expansion of gay rights and hold positions of power or influence in the polity (e.g., Eldersveld 1989). While elites occupying different positions fulfill different roles, we generally see three levels of elites who design and implement strategies and mobilize opposition to gay rights. One tier consists of the founders, leaders, organization heads, and major contributors dedicated to opposing gay rights nationally by funding and coordinating strategy across and within states and, in some cases, countries. These include billionaire funders like Phillip Anschutz, Richard DeVos, and the Mayer Family Foundation, and people like James Dobson, the founder of Alliance Defending Freedom, the Family Research Council, and Focus on the Family, as well as people like Anita Bryant, who founded Save Our Children, and Tony Perkins, president of the Family Research Council (e.g., Bull and Gallagher 1996; Capehart 2016).[5] In many cases the positions held overlap with leaders of the religious groups, like Jerry Falwell and Pat Robertson, who, along with others, founded the Moral Majority. These leaders work to link political and religious activity. In January 2000, for instance, Gordon Hinckley, president of the Church of Jesus Christ of Latter-day Saints, ordered that a letter asking congregants to redouble their efforts to pass California Proposition 22, banning gay marriage, be read in every Mormon church (Lattin 2000).

A second tier of elites includes the heads of affiliated state and local organizations with ties to the national organization, the spokespeople for these organizations at all levels, and the political strategists and lobbyists who develop strategies and write legislation and referenda and who work to mobilize still other elites. This group includes people like David Lane, a born-again Christian who travels the country to build local political coalitions that politically organize and mobilize pastors to lead from the pulpit (Eckholm 2011).

A third group includes those who exert influence on the local level, including local religious leaders such as pastors who preach politics from the pulpit, local political candidates and their volunteers, and activist church members, all of whom work to mobilize the like-minded, to educate people about the message, to organize them politically, and to mobilize them to get their family and friends to participate. These elites can be especially powerful, as research shows that feedback that threatens self-perceptions of religious group membership can be especially effective in inducing behavior consistent with religious stereotypes (Burris and Jackson 2010). The implication here is that owing to the strength of religious identities (Ysseldyk, Matheson, and Anisman 2010), religious leaders may have disproportionate ability to motivate participation.

Coordinated campaigns by elites cultivate and mobilize those who either already oppose gay rights or those who are predisposed to do so (e.g., Bull and Gallagher 1996; Burack 2008; Fitzgerald 2017). People who feel strongly, either because they feel a sense of loss or threat or because they have strong religious identities, are more likely to be receptive to appeals to vote, to approach others to vote, and to contribute resources to support their views (e.g., Bishin 2009). Those with religious identities are especially likely to be sensitive to intergroup conflict and to react strongly in response to it (Ysseldyk, Matheson, and Anisman 2010). They are also more likely to act to bolster self-perceptions of religious group membership when that identity is threatened (Burris and Jackson 2010). Moreover, those in conservative religious organizations are more likely to share the same attitudes about gay rights. Membership in these hierarchical religious organizations makes them easier to access, inform, and mobilize. In short, appealing to those with strong feelings is a highly efficient way for these organizations to cultivate support.

In much the same way that white evangelicals came to embrace Catholic groups' opposition to abortion, there is a long history of Elite-Led Mobilization and coordination against gay rights by various religious advocacy groups (e.g., A. Lewis 2017). For example, in January 1996, elites mobilized to create the National Campaign to Protect Marriage, in which major conservative organizations worked to write, introduce, and lobby for passage of state-level Defense of Marriage laws. By the end of that year, 82 percent of states were considering such legislation (Haider-Markel 2001). Some of these advocacy organizations, like the Family Research Council, were among those that twenty-four years later would work to defeat the judges in Iowa (Paulson 2004).

Where possible, these elite campaigns both build broad coalitions across both groups and tiers and coordinate closely with candidates and parties. In June 2003 the most prominent leaders of the Christian Right met and formed what would become known as the Arlington Group to address the policy losses the Christian Right had suffered over the last few years (Fitzgerald 2017). Their central goal was to refocus the movement on the issue of gay marriage, work to pass the Federal Marriage Amendment, and attempt to place constitutional amendments banning gay marriage on the ballot in thirteen states (Fitzgerald 2017). The group, which would eventually grow to include seventy distinct religious advocacy groups, included evangelicals, Muslims, Catholics, Mormons, and African American groups who opposed gay marriage (Fitzgerald 2017). Working in close coordination with the Bush/Cheney campaign, they used gay marriage to mobilize religious conservatives, especially evangelicals, to the polls. The Bush/Cheney campaign hired prominent evangelical Ralph Reed, former executive director of the Christian Coalition, to establish credibility and to facilitate coordination with the Arlington Group and other religious activists, and held weekly strategy calls with top campaign officials, including chief political strategist Karl Rove (Fitzgerald 2017).

Strategies of Elite-Led Mobilization

Conservative religious organizations use a variety of tools to mobilize supporters. Initially the strength of the religious right was cultivated through targeted direct mail campaigns and radio and television shows that were used to publicize their message and raise money (e.g., Bull and Gallagher 1996). With time, the strategies evolved to include targeted online web advertising. Perhaps the most significant innovation, however, has been the campaign to politicize religious officials. Historically, white evangelical churches were reluctant to get involved in politics. Today anti-gay organizations work to politicize pastors and encourage them to preach on their core issues and tie them directly to contemporary politics and elections (Fitzgerald 2017). Potential supporters are identified and mobilized through petition drives, voter registration drives, the sharing of membership information across conservative Christian groups and, in some controversial cases, by obtaining church directories (Fitzgerald 2017). Lower-level elites contact and mobilize potential supporters, often at the urging of activist pastors and fellow parishioners (e.g., Schulte 2010; Eckholm 2011). Grassroots mobilizing techniques employing micro-targeting range from phone calls to targeted web advertisements during political campaigns in order to mobilize those who are sympathetic to their cause (Pettys 2011; Fitzgerald 2017).

These organizations and the elites who run them pursue their policy goals in three primary ways. First, they identify key issues and work to enact policy about those issues. They do this directly by writing and lobbying for legislation, by sponsoring or supporting policy referenda that limit gay rights, and by lobbying sympathetic federal, state, and local elected officials to work for their policy. They also pursue political objectives indirectly, as when they recommend or support political appointees or judges charged with creating, deciding, or enforcing laws. Since the late 1990s, as public opinion became increasingly supportive of gay rights, the religious right has increasingly prioritized the importance of court appointments to help neutralize the laws written by state legislatures they view as becoming increasingly hostile to their positions (Fitzgerald 2017).

Second, in order to achieve their instrumental goals, these organizations and elites seek to sway opinion, mobilize supporters, and build public opposition to gay rights. They seek opportunities to publicize their organizations and to make their positions visible and relevant (Lesage 1998). Publicizing their views signals the public that the issue is important, raises the visibility of the issue for both current supporters and potential confederates, and helps foment opposition to gay rights. Cynthia Burack (2008) shows that broad public appeals also help inform and educate existing supporters about key issues. Publicity is important because, as Fred Fejes (2008) notes, historically few Americans had been exposed to gays and lesbians, as they were only publicly out in large numbers in a handful of cities. Absent their visible presence as a threat, anti-gay positions must be cultivated and widely publicized to build support for their socially conservative mission (Frankl 1998). As a consequence, elites look for opportunities to generate positive coverage for their positions (Fetner 2008). One way they do this is by exploiting current events to achieve these instrumental goals. When a city or state considers legislation advancing gay rights, for instance, these organizations can use that policy as an opportunity to remind supporters that an immediate threat to their values exists, to fund-raise among their supporters, and to have them mobilize and reach out to the appropriate government officials.

Third, conservative religious organizations work to identify, recruit, mobilize, organize, and support allies and to dissuade and defeat opponents of their agenda. Most directly, they work to help ensure the election of like-minded officials and to defeat those who oppose them (Lesage 1998). Publicizing their views and their support for candidates not only lets potential opponents know that the issue is contentious and potentially costly but also incentivizes politicians to support them (Segal 2018). In short, publicizing their views lets people know where they stand, makes the issue appear more salient to potential confederates, and signals to political and other elites that prominent opposition exists.

Why and When Elites Mobilize

The history of the politics of gay rights suggests that anti-gay elites mobilize in two circumstances and are likely driven by some combination of political opportunism and psychological factors. Anti-gay elites mobilize reactively when they perceive a threat to the status quo by gay rights advocates working to obtain recognition, power, status, or policy. In these cases, mobilization is primarily designed to help achieve their goal of preventing the advancement of policies that benefit the LGBT community and acceptance of gays and lesbians. Alternatively, anti-gay elites also mobilize proactively, for strategic purposes, when the opportunity to publicize their positions can achieve policy goals, enhance their power, prestige, relevance, or legitimacy, or provide an opportunity to garner financial or other resources.

Reactive mobilization typically occurs in response to gay rights advocates' challenges to the status quo proscriptions on gay rights. Historically,

LGBT people experience high levels of discrimination across issues ranging from employment and survivorship rights to military service and adoption, as state and federal policies typically reflect the preferences of anti-gay elites (e.g., C. Smith 2007). Beginning in the mid-1970s, laws protecting gays and lesbians from employment discrimination were considered and passed by a small number of local governments. Before the consideration of nondiscrimination ordinances, anti-gay elites had little need to mobilize in opposition. In response to the challenges to the status quo that nondiscrimination laws represented, elites opposing gay rights began to mobilize against advances in gay rights by using the evangelical organization (Fejes 2008; Fetner 2008).[6]

What leads these elites to organize against gay rights? Keep in mind that challenges to the status quo on gay rights were rare prior to the last few decades. As a consequence, challenges that did occur may have been particularly startling to those who oppose gay rights. Research on social identification shows that people who care strongly are much more likely to notice events or changes related to issues they see as important (Tajfel and Turner 1979). And those who care strongly may be motivated to act because losses are felt more strongly than gains (Kahneman and Tversky 1973). Intergroup conflict over religious beliefs may lead to an especially strong reaction, as religious group membership provides a social group identification that is grounded in a system of beliefs often seen as sacred (Ysseldyk, Matheson, and Anisman 2010). Importantly, the sense of threat or loss or the transgression of a central group identity can motivate people on both sides of an issue such that anti-gay Elite-Led Mobilization may lead to losses that galvanize gay rights advocates to act.

Conservative Christian groups also organize and mobilize on gay rights issues proactively in order to take advantage of political opportunities to help their organizations. After a series of policy losses in the late 1990s, and faced with increasingly permissive social attitudes as well as declines in the number of religious adherents, conservative religious organizations began looking for issues that would help galvanize members and allow them to achieve policy victories (Fitzgerald 2017). The issue of gay rights appeared to be promising for achieving policy success and enhanced their groups' status given widespread public opposition to gay rights, especially to gay marriage (Fitzgerald 2017). Indeed the issue of gay rights is just one of several historical examples of the Christian Right, and white evangelicals in particular, adopting or emphasizing an issue in order to achieve strategic objectives (Fitzgerald 2017; A. Lewis 2017).

Proactive strategic decisions aren't limited to the choice of which issues to emphasize; they also extend to questions about how to best pursue policy objectives. One example of how anti-gay elites employ new strategies is seen in white evangelicals' shift to a "rights-based" approach to policy arguments. Andrew R. Lewis (2017) demonstrates that the shift from the position that religion serves as the enforcer of community morality to one in which white evangelicals promote and protect individual (religious) rights was driven by strategic considerations. White evangelicals came to accept rights-based arguments owing to their relevance in advancing their position on abortion and effectiveness in opposing other minority groups (A. Lewis 2017). This led white evangelicals to increasingly employ rights-based arguments to promote their position on other issues. On gay rights, for instance, the Christian Right initially argued that prohibitions were necessary to protect community standards, but over time they have shifted to emphasize the importance of religious liberty (A. Lewis 2017). In particular, white evangelicals came to realize that issues related to rights-based arguments, such as religious liberty and free speech, are more winnable than those based on policing community morality (e.g., sodomy) (A. Lewis 2017).

Importantly, Lewis documents how the shift in rhetorical and legal strategies to embrace rights-based arguments was driven by evangelical elites, who borrowed from Catholics' long-standing use of individual rights–based arguments against abortion. Evangelical elites' embrace of individual rights-based arguments was accelerated by their self-perceived decline in religious hegemony, as they could no longer rely on majority public opinion to countenance their views. As their relative power declined, white evangelicals increasingly emphasized a frame portraying Christians as subject to discrimination and entitled to constitutional protections of the individual's right to behave consistent with religious beliefs (A. Lewis 2017). The embrace of individual rights was further facilitated by pastors' and legal strategists' recognition of the success that rights-based arguments have had on issues of civil rights and liberties (A. Lewis 2017). Today, individual rights–based arguments are used to oppose a wide range of positions, including "seeking to reduce contraceptive coverage, fight non-discrimination provisions, and protect the role of religion in public life" (A. Lewis 2017, 4).

Another important strategy employed by anti-gay elites is the policy of preemption, in which laws designed to limit the ability of local governments to protect gay rights are passed at the state level. Preemption laws limit local regulation on issues that include fracking, sanctuary cities, and the minimum wage. Preemption has been used perhaps most successfully—laws have passed in more than forty states—by the National Rifle Association, which has worked since the 1990s to prevent local governments from imposing various aspects of gun control (Riverstone-Newell 2017). On gay rights issues, three states currently use preemption to prevent local governments from passing laws addressing antidiscrimination ordinances, bathroom bills, and bans on conversion therapy. Moreover, as of this writing, state legislation banning bathroom bills is pending in at least twenty more states (Movement Advancement Project 2018). These preemption laws are typically passed in conservative state legislatures and are coordinated by elites, often led by state branches of national anti-gay organizations, such as the Family Action Council of Tennessee, as well as national organizations, such as the American Family Action Association and the Southern Baptist Ethics and Religious Liberty Convention (Reiner 2016; Wang, Geffen, and Cahill 2016).

These strategies are examples of how anti-gay groups tailor their strategy to the various institutions available in each state. Social conservatives work to overcome court rulings or state legislative action by using other venues to oppose gay rights (e.g., Hume 2013). The ability to effectively do so, however, depends in large part on the institutions that exist in a state and their ideological orientation (Bull and Gallagher 1996). In California, for instance, gay rights opponents typically exploit the referendum process—a process not available in every state—in response to losses in the courts and opposition in the legislature. In other states, conservative control of state legislatures fosters legislative action, as occurred in Ohio, which banned gay marriage in 2004 (Fitzgerald 2017).

Today restrictions on gay rights are widely contested. Anti-gay elites and their organizations constantly look for opportunities to make policy advances across issues, either by promulgating new policy (e.g., anti-trans bathroom laws) or opposing attempts by pro–gay rights groups to advance policy (e.g., gay marriage). While Elite-Led Mobilization Theory differs from and elaborates on existing theories of elite behavior like frontlash, which suggests that opponents embrace their losing positions in order to gain credibility on other issues (Weaver 2007), it is also consistent with aspects of other theories in which elites seek to expand the scope of issues on which they pursue their policy goals (e.g., Weaver 2007; Dorf and Tarrow 2014). The decision to emphasize opposition to gay marriage, to shift to a strategy of making rights-based arguments, and to employ preemption are important examples of how anti-gay elites employ new strategies to achieve policy success. In doing so, they also look for opportunities to gain visibility, popular support, and enhance perceptions of their relevance and legitimacy.

Implications

Mass Opinion Backlash and Elite-Led Mobilization Theory explain opposition toward gay rights in very different ways. While a handful of studies examine the extent to which favorable court rulings have ignited opinion backlash against gays and lesbians, the theory of Mass Opinion Backlash has yet to be evaluated in a rigorous and systematic manner. Importantly, existing research has not considered the extent to which the reactions attributed to mass backlash are better explained as a product of Elite-Led Mobilization. Evaluating these two theories is the task to which the remainder of the book turns. Doing so requires identifying key implications of the theories. By identifying empirical claims that must be true if the theories are correct, we can then locate cases appropriate for testing these theories.

Mass Opinion Backlash holds that challenges to the status quo on gay rights elicit a sense of loss or threat that trigger a shift in attitudes against the policy or group. Specifically, challenges to the status quo on gay rights create large, negative, and enduring opposition to gay rights among the broader public. Importantly, the status quo being challenged is one in which gays and lesbians are traditionally hidden from view and in which policy that discriminates against gays and lesbians is the norm. Consequently, challenges to the status quo sufficient to trigger a sense of loss or threat are likely to be those that increase the visibility of gays and lesbians or that propose policy changes that benefit them. Opposition to gay rights typically takes the form of opinion change but may also be reflected by an increased propensity to engage in political activity by those who previously opposed the policy, those who are indifferent, or among the apathetic.[7] Crucially, the theory is a reactive one in which backlash is incited by the actions of gays and lesbians as the expression of threat or loss among the masses.

Three implications follow from Mass Opinion Backlash. If reactions are incited by backlash, then we should see each of the following: First, large, negative, and enduring shifts in opinion should follow attempts by gay rights advocates to advance policy or in response to increased visibility of gays and lesbians who threaten the status quo. Second, opinion change should occur broadly, not just among those who either previously held supportive views or who lacked meaningful preferences. Third, as a mass-driven rather than elite-driven theory, following salient challenges to the status quo, public reaction opposing pro-gay policies or decreased acceptance of gays and lesbians should precede elite action. That is, challenges to the status quo should reduce support for the policy or group among the masses before elites mobilize to oppose it.

Elite-Led Mobilization Theory, in contrast, holds that prominent events or organized campaigns to oppose gay rights are driven not by mass reactions stemming from gays' and lesbians' challenge to the status quo but by anti-gay elites who oppose the acceptance of LGBT people as legitimate members of society. They use issues of gay rights to advance their moral and

political agenda and enhance the reputations and influence of their organizations and movements. Opposition to gay rights is the product of calculated political decisions about how, when, and where to act in order to
prevent increased acceptance of gay rights. Specifically, opposition to gay
rights occurs not only reactively, to frustrate attempts by gays and lesbians
to make policy advances, but also proactively, even when challenges to the
status quo do not occur, if other opportunities to advance their political or
moral agenda arise. Here, elites act any time that doing so may help advance
their policy goals, enhance their reputations, or help them obtain resources,
whether those are donations, increased visibility, or enhanced legitimacy.
In some places anti-gay elites pursue policy through the courts, in others
through national or state legislatures, or in still others through referenda,
depending on which political environment is most likely to be most accom-
modating. Irrespective of the venue, anti-gay elites often seek to mobilize the
like-minded and those predisposed to agree with them. Mobilization should
be especially strong among religious conservatives, as anti-gay elites have
close ties to these organizations, in some cases serving as their leaders.

Three key implications follow from Elite-Led Mobilization Theory:
First, political opposition to gay rights is led by elites who organize and
mobilize opposition to gay rights. Second, elites organize and mobilize
to oppose gay rights both reactively, in response to challenges by pro–
gay rights groups, and proactively, even in the absence of gay and lesbian
rights groups challenging the status quo to advance their goals. Third,
anti-gay elites focus on mobilizing the like-minded, particularly religious
conservatives.

What sorts of contexts are most fertile for evaluating these theories?
As each of the theories make claims about different actors (i.e., elites and
masses), with different motivations (e.g., emotional vs. strategic), who may
act at different times (proactively and reactively), the ideal contexts for
evaluating them vary. In chapters 3, 4 and 5, we evaluate the central claim
of MOB by examining how individuals respond to salient challenges to the
status quo. Specifically, we conduct online experiments to create threats,
and we administer surveys to capture natural challenges to the status quo
in order to examine the effect of a policy threat under which backlash is
expected to occur. Then we look to validate these results by gathering
large sample surveys of opinion and examine the extent to which opinions
shifted following salient events in the gay rights movement.

The history of the gay rights movement provides a context for assessing the extent to which the competing theories comport with the signal
historical events in chapter 6. In order to evaluate the extent to which the

theories explain opposition to gay rights over time, we also examine major controversies about gay rights after World War II through contemporary controversies. This provides historical leverage to assess the extent to which the theories help explain the struggle for gay rights during a period when we might expect to observe little elite behavior, given that gays and lesbians were largely hidden and social policy uniformly discriminated against them. Specifically, we examine whether challenges to the status quo on questions of gay rights led to negative opinion changes and whether and under what circumstances elites sought to mobilize against the gay rights movement. While elite behavior is often more difficult to document because it often occurs in private, some actions elites take are quite visible. Specifically, Elite-Led Mobilization implies that we should see little mobilization against gay rights until after gay rights advocates show some ability to actually obtain rights and thereby make their movement a threat to those defending the status quo. In contrast, according to Mass Opinion Backlash, we should expect challenges to the (repressive) status quo to be met by increased hostility toward gay rights among the mass public.

Our final test seeks to evaluate a key distinction between the theories in the contemporary era—whether political events opposing gay rights are led by elites or masses, and whether elites effectively mobilize the like-minded, or whether these events are characterized by widespread opposition to gay rights. The study of campaigns and elections in which gay rights issues are central to the campaign allows for this assessment. Specifically, in chapter 7 we employ an original data set of campaign contributions in judicial retention elections to compare states where there were no reports of anti-gay backlash with states where backlash was said to occur (Iowa). Iowa is a difficult case for Elite-Led Mobilization Theory as it is widely considered a classic case of opinion backlash in which an angry public punished the justices who contravened their will. Moreover, we also examine voting data from the 2009 Iowa judicial retention election in order to compare the theories' expectations against one another. Specifically, we examine whether the mobilization against the judges was a broad-based phenomenon, as Mass Opinion Backlash predicts, or whether it was largely limited to the like-minded opponents of gay rights, as Elite-Led Mobilization Theory predicts.

THREE

In Search of Backlash

The Experiments

The folk story about the "backlash" to same-sex marriage is perhaps best illustrated by popular narratives surrounding the referendum on California's Proposition 8. Indeed, the complete history of Proposition 8 includes not one but two alleged instances of mass-level backlash. The first occurred in 2000, with the passage of Proposition 22. Proposition 22, part of the national movement to pass state "defense of marriage acts," was an extension of the movement to limit marriage to opposite-sex couples, which began with passage of Hawaii's Amendment 2 (1998). While heralded as a backlash against efforts to redefine "traditional marriage," the movements to restrict marriage in Hawaii and California are in fact examples of the phenomenon we have labeled "elite-led mobilization" in the preceding chapters.

Proposition 22 was overturned by the California Supreme Court in 2008. In response, anti-gay elites activated and were able to place a proposition on the ballot that provided for a constitutional amendment prohibiting same-sex marriage. This effort to constitutionally prohibit same-sex marriage would be more difficult to challenge in courts or to reverse legislatively. This effort, known as Proposition 8, was again held up as an example of organic, mass-driven backlash, but it was actually a coordinated effort among religious leaders and other anti-gay elites. The challenges faced by gays and lesbians when they attempt to ensure or expand their rights in the face of majority opposition have routinely been labeled "backlash," despite nearly always being spearheaded by elites.

The struggle for gay and lesbian rights beginning in the 1950s raises an important question: How can we determine whether the reactions that follow challenges to the status quo on gay rights are more consistent with backlash or some other explanation, such as elite-led mobilization? We begin to answer this question by assessing the extent to which backlash occurs under conditions typically seen in contemporary politics. Specifically, we conducted experiments that allow us to test the central tenet of Mass Opinion Backlash—that in the absence of opinion leadership by elites, salient threats to the status quo cause individuals to change their opinions and lash back against minority groups seeking to expand their rights.

Experiments are an especially powerful tool because they allow us to examine behavior under conditions thought to be most conducive to backlash. Specifically, by randomly exposing some citizens to news about the expansion of gay rights while withholding that news from others, we can be sure that learning of challenges to the status quo on gay rights—and not some other factor like partisanship, ideology, religiosity, socioeconomic status, other predispositions, or varying exposure to elite appeals—provokes backlash. Employing experimental analysis allows us to control which factors people are exposed to and thereby allows us to be certain that the conditions necessary for Mass Opinion Backlash are met. Moreover, the absence of opinion change under such conditions raises significant questions about the theory of Mass Opinion Backlash.

One benefit of testing for backlash using an experiment stems from the fact that most Americans are not close followers of politics and current events. Because so many Americans may never receive information about gay rights, studies of anti-gay backlash may be prone to underestimate opinion change by those who miss the news or message. Employing experiments allows us to simulate an environment in which Americans both receive and understand or accept information about an expansion of rights. More specifically, by exposing people to news about gays and lesbians, we can reliably estimate the effect of exposure, even among those who might not typically notice events expected to stimulate backlash. Additionally, we can refine our analysis to focus only on those who can correctly recall the information to which we expose them, allowing us to reliably estimate the effect of receiving information about gays rights.

Triggering Backlash

Recall from the introduction that we define "backlash" as a sharp, negative, organic, and enduring change in opinion about gays and lesbians and their policy preferences by members of the public in response to challenges to the status quo. We refer to this process of opinion change as the theory of Mass Opinion Backlash. Mass Opinion Backlash, or MOB, occurs following either an actual change in policy (such as the passage of a bill or after a court decision) or threat to the status quo that upsets one's worldview, power relations, or sense of propriety (i.e., a symbolic shift in what behavior is considered acceptable). To study and elicit backlash, we presented respondents with contrived newspaper articles designed to stimulate various types of challenges to the status quo. We differentiate between different types of threat by changing the content of the stories. Specifically, a story announcing the passage of same-sex marriage in Oregon provides a direct policy threat that is consistent with academic and journalistic accounts of backlash. In order to test for the possibility that backlash against LGBTs can manifest simply by making their presence better known (and to measure whether opposition to same-sex marriage is based on opposition to the policy itself or animus toward LGBT Americans), we employ an article about an LGBT pride parade in Oregon that should elicit symbolic and non-policy threats. An article about the passage of a gun control measure is our control condition.[1]

Recall that backlash can take the form of a negative shift in opinion toward a particular policy or minority group, or it can take the form of increased importance or intensity one places on an issue. Since each of these represents a negative, sharp, and enduring opinion change following some challenge to the status quo and existing power arrangements, we consider evidence of any of them as evidence of backlash.

Who lashes back? While the central argument underpinning MOB is that backlash occurs among the general public, some argue that it occurs among specific subgroups that are disproportionately sensitive to the group or issue. It is worth noting that backlash among these groups seems disproportionately likely to be reflected by increased intensity about the issue, if only because members of these groups tend to already hold strongly negative opinions prior to any events occurring. After all, if one already opposes, for example, gay marriage, it is not possible to become more negative in policy terms. Provided that person does not already see the issue as being of the highest possible importance, however, there may be room to move on the intensity scale.

To summarize, MOB predicts that respondents, both from the general public and from groups with a proclivity to lash back, will display a sharp, negative, and enduring change in opinion toward same-sex marriage and toward gays and lesbians as a group after hearing about its passage or the threat of its passage. Additionally, respondents will be more likely to indicate that same-sex marriage is important to them after exposure to information about it.

While journalistic and scholastic accounts of MOB are common, there are good reasons to question its occurrence (e.g., McGuire 1968; Zaller 1992). Foundational studies in public opinion indicate that opinion change should be rare. Specifically, research suggests that those who have firm opinions are unlikely to change them, as the considerations on which their opinions are based tend to be populated by those that reinforce one's existing attitudes, while those who hold weak opinions are unlikely to notice or accept new information that might lead to the creation of or change in opinions in a direction that penalizes the group (e.g., Zaller 1992). The central implication of this literature is that instead of widespread opinion backlash, shifts in opinion or intensity should be most likely to occur among individuals who lack well-formed opinions on an issue. These individuals could be political independents, perhaps because they lack a strong partisan cue to inform their opinions, or the politically unsophisticated—those who do not pay much attention to politics or have very low levels of political knowledge. Moderates and the unsophisticated are less likely to consume political news, take cues from political elites on the issue, or retain information about politics than Americans with stronger ideological or partisan convictions (Zaller 1992).

Measuring Mass Opinion Backlash

In order to examine mass opinion backlash, we employ three measures of opinion. We begin by assessing policy opinion. Among the most controversial of policies related to gay rights is gay marriage. The most straightforward way of measuring favorability toward same-sex marriage is to ask about the policy directly. We ask respondents to report their support for gay marriage on a four-point scale, ranging from strongly support (4) to strongly oppose (1).[2] We refer to this measure as "policy support" or "favorability toward gay marriage."

To account for the possibility that opinion backlash manifests as a change in the intensity or importance of the issue, we ask respondents to indicate how important they feel gay marriage is on a scale from 0, indicating they don't care at all, to 10, indicating that gay marriage is the most important issue to them. We refer to this measure as "issue importance" or the "importance of gay marriage opinion." It is also possible that opinion backlash may spill over into non-policy areas and affect attitudes about gays and lesbians themselves. To account for this, we use a feeling thermometer, a scale that asks respondents to rate gays and lesbians on a scale from 0 (completely cool or negative) to 100 (completely warm or positive).[3] We generally refer to this measure as "attitudes toward gays and lesbians."

Mass opinion backlash should manifest through a sharp decline in favorability toward gay marriage or in the feelings one holds toward gays and lesbians after hearing news that same-sex marriage rights have expanded. Similarly, respondents experiencing a backlash against gay marriage will view the issue of same-sex marriage as more important (or have more intense attitudes about gay marriage) after learning that same-sex marriage rights have expanded. A sharp decline in warmth toward gays and lesbians after being informed that same-sex marriage rights have expanded indicates backlash against gays and lesbians as a group.

Opinion backlash may manifest in any combination of these three ways. By including robust and varied measures of policy support for same-sex marriage, issue intensity of same-sex marriage, and attitudes toward gays and lesbians as a group, our study is sufficiently open and flexible to detect opinion backlash in any form.

What Causes Backlash?

Mass Opinion Backlash occurs in response to actual, threatened, or perceived changes to the status quo but also regarding the expansion of any rights. Although extending new rights and legal protections to gays and lesbians imposes imperceptible tangible burdens on citizens, their psychological effects may be substantial, as they alter the balance of power on a highly symbolic issue and signal a change from what could be considered "traditional" values or long-standing social institutions. Consequently, there are several potential causes of backlash, including psychological factors, religious beliefs, and preferences for preserving the status quo. Each of these factors provides different implications for which groups are most likely to lash back.

Most accounts presume that backlash is a widespread phenomenon; previous studies of backlash and references to backlash in the media indicate that we should expect to see backlash among the general public (D'Emilio 2006; Egan et al. 2008; DeVogue 2013). It is not clear, however, whether one citizen's reasons for reacting to the expansion of gay rights are the same as another's. Consequently, in some cases backlash may be more concentrated among particular social groups who are especially prone to react or are especially sensitive to one or more causes.

Backlash could be the result of a psychological threat that manifests as outgroup antipathy toward gays and lesbians or opposition to same-sex marriage. We take a general approach to operationalizing psychological threat by employing Integrated Threat Theory (ITT), which encompasses four prominent and interrelated explanations for psychological threat (Riek, Mania, and Gaertner 2006; Stephan and Stephan 2000). Real Group Conflict Theory attributes negative attitudes between groups to intergroup competition over resources (Sherif et al. 1961). These resources could be material, such as money, jobs, or connections, but they could also include political influence, such as the ability to shape policy or wield power over institutions. With respect to same-sex marriage, the majority of realistic group threat is of this influential form. Some individuals may be particularly threatened by the ascendency of LGBT Americans to public office, their inclusion in the institution of marriage, their increased visibility as a political subconstituency, and their ability to make policy gains.

Another dimension of Integrated Threat is the notion that some outgroup members violate important norms and do not share the in-group's beliefs and values. This dimension, referred to as Symbolic Threat (Kinder and Sears 1981), is prominent in the literature on racial antipathy but could also apply to attitudes about gays and lesbians. Symbolic threat holds that out-group members need not present a physical or material threat to the dominant group in order to be perceived negatively; out-group members need only possess different values and present themselves as a moral threat to the dominant group. Americans who see gays and lesbians as morally lacking or contrary to their values will demonstrate higher levels of symbolic threat.

Fear of contact with out-groups and a particular anxiety about how to behave in interactions with out-group members is another source of integrated psychological threat. Intergroup Anxiety Theory claims that this anxiety results in a strong desire to avoid contact with out-group members and contributes to hostility and prejudice against them (Plant and Devine 2003).[4] Individuals who harbor this sort of anxiety are psychologically threatened by increased visibility of LGBT Americans and news that gay rights have expanded.

Finally, Stereotype Threat holds that some individuals develop negative expectations and attitudes about out-group members (Stephan and Stephan 1996). Individuals who subscribe to negative and stereotypic beliefs about gays and lesbians believe that they are amoral, promiscuous, decadent, or even sexual predators, and display negative attitudes about gays and lesbians because of stereotype-based perceptions of threat. Individuals who ascribe positive stereotypes to gays and lesbians believe that they are creative, honest, or hardworking, and display more positive attitudes toward them. We expect that these attitudes and expectations will influence not only attitudes toward gays and lesbians as a group but policy support for same-sex marriage as well.

On their own, any of these sources of psychological threat might cause backlash. Because threat along one dimension predicts threat along the other dimensions, Integrated Threat Theory is an appropriate way to examine a major psychological cause of backlash. An individual who believes that gays and lesbians do not share the same values as heterosexuals, for example, is also more likely to believe negative stereotypes about gays and lesbians. Because these beliefs work together to create prejudice against gays and lesbians, we include measures of all four ITT dimensions by combining them into a single dimension using factor analysis.[5] Individuals who score particularly high on our measure of integrated threat should be more likely to lash back than individuals who score low on this measure.

The causes of backlash are not confined to one's perception of threat and may also follow from one's social perspective. One example of such a perspective is authoritarianism, in which a desire for stability, order, uniformity, and sameness produces prejudice against individuals who are perceived as violating that order (Stenner 2005). By pressing for rights, authoritarians view gays and lesbians as violating the societal order, making the authoritarians more prone to lash back.

Individuals with an overall preference for hierarchy in society will similarly be more likely to lash back. Social Dominance Orientation (SDO), the perception of and desire to make one's in-group superior to other groups, could cause backlash when a group perceived as subordinate presses for equal rights (Pratto et al. 1994; Hetherington and Weiler 2009). While neither authoritarianism nor SDO are explicitly connected to gay rights, individuals who exhibit high levels of one or both traits are likely to be more prone to lash back. In sum, one's views about the social position of groups are another potential psychological cause of backlash, alongside threat.

Opposition to same-sex marriage and antipathy toward gays and lesbians can also be the result of religious beliefs that emphasize "traditional" values and expressly forbid same-sex marriage. While some mainline Protestant denominations are fairly welcoming to gays and lesbians and may recognize or even perform same-sex marriage, evangelical congregations remain in steadfast opposition to same-sex marriage and most expansions of gay rights (Burack 2008; Fejes 2008). White evangelical Christians or individuals who identify as "born-again" Christians are significantly more likely than other Americans to oppose same-sex marriage (Barclay and Flores 2014). Therefore, one potential cause of backlash could be religious beliefs, which tend to be acquired early in life and remain fairly stable over time. We expect white evangelicals to be especially prone to backlash.

In contrast to MOB, research on public opinion suggests that attitude change should be rare. The process by which opinion changes, the *Receive, Accept, Sample* model suggests that people must first be exposed to and receive new considerations about an issue, psychologically accept these new considerations (i.e., not reject them outright because they run counter to their predispositions), and then sample from the considerations at the top of their heads (Zaller 1992). Those who care deeply about an issue, perhaps because they fall into one of the groups described in the preceding sections, may receive information that contradicts their views, but are less likely to accept it, but the considerations from which they sample tend to reinforce their existing views.

In contrast, those who pay little attention to politics tend to know very little about current events and issues, including how they feel about these issues. In particular, they are unlikely to notice (receive) or accept the information needed to form or change their opinions on an issue. When they do receive and accept the information, however, the lack of strongly held considerations should make them more open to changing their opinion. As politically unsophisticated individuals tend to have weak or inchoate attitudes about politics, they are therefore more likely to be moved or persuaded by new information, particularly because that information has few other considerations with which to compete. This is especially likely in our experimental test of backlash, because we are forcing individuals to receive and accept information about the expansion of same-sex marriage, something they may otherwise be able to miss or avoid if they spend little time thinking about or following politics.

Another group of weak attitude holders can be identified through partisanship. Few stronger influences exist on our attitudes and beliefs than our partisan identities. For many Americans, partisan (or ideological) attachments dictate how they feel about a multitude of issues, including new issues or issues to which they haven't given much thought (Mason 2018). Signals from trusted elites provide clear partisan cues that shape and inform political attitudes (Zaller 1992). Historically, the Democratic Party and its members have been more in favor of gay rights than the Republican Party and its members, which remains the case in contemporary politics. However, some

Americans lack a strong partisan identity and therefore are less receptive of cues given by party elites. These political independents may have poorly constrained ideologies or lack especially strong beliefs about politics (but see Petrocik 1974 or Keith et al. 1992). As a result, we expect the negative opinion change that is characteristic of backlash to be more likely among political independents as a consequence of their weak prior beliefs.

In sum, identifying sources of opinion reaction allows us to identify individuals who should be especially prone to backlash. While the literature on backlash suggests it is a general phenomenon, identifying individuals and groups most likely to change opinions and lash back allows us to conduct the most comprehensive tests possible for backlash. Failing to find backlash among even those most likely to display it raises serious questions about the existence of MOB.

Stimulating Backlash: Data and Methods

We begin to assess Mass Opinion Backlash on same-sex marriage by conducting an original online survey experiment. Employing experimental methods to study MOB allows us to examine whether policy change causes backlash. Importantly, using experiments allows us to overcome a central challenge that hinders other methods of evaluating the theory. In the real world we are typically unable to evoke or observe the threat to the status quo necessary to elicit the sharply negative change in opinion that is characteristic of backlash. Moreover, since research holds that opinion formation and change are fostered by receipt and acceptance of information, only by forcibly exposing people to a threatened change in the status quo can we be sure the conditions preceding opinion change are met.

To estimate the effects of a change to the status quo on gay rights, we randomly assign some individuals to read a news story about an expansion of gay rights, and some individuals to a control condition where they read a news story that does not pertain to gay rights. The stories are designed to elicit a strong reaction while reflecting changes in policy similar to those actually observed in contemporary American politics. Opinion and intensity differences between those who read the gay rights stories and those who do not can be viewed as causal effects of a perceived or threatened change to the status quo. Differences that are sharply negative are evidence of backlash. Note that this round of the experiments was conducted before the U.S. Supreme Court weighed in on marriage equality.

We randomly assign individuals in our sample to one of five experimental conditions—three policy-relevant conditions that discuss the expansion of same-sex marriage, a non-policy condition that discusses a gay pride parade, and a control condition that discusses gun control and makes no mention of gays and lesbians or same-sex marriage. In order to detect backlash, we compare respondents in each of the four conditions that pertain to gays and lesbians with respondents in the control group.

Three conditions (conditions 1–3) contain information that is both policy-relevant and pertains to same-sex marriage. In each condition, which takes the form of a short, contrived news article meant to resemble a real excerpt from a newspaper, respondents read about an expansion of same-sex marriage in the state of Oregon. In all three conditions, same-sex marriage passes by a two-thirds majority. The purpose of conditions 1–3 is to elicit backlash. If respondents in conditions 1–3 are significantly more opposed to gay marriage or hostile to gays and lesbians than respondents in the control condition, then we can conclude that we have found evidence in favor of MOB.

The articles in conditions 1–3 are identical but for one key detail: we vary the institution that approves the expansion of same-sex marriage in Oregon. Condition 1 identifies the state legislature as the institution responsible for overturning a previous ban on same-sex marriage. Condition 2 reports that the state supreme court expanded same-sex marriage to Oregon by overturning the ban. This condition is similar to the circumstances under which same-sex marriage became law in Iowa, beginning the process of judicial recall that many have labeled backlash. Condition 3 reports that Oregon voters expanded same-sex marriage directly through a referendum. Varying the institution responsible ensures that our results are not an artifact of dislike of a particular institution and allows us to test for the possibility that backlash is more intense following an expansion of minority rights through a counter-majoritarian institution such as the courts, a question we take up in chapter 5.

The news article used in condition 4 describes a gay pride parade in Salem, Oregon, which concerns gays and lesbians but does not include any mention of same-sex marriage. Gay pride parades are regular events in many cities and often include political themes, but condition 4 includes no mention of any political institutions. Including this condition in our study provides us with a richer understanding of the dynamics of backlash—that is, it allows us to control for general antipathy toward gays and lesbians that has nothing to do with changes or threatened changes to the status quo. Consequently, any differences we observe between respondents in condition 4 and respondents in our control condition are due to this group threat and not policy change, since condition 4 is not policy-relevant. By comparing the policy-relevant conditions (1–3) to condition 4, we can test for backlash following expansions of gay rights, as opposed to backlash to the mere mention of gays and lesbians openly celebrating their identities.

Finally, our control condition (condition 5) once more takes the form of an excerpt from a news article but describes the Oregon Supreme Court overturning a policy that permitted the carrying of concealed weapons on college campuses in the state. While this vignette does include policy-relevant details, it does not concern same-sex marriage or gay rights in any way. Our logic in using gun control for the baseline condition is that it is entirely unrelated to gay rights and does not activate any of the considerations or theorized causes of backlash that we identified earlier in this chapter. Also, we are careful to include a policy change that moves the status quo in a more liberal condition in order to make this control condition comparable to our policy-relevant conditions.[6] For convenience, we summarize the experimental conditions in table 3.1. The experimental vignettes themselves appear in an appendix to this chapter.

By comparing conditions 1–4 to the baseline condition, we can recover the causal effects of the expansion of gay rights (or the threatened expansion of gay rights) on attitudes about gays and lesbians and support for same-sex marriage. If these effects are negative and large, then we have found evidence in favor of opinion backlash.

Our experiment relies on stylized but highly realistic newspaper excerpts in order to accurately and convincingly portray an expansion of same-sex marriage rights in Oregon. (Participants were given a full debriefing at the end of the experiment and were told that any news stories they read were fictional.) We chose to use Oregon because at the time of our experiment, same-sex marriage, while expanding state by state, had not yet reached Ore-

TABLE 3.1. Summary of experimental conditions

Condition	LGBT Content	Policy–Related	Institution	Article Headline
1	Yes	Yes	Legislature	"Legislature Overturns Gay Marriage Ban"
2	Yes	Yes	Courts	"Court Overturns Gay Marriage Ban"
3	Yes	Yes	Referendum	"Referendum Overturns Gay Marriage Ban"
4	Yes	No	n/a	"Thousands Attend Gay Pride Parade"
5	No	Yes	Courts	"Court Overturns Concealed Carry Policy"

gon. So an article describing the expansion of same-sex marriage in Oregon was plausible. In addition, Oregon is a fairly progressive state, and it is conceivable that the Oregon Supreme Court, the Oregon state legislature, or the citizens of Oregon could vote to expand same-sex marriage, which would not be the case for more conservative states. Finally, Oregon has a relatively small population, and we wanted to avoid the problem of having a high proportion of respondents from the state we used for our contrived news articles, for fear that someone familiar with state politics would realize that they were reading a contrived article. Because of its policy status quo at the time of the experiment, its political climate, and its population size, Oregon is an ideal setting for our key experimental test of backlash.

We began administering the survey on June 7, 2013, and stopped the survey on June 17, 2013. We intentionally chose this time frame in the hopes that the U.S. Supreme Court would release one or more opinions about gay rights shortly after the conclusion of our survey. Thankfully, the Supreme Court was kind enough to wait until our survey was out of the field to release its opinions in the cases of *Perry v. Schwarzenegger* and *United States v. Windsor* (both cases 2013). This allowed us to conduct a "natural experiment" in which we interview a new sample but withhold any experimental treatment from the subjects (subjects were all assigned to the control condition) until after the release of the opinions, which received significant media coverage. By comparing subjects in the control condition who were interviewed just before the release of the opinions, and subjects in the control condition who were interviewed just after the release of the opinions, we are able to test for backlash in the "real world" following a major extension of gay rights.

We use Amazon Mechanical Turk (AMT) to recruit subjects for our experimental study of opinion backlash. AMT is an online marketplace for small tasks that require human input. In recent years it has become a valuable tool for social inference as it is a cost-effective and flexible platform for recruiting survey respondents. Using AMT to recruit subjects allows us to put together a fairly representative sample from across the United States cheaply. The sample is not perfectly representative—AMT samples tend to be younger and more liberal than nationally representative samples—as we are interested in average treatment effects rather than accurate forecasts of the national electorate, these samples are appropriate. Studies examining the validity of AMT surveys consistently show it is appropriate for such research (Berinsky, Huber, and Lenz 2012). AMT served only as a subject recruitment platform; our respondents filled out their online surveys using an industry standard survey platform. Using AMT proved to be a huge advantage, as it enabled us to readminister our survey the next day after the *Perry v. Schwarzenegger* and *United States v. Windsor* opinions were released without having to coordinate with a survey research firm. This also allowed us to prevent individuals from taking our survey twice, before and after the release of the opinions.

Through AMT we recruited 2,402 participants to complete our short survey, which they were told was about current issues. Respondents received seventy-five cents for completing the survey, which took only a few minutes. Our use of AMT allowed us to complete this project much more cheaply than the costs of recruiting a nationally representative sample through a polling company; it also afforded us the flexibility to readminister our survey a day after the historic Supreme Court decisions. In addition to our main analyses, we reanalyzed all of our experimental data using weights to estimate a nationally representative sample, and the results are unchanged.

We begin by ensuring that our experimental design and survey instruments are valid by conducting a randomization check, which ensures that the characteristics of our sample are balanced or similar across conditions. The results of this check are presented in table 3.2 and show that the demographic, religious, and political characteristics of our sample are comparably represented in each experimental condition. We can be confident that any differences in opinions that we measure can be attributed to the treatment vignettes that respondents in each group read, not because different kinds of respondents fell into each experimental condition.

Assessing Antipathy: Identifying Those Most Likely to Lash Back

Backlash occurs among those threatened by change to the status quo. Recall that in order to provide the most comprehensive assessment possible, we not only consider backlash among the general public, but we also identify the individuals in the groups most likely to lash back.

TABLE 3.2. Randomization check

Variable	Court	Legislature	Gun Control	Parade	Referendum
Female	51%	50%	52%	54%	54%
Evangelical	12	10	12	14	10
Republican	17	16	15	15	15
Conservative	24	21	23	24	21
African American	7	7	7	8	6
Hispanic/Latino	5	4	6	4	6
College degree or higher	46	47	45	43	43

Research on *religious affiliation* shows that white evangelical Protestants—the "born again"—are perhaps the staunchest political opponents of gay rights (Lugg 1998; Fejes 2008). In our survey, respondents who identify both as white and evangelical or "born again" are coded as white evangelicals. This group comprises about 12 percent of our overall sample and self-reports high frequency of church attendance and prayer.

Individuals with weak party attachments or with little political knowledge are also potentially prone to backlash. We identify the weakly attached by asking a standard party-identification question and noting which respondents identify as independents—about 28 percent of respondents. To measure *political sophistication*, we use a five-question battery of political knowledge items and create a scale that ranges from 0 to 5, with one point for each correct answer. The questions are included in the appendix to this chapter. Roughly one-quarter of our sample correctly answered three or more questions correctly, so we use this as the cutoff for political sophistication. Respondents who answered fewer than three knowledge questions correctly are coded as "unsophisticated."[7]

To measure Social Dominance Orientation, another potential source of backlash, we use a six-item battery of questions that is standard in the social psychology literature, included in the appendix to this chapter (Sidanius and Pratto 1999). We define high-SDO individuals as respondents scoring in the top third of our social dominance orientation scale. This results in roughly 18 percent of respondents coded as "high-SDO."

Finally, we identify individuals who have high scores on our Integrated Threat Theory (ITT). We use multiple survey items to measure realistic group conflict, symbolic threat, intergroup anxiety, and stereotype threat and combine these items into a single scale using factor analysis. The threat items combine to form a single scale that captures integrated threat quite nicely.[8] Once more, we take the top third of the scale as our cutoff for high ITT. Examining each of the four types of threat that comprise integrated threat separately does not substantively change any of the results in this chapter.

Validating the Measures

We begin our analysis by validating the measures to ensure they comport with our expectations and previous research. Specifically, we examine members of groups who: exhibit high levels of social dominance (SDO), or exhibit high sensitivity to intergroup threat (ITT), are politically unsophisticated, independents, Evangelicals, and the general public. Specifically,

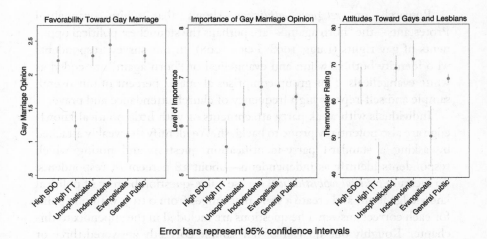

Figure 3.1. Attitudes toward gay marriage, opinion intensity by group, and thermometer ratings

figure 3.1 shows the mean score on each of our three measures (indicated by a dot) for each group, where the lines above and below each dot are the 95 percent confidence interval around this estimate.

The results displayed in figure 3.1 are consistent with our expectations. The groups we have identified as most susceptible to backlash are also most opposed to same-sex marriage. White evangelicals and high-ITT respondents are significantly more opposed to same-sex marriage than the other groups, particularly independents and the general public. Evangelicals rate the issue of same-sex marriage as more important than any of our other key groups rate it. Additionally, evangelicals, high-ITT respondents, and high-SDO respondents report feeling much less warmly toward gays and lesbians than do other groups.

One possible concern is that our results might understate the amount of backlash if white evangelicals in our sample are more progressive than those in the public at large. We investigated thermometer ratings of gays and lesbians from a recent national sample, the 2008 American National Election Study. The average thermometer score among white evangelicals in 2008 was 46.5 versus 50.4 in our sample in 2013. Given the dramatic increases in warmth toward gays and lesbians across society over this period, these similar results suggest that our sample does not likely overstate warmth toward gays and lesbians during the time it was fielded. Having determined our survey measures are valid, we can now use them to test for public opinion backlash.

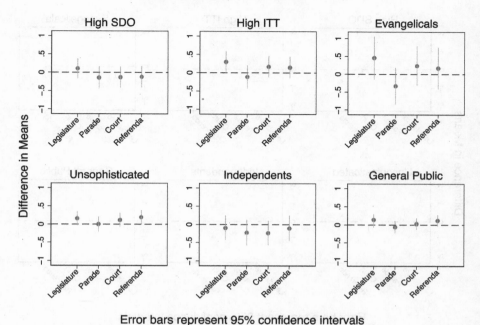

Error bars represent 95% confidence intervals

Figure 3.2. Differences in support for gay marriage (treatment vs. control)

Results: Does Backlash Occur?

Backlash is the negative, large, organic, and enduring shift that occurs in response to a threatened change to the status quo. We measure backlash by subtracting the average opinion in the baseline condition (the gun control vignette) from mean opinion in each treatment condition. Negative scores indicate backlash, while positive scores are inconsistent with backlash. Additionally, predicted values in which the error bars cross the zero line are also inconsistent with backlash, as this indicates a result that is not statistically significant. The plots in figure 3.2 show the difference in mean support for gay marriage for each of the groups.

The results in figure 3.2 depict no evidence of backlash. The one significant effect we observe happens to be positive. Among the general public, the differences in opinion relative to the baseline condition are small and not statistically significant. We see similar results among high-ITT and unsophisticated respondents. Only among evangelicals exposed to the parade story do we see even a modest-size negative effect, but even here it is neither significant nor large. Despite our efforts to induce opinion back-

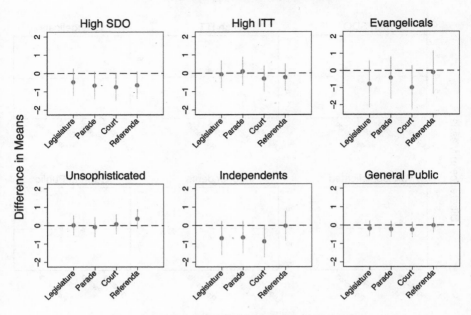

Error bars represent 95% confidence intervals

Figure 3.3. Differences in the intensity of feelings about gay marriage (treatment vs. control)

lash on support for same-sex marriage, we are unable to do so, even among groups most prone to lash back.

Having found no evidence of backlash on policy support for same-sex marriage, we next examine the importance people ascribe to same-sex marriage. After all, it is possible that instead of changing minds about same-sex marriage, salient threats to the status quo reframe priorities and make the issue more important to some Americans. Figure 3.3 plots the changes in intensity of opinion for each group. Unlike the previous figure, backlash is indicated here as a *positive* change over the baseline, reflecting an increase in intensity.

The results in figure 3.3 are similar to those in the preceding analysis, as we see no evidence of backlash. All of the differences in issue intensity are very small, as none crack even one point on a ten-point scale, and only one is clearly positive. In all, we find little change in issue intensity following exposure to LGBT-related information.

Rather than occurring through opinion change on policy, or through a shift in the importance ascribed to the issue, backlash may be directed toward the group advocating the policy change. After all, research shows

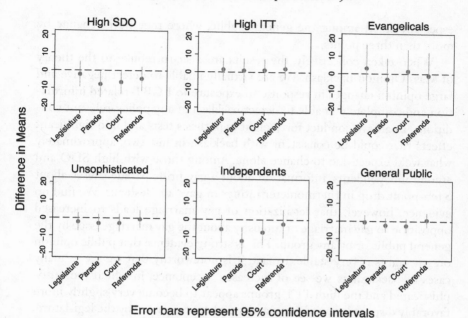

Error bars represent 95% confidence intervals

Figure 3.4. Differences in thermometer rating of gays and lesbians (treatment vs. control)

citizens have low levels of political knowledge, especially about specific issues. Moreover, as few people in our study reside in Oregon, they are unlikely to be directly affected by the policy, but they may see such change as a symbolic threat. To account for this possibility, we examine backlash as antipathy or hostility toward gays and lesbians as a group. More specifically, we look to our feeling thermometer measure for gays and lesbians to address this possibility. Figure 3.4 plots these measures across treatment conditions, with negative values indicating increased antipathy against gays and lesbians consistent with backlash.

The results in figure 3.4 demonstrate little evidence of decreased warmth toward gays and lesbians caused by exposure to LGBT-relevant information. Across the board, all changes in warmth are small; in only one case do we see even a ten-point change in warmth. We see significant and negative treatment effects in just two cases: among high-SDO respondents and among independents. Interestingly, both of these treatment effects occur in response to the parade condition, meaning that we see no evidence of backlash in any of our policy-relevant conditions across any of our outcome measures. It is worth emphasizing that the effects are especially small among the general public, where they never change by more than three points.

When taken collectively, the results are a sharp rebuke to the theory of Mass Opinion Backlash. We are virtually unable to detect negative and large opinion changes in response to exposure to LGBT-related information and completely unable to detect backlash in any policy-relevant conditions. In all, we conduct forty-eight hypothesis tests and find significant effects that could be consistent with backlash in just two, approximately what we'd expect due to chance alone. Among those with high SDO and among independents, information about a gay pride parade causes about a ten-point drop in thermometer ratings of gays and lesbians. We find no evidence, however, that legalization of gay marriage leads to increased opposition to gay marriage or intensity about the gay marriage issue by the general public or by any group. This is strong evidence that public opinion on gay rights is very stable. In fact, it is noteworthy that we see as many cases of backlash as we see of increased acceptance, in which the unsophisticated and the high-ITT groups appear to become very slightly more favorably disposed toward gay marriage when it is passed by the legislature.

While there are good reasons to question the existence of backlash, given all of the attention it has received, it is worth considering how and why the results came up empty. We can rule out a few potential challenges to our approach rather easily. One possibility is that our experiment lacked enough participants to detect opinion changes that could constitute backlash, particularly in some of our subgroup analyses. This is unlikely. Recall that Mass Opinion Backlash requires a large shift in opinion, but the effects that we observed across conditions were nearly always tiny and often signed incorrectly. Nonetheless, we investigated this possibility by conducting power calculations for each of our key measures, which indicate that the samples are sufficiently large to detect changes consistent with backlash. Specifically, for all but three of the groups we examine, our analyses are sufficiently large to allow for 80 percent power in our tests, thereby meeting conventional levels required to assess significance. These results are seen in the appendix to the chapter.

Another potential limitation is that the respondents did not read and absorb the information in the vignettes. Lately there has been increased concern about the use of bots to fill out online surveys, in addition to concern that AMT survey takers do not pay close attention to surveys and try to click through as quickly as possible to receive payment. In order to ensure the subjects actually received and accepted our treatments, we asked questions about the content of the vignettes and then limited our sample to those respondents who answered them correctly. The results are substantively unchanged and we present this reanalysis in the appendix to this chapter.

Discussion

The results of our analyses are striking. Across multiple experiments, examining a wide range of groups that past research indicates should be especially prone to lash back, we fail to observe almost any consistent reaction at all. In fact, people's views are as likely to become more positive toward gay rights as they are to become more negative. Taken together, the results are much more consistent with the political science research on opinion change than they are with journalistic and scholastic accounts of backlash. Given these findings, is it possible that backlash not only exists but is also widespread? What might explain these results?

There are several possible explanations for these findings that might still allow for backlash. First, it is possible that our experiments failed to trigger a threat to the status quo that was strong enough to elicit backlash. In particular, while our stimulus focused on the legalization of gay marriage, a strong and contentious policy shift, it is possible that some subjects did not view it as a significant threat because it was centered in Oregon, which for most is a distant state. While extensive reports suggest that the national movement to ban gay marriage through passage of the 1996 Defense of Marriage Act was triggered by the mere possibility that a judge in an even more distant state, Hawaii, might legalize gay marriage there, differences between our contrived policy shift in Oregon and the actual threat seen in Hawaii (e.g., the absence of media coverage on the contrived Oregon policy change) may have led our subjects to view it less seriously. In other words, while the Backlash Hypothesis allows for the salient threat of a remote policy change to trigger Mass Opinion Backlash, it is possible (but by no means certain) that our test is somewhat weak due to its use of Oregon as a test case.

Alternatively, it is possible that some form of attitude change did occur but that our research design, comparing averages across groups of different people, might obscure these differences, making them difficult to detect. Hypothetically, backlash, or negative movement, among some subjects might be offset by positive movement among others, leading to no average difference across treated and untreated groups. While we have no theoretical explanation to identify or explain which groups might have shifted, we are unable to rule out this possibility based on these experiments.

Another possibility is that the absence of backlash could be due to when our experiments were conducted. Although we conducted experiments in order to control the flow of gay rights information to respondents, we may not have reached the most receptive audience. Because we conducted the experiments in 2013, we look at gay rights relatively late in the issue cycle. The period between 2010 and the present has seen one of the most dramatic shifts in public attitudes in modern American history, with opinion rapidly shifting in favor of both gay rights more generally as well as gay marriage specifically (Garretson 2018). It is therefore possible that, despite extensive media and scholastic references to backlash during this period, attitudes were hardened by the time we studied them and that had we examined them earlier, people might have been more open to backlash. Still, our use of an experimental approach is very powerful, as it permits us to provide information that the backlash hypothesis predicts should induce a backlash without having to worry about the confounding effects of the media environment or a general growing acceptance of gay rights. Moreover, if there is no backlash in response to the most visible and controversial policy on gay rights, to the extent that backlash exists elsewhere regarding some other issue, its consequences are likely to be much less important than scholars and pundits imply.

Interestingly, the experimental condition that came the closest to inducing effects consistent with backlash included no policy-relevant information. The parade condition contains just the mere mention of gays and lesbians openly celebrating their identities in a proud manner. While gay pride parades are by no means new or unfamiliar, many Americans remain uncomfortable with them, despite the fact that they are primarily symbolic and present no meaningful challenges to the policy status quo. This increased visibility of gay and lesbian Americans may induce feeling of prejudice among citizens or may conjure up latent feelings of homophobia. Further research is needed to unpack whether lingering antipathy toward gay and lesbian Americans is driven by these feelings, but this evidence remains entirely inconsistent with backlash due to real or perceived threats to the policy status quo.

Finally, it is possible that despite all of our efforts to ensure the validity of our samples, stimuli, and estimates, the results we obtain are a product of some unobservable problem with our experiments and, hence, don't translate well to the real world. In short, it may be difficult to replicate the kind of threats and conditions that lead to backlash in the real world by using an online experiment. We address these potential challenges, as well as others, in the next chapter.

Conclusion

Despite a series of careful experimental tests, with a specific focus on groups that should be prone to backlash, we cannot induce the sharp and negative changes in opinion that are necessary conditions of Mass Opinion Backlash. We find little support that backlash is an organic, bottom-up phenomenon that can be directly stimulated by the expansion of minority rights or even the mention of an unpopular minority becoming more visible in society. While we have yet to resolve the central puzzle underpinning this chapter—whether opposition to expansions of gay rights is driven by mass backlash or by elite mobilization—the evidence presented in this chapter does not support the argument in favor of mass opinion backlash. In the next chapter, we continue to examine whether backlash occurs in the "real world," this time using a variety of high-profile expansions of gay rights as test cases. In doing so, we address some of the key limitations of this chapter's experimental approach and provide a holistic examination of whether there exists a mass opinion backlash to the expansion of gay and lesbian rights in the United States.

FOUR

In Search of Backlash

Observational Evidence

In the summer of 2015, the U.S. Supreme Court issued its ruling in the *Obergefell v. Hodges* case. The court ruled that the Constitution guarantees the right to marry for same-sex couples and barred states from banning same-sex marriage. This decision legalized same-sex marriage across the United States, a move that seemed unthinkable even a few years before (Liptak 2015). One would be hard-pressed to find a greater change to the status quo or event that provoked a feeling of loss among opponents of marriage equality. Despite this, almost three years after the ruling, public opinion in support of gay marriage reached a record high at 67 percent in favor (Gallup 2018). While it now seems clear that no public opinion backlash occurred in response to this ruling, the threat of public opinion backlash was ever present in the political debates leading up to the decision.

Through the use of multiple experiments across a number of groups that past research suggests are most prone to backlash, the preceding chapter presented substantial evidence that undermines the assertion backlash occurs. The somewhat surprising results discovered in chapter 3 naturally raise questions about the extent to which backlash occurs in contemporary society and the potential limitations of the experimental approach. Under a variety of experimental conditions, we were unable to detect evidence of public opinion backlash. While our experimental conditions did not elicit backlash among the public, it is possible that prominent real-world events—such as major Supreme Court rulings, *would* galvanize opinion.

Thus, we are interested in examining whether backlash occurred not just in experimental contexts but also in real-world cases.

This chapter seeks to examine the public reaction to important events that have led to the granting of equal rights to gays and lesbians and to thereby overcome some of the limitations of the experiment-based evidence in the previous chapter. That is, while our experimental results fail to uncover evidence of backlash, even among those groups that past research suggests are most likely to lash back, our experimental stimuli may poorly reflect the conditions that elicit backlash that occurs in actual contemporary politics.

In this chapter we examine how the public reacted to three of the most prominent and controversial challenges to contemporary gay rights policy. First, we examine public opinion during a time when the issue of gay marriage was just beginning to make national headlines as a number of state courts overturned bans on gay marriage and President Bush announced support for the Federal Marriage Amendment, which would have effectively banned gay marriage nationwide. Second, we examine whether backlash occurred following the two salient Supreme Court rulings of *Perry v. Schwarzenegger* and *United States v. Windsor*, which overturned California's ban on gay marriage and the federal Defense of Marriage Act respectively. Finally, we analyze public opinion after the nationwide recognition of same-sex marriage in the Supreme Court case of *Obergefell v. Hodges*. Examining these cases allows us to answer a central question driving this chapter: To what extent do we observe backlash in contemporary politics?

Explaining the Absence of Backlash

The striking findings presented in chapter 3 raise two pressing questions: First, to what extent are these findings reflected in contemporary American politics? Second, to what extent are the limitations of the experiments we conduct responsible for the findings? Several factors may limit the validity and generalizability of those results. One factor is that our contrived events (i.e., experimental stimuli) occur in Oregon. It is possible that events in a small northwestern state do not adequately trigger a sense of threat commensurate with the major challenges to restrictions of equality to gays and lesbians over the years. To the extent to which the average American might know something about the state's politics, it might be seen as a generally liberal/progressive state; thus actions to grant gays and lesbians equal rights might be unsurprising and inconsequential and fail to be seen as a real challenge to the status quo. Moreover, the challenges to gay rights that occur are not as isolated as a single policy in a single state; more typically they reflect constant challenges to laws and policies over a long period of time. As media coverage and elite cues may vary across issues and contexts, we might not expect backlash in a situation where the challenge to gay rights is not also accompanied by these other phenomena.

A second concern about our experimental results is a product of societal attitude change. The experiments in chapter 3 were conducted relatively late in the issue cycle, during a period when public opinion had already shifted in favor of gay rights. Examining attitudes during this time may limit the number of people susceptible to changing their views and could diminish the amount of backlash that any experiment could induce.

A third concern is that the sample on which the experiments were conducted is unrepresentative in some important way. Recall that we recruited respondents using online surveys recruited from Amazon's Mechanical Turk subject pool. While this program is widely used by survey researchers it differs from nationally representative surveys (e.g., ANES or CCES). Despite our best efforts to make sure we had a representative sample (and employing multiple strategies to validate and weight the data to closely mirror the American population), it is possible that our respondents differ from the general American public in some important but unobserved way. This could occur with the survey respondents overall or among groups that are most likely to exhibit backlash (e.g., perhaps Republicans in the AMT sample may be more libertarian than in the general American population).

A final limitation of the experimental analysis in the previous chapter concerns the way we examine opinion change. Perhaps backlash is occurring and individual opinions are shifting but changes are concealed by taking averages of opinions and intensity across groups. Using averages might disguise substantial intergroup variation and could be detected only by measuring an individual's attitudes at multiple points in time.[1]

To address these concerns and to examine whether contemporary politics are characterized by anti-gay backlash as journalists, activists, and scholars suggest, we conduct a series of studies examining public opinion surrounding several of the most salient and important challenges to the status quo on gay rights. Doing so allows us to both evaluate these claims of backlash and assess the extent to which, and when, backlash occurs. Specifically, by conducting three separate studies, it also allows us to overcome the potential limitations of the experimental studies conducted in the preceding chapter.

Did Backlash Occur Earlier in the Issue Cycle?

Few issues have seen as much opinion change over the past decade as attitudes toward gay rights. According to Gallup, between 2003 and 2018, support for gay and lesbian relations being legal moved from around 43 percent in favor to 75 percent in favor. Similarly, support for gay marriage rose from less than a majority (42 percent) in 2004 to a clear majority in 2018 (67 percent) (Gallup 2018). Moreover, there have been changes among all ages but no more so than among the millennial generation, with three-quarters of this group now in favor of gay marriage (compared to 44 percent in favor in 2004) (Pew Research Center 2018). This change has important implications for gay rights in that it suggests policy is likely to become much more favorable.

Thus, one possible explanation for these changes is that the lack of backlash from the experimental results in chapter 3 stems from the increasingly positive attitudes exhibited by the general public over the last few years. Perhaps attitudes were well formed by the time our experiments were conducted. One reason for this may be that backlash only occurs early in an issue's life cycle. While such a phenomenon seems unlikely given the changing opposition to gay rights, we note that such an argument has important implications. The tangible and normative implications of backlash are less threatening if there is a short window during an issue's life cycle in which it can occur. Of course, it is also possible that despite our validity checks and the extensive research validating the Mechanical Turk sampling process, those in our sample still differ from the American public in some important but unobservable way that affects our results.

In order to assess these possibilities, we examine public opinion well before it had shifted in favor of extending rights and during a time when there were three salient events relating to gay marriage—2003 and 2004. On November 18, 2003, the Massachusetts Supreme Court ruled that banning gay marriage violates the state constitution. This ruling was the first in the nation that granted same-sex couples a legal right to marry. Previously, states such as Vermont had allowed only civil unions for these couples. The ruling led Massachusetts to be the first to allow actual marriage licenses to same-sex couples (Burge 2003).

Shortly after the Massachusetts ruling, on February 24, 2004, President Bush announced his support for the Federal Marriage Amendment (FMA), which would have banned gay marriage nationwide. The president's endorsement of a constitutional amendment on the heels of the Massachusetts ruling came in the form of a live television address from the

White House to the nation (CNN 2004). Finally, on March 11, 2004, the California State Supreme Court ordered officials in San Francisco to stop performing gay marriages.[2] The mayor of San Francisco, Gavin Newsom, had begun granting marriage licenses to same-sex couples in February of that same year. While the granting of licenses in California did not last long, it did lead to a salient court challenge.

These events provide insight into the effect of visible challenges to the status quo on opinion during a time when gay marriage had just entered the national arena. As Bush's announcement and the California Supreme Court ruling were highly salient events that kept the issue at the forefront of media attention, each could serve as a strong provocation that challenged the status quo and could spur backlash. Importantly, examining public opinion during this time allows us to test the generalizability of our experimental findings from the previous chapter. These real-world events, and the public's reaction to them, provide important opportunities to examine whether backlash occurred following salient events. The Massachusetts ruling also represents a typical example of what is often seen when a state makes a controversial policy. Often there is widespread media attention in which other elite actors (e.g., the president) may become involved.

One happy coincidence is that excellent data are available for assessing opinion change during this time. The 2004 National Annenberg Election Survey (NAES), a representative national public opinion poll, was in the field before and after these events occurred. At the time only about 21 percent of Americans favored granting gays and lesbians the right to marry. The NAES surveyed about two hundred respondents daily, between October 2003 and November 2004, on questions about attitudes toward gay groups and on gay rights policy (NAES 2004). Because questions were asked over a long period of time, the duration of opinion change can also be examined. Moreover, because the surveys were randomly administered, the NAES data allow us to approximate a natural experiment by treating subjects as if they were randomly assigned to pre- and post-treatment groups. While we cannot tell whether respondents were aware of these events, we can examine whether attitudes changed following their occurrence.

Building on our work in the previous chapter, we test the mass opinion backlash perspective, which predicts a negative and enduring response to a salient event or another visible threat to the status quo. Mass Opinion Backlash predicts that the general public and groups with particular proclivity to hold anti-gay biases (i.e., Evangelicals, those scoring high on the social dominance scale) or feel psychologically threatened (those scoring high on the ITT scale) will display a sharp, negative, and enduring change in opinion about same-sex marriage and gays and lesbians as a group.

Did Backlash Occur in Response to Presidential Support of the Federal Marriage Amendment?

In order to examine whether backlash occurred earlier in the issue cycle, we use the National Annenberg Election Study, which conducted a representative national public opinion poll at a time when majority opinion was much more opposed to gay marriage. For short, intermittent periods of time, the NAES administered questions that asked whether gay marriage should be legalized by the state and whether the respondent supported the Federal Marriage Amendment. These questions allow us to examine whether significant public opinion change occurred. Specifically, we look to see if the public's attitudes toward gays and lesbians shifted in response to these court cases and announcement. To do so, we pool respondents to the 2004 NAES into weeklong periods before and after the court rulings were made.

In table 4.1 we compare attitudes toward the Federal Marriage Amendment and toward legalizing marriage in the state before and after the rulings for each group for whom data are available. For the Massachusetts ruling we employ only the FMA measure, as the state opinion question was not asked during this time, but for Bush's FMA announcement and the California ruling we employ both measures.[3] If backlash occurs, then attitudes should become less favorable after the court rulings.

Table 4.1 presents the differences in opinion observed before and after

TABLE 4.1. Change in support for marriage before and after court rulings

	Massachusetts Ruling	Bush Announcement	California Ruling
Federal Marriage Amendment			
General Public	0.02	−0.03	0.03
Evangelicals	0.12	−0.05	0.10
Independents	0.03	−0.07	−0.10
Unsophisticated	0.04	0.08	−0.14
State Marriage			
General Public		−0.10	0.04
Evangelicals		0.21	0.03
Independents		0.10	−0.04
Unsophisticated		−0.18	0.32

the Bush announcement and the Massachusetts and California court rulings for the general public, white Evangelicals, independents, and the unsophisticated. Despite high absolute levels of opposition to expansions of gay rights (which we do not report in this table but help explain the prevalence of so much anti-gay policy during this time period), the differences in support for these issues are tiny. In no case do we observe large negative shifts in attitudes, as the estimates hover around zero, suggesting very little opinion change followed these events.[4]

These differences suggest little opinion backlash, though it is hard to be sure that the differences we observe are not the product of some other set of factors that might be peculiar to respondents' political or background characteristics. To investigate the possibility that the (null) results we observe are driven by samples that have disproportionate numbers of respondents who hold pro-gay attitudes, for instance, we employ regression analyses that control for political and demographic factors thought to correlate most highly with attitudes toward gays and lesbians.[5]

The independent variables in our analyses consist of demographic and political factors. Partisanship is widely shown to be associated with attitudes toward gays and lesbians, so we control for whether the respondent identifies as Republican or Democrat as well as their ideological liberalism. Similarly, we also control both for religious affiliation and how often they attend church as a measure of religiosity. Finally, we account for a series of demographic variables that past research indicates are related to LGBT attitudes, which include race, gender, and age.

Our central interest in these analyses is whether or not the ruling led to a shift in people's attitudes. To test this, we create an indicator variable, called *ruling*, scored 0 if the respondent was surveyed in the eight days that preceded the court ruling or announcement and 1 if they were surveyed in the eight days after the court ruling. We then examine whether this variable is large and significant for each of the groups most likely to exhibit backlash on the rulings. If backlash drives attitudes, we would expect to find large, statistically significant, negative coefficients for the ruling variable after controlling for all of the other possible influences on attitudes. To estimate these models, we employ Ordered Logistic Regression to estimate support for the Federal Marriage Amendment. The results of these analyses (with cut points suppressed) are seen in figure 4.1, which plots the coefficients of the logistic regression (full results in the appendix).

The results in figure 4.1 are entirely consistent with our previous findings. While we do find the occasional negative coefficient, in no case are the effects significant or large. Similar results are observed when we exam-

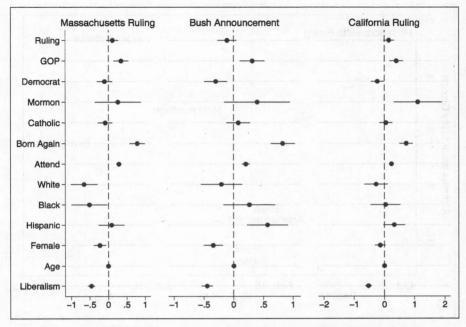

Figure 4.1. Coefficient plot of ordered logistic regression estimating support for Federal Marriage Amendment

ine changes in attitudes toward gay groups as our dependent variable (see the appendix). These results suggest that the null findings observed in the difference of means tests are not likely the result of differences in sample demographics between the respondents who completed the survey before and after the rulings and announcement.

We can also examine attitudes toward gays and lesbians as a group and whether any change in attitudes is enduring by comparing responses over time for the general public, the unsophisticated, independents, and white evangelical Protestants to the question "On a scale of zero to 10, how favorably do you rate gay and lesbian organizations?" which was asked before and after all three of the salient events.[6] The data we employ are average responses by week for the entire period during which the question was asked, which corresponds roughly to the year preceding the 2004 presidential election (i.e., Oct. 7, 2003, to Sept. 19, 2004). The horizontal lines in figure 4.2 show the degree to which attitudes toward gay groups were favorable during late 2003 and most of 2004.

To assess backlash against gay groups, we examine whether there is a

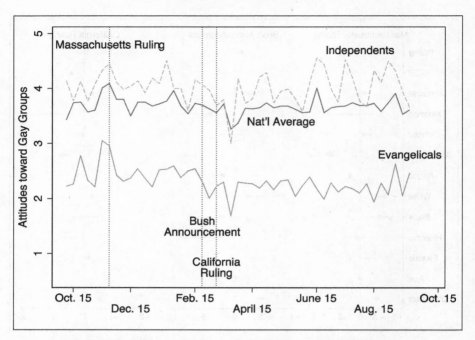

Figure 4.2. Favorable attitudes toward gay groups during 2003–2004 (10-point scale)

negative, large, and enduring drop in opinion. For each of the three groups, we observe small negative responses to the Massachusetts and California court rulings and President Bush's announcement. The results differ somewhat across rulings in that opinion at the time of the Massachusetts ruling was at approximately its highest point during the series, making the drop that followed appear especially pronounced. A close look, however, shows that in every series, the attitudes just after the ruling are comparable to those expressed just a few weeks before the ruling. The small drop we observe at the time of the ruling is neither large nor sustained.

The California ruling and President Bush's announcement are noteworthy because, in contrast to the Massachusetts ruling, they threatened gay rights by stopping or proposing to outlaw marriages. Despite this, the pattern we observe is similar to the pro–gay rights ruling in Massachusetts except that we see a tiny positive uptick in attitudes toward gay groups following the court ruling before we see a small drop the following week. To the extent that a negative reaction occurs, it is slightly delayed, and even then it is very short lived. Here, too, opinion seems to revert to pre-ruling levels within just a couple of weeks of the ruling. The changes in aggregate opinion seem to be little more than short-term spasms.

Overall, we find no evidence of mass opinion backlash following these events. The fall of 2003 and spring of 2004 were an incredibly active time for those concerned about the issue of gay marriage. The Supreme Court's ruling led to Massachusetts becoming the first state to legalize gay marriage (as opposed to civil unions). The implementation for the ruling was followed both by President Bush publicly supporting the Federal Marriage Amendment and Mayor Gavin Newsom issuing marriage licenses in San Francisco. In combination these events made gay marriage incredibly salient nationally; thus, it would seem to constitute precisely the type of threat to the status quo that backlash proponents argue should trigger the effect. Despite this, looking for effects on a variety of measures, for a wide range of groups that past research suggests should be most likely to lash back, we are unable to find any evidence that they shifted opinion. Thus, the results from the first study examining an earlier time frame exhibit no support for the Mass Opinion Backlash Perspective. Instead, opinion seems quite stable during this time of high-salience events relating to gay marriage.

Testing Backlash Using the Supreme Court Rulings of *Perry v. Schwarzenegger* and *United States v. Windsor*

Perhaps the fact that marriage was legalized in Massachusetts—among the most liberal states in the nation—combined with the widespread opposition to gay rights by politicians of both parties and strong opposition from the public more broadly, allowed most Americans to ignore the court's ruling or President Bush's support of the FMA. After all, these events had little tangible effect on the vast majority of the nation. The 2013 U.S. Supreme Court's multiple rulings on gay rights, however, had much more profound and wide-reaching implications.

In the summer of 2013, the U.S. Supreme Court ruled on two prominent issues related to gay rights. The first ruling (*Perry v. Schwarzenegger*) concerned Proposition 8, which prevented gays and lesbians in California from marrying even after same-sex marriage had previously been legalized. The second ruling (*United States v. Windsor*) concerned some of the federal government's restrictions on marriage recognition and the limitation of government benefits to same-sex married couples in the Defense of Marriage Act. These two rulings served to legalize gay marriage in California, marking a major step toward nationwide recognition of same-sex marriage (and providing the legal basis for it). The *Windsor* ruling made parts of DOMA unconstitutional nationwide, marking a dramatic expansion of gay rights, which could have activated a significant threat to the status quo for those susceptible to backlash. Both rulings were issued on the same day, minutes apart. Indeed, one would be hard-pressed to create a stimulus stronger than a Supreme Court ruling that expanded both gay marriage and gay rights on a national and state level.

To examine the effects of this powerful real-world stimulus on opinions about same-sex marriage and gays and lesbians, we went back into the field with the baseline condition of our survey, which contained an article about gun control and did not pertain to gays and lesbians. This natural experiment allows us to externally validate our previous results by comparing attitudes before and after the landmark Supreme Court rulings. We exclude the high-ITT group because we are concerned that the court's ruling may have heightened one's sense of threat or discomfort with gays and lesbians and hence their ITT score and group membership. The results of this analysis are presented in figure 4.3.

Yet again, our results do not support the predictions of backlash. Despite an extremely strong stimulus that actually happened in the real world, had national significance, and received a great deal of media coverage, any observed opinion change is very small and statistically insignificant. We find no difference in opinion on gay marriage, intensity of feelings about gay marriage, or warmth of feelings before versus after the rulings. These results are also small in relative terms, as Jeremiah J. Garretson (2014b), for instance, finds that exposure to a television show with a gay character increases warmth toward gays and lesbians substantially more than any of the stimuli we employ.

Examining Public Reaction to the Nationwide Recognition of Same-Sex Marriage in the Landmark *Obergefell* Decision

Our failure to detect any significant results that support the backlash perspective is not likely the product of a failure to treat some or all of the subjects, the use of weak treatments, an unrepresentative sample, or of low statistical power. Both in the controlled environment of our online experiment and in the natural context of the real world after historic expansions of gay rights, we find no backlash. However, in order to effectively rule out the possibility of backlash, we conduct one more test using both the strongest possible stimulus and the strictest possible survey design.

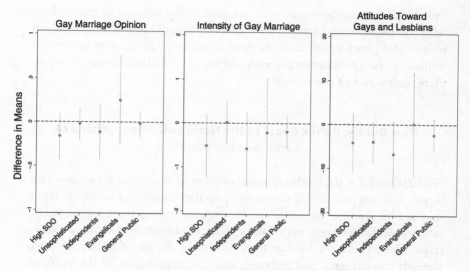

Figure 4.3. Differences in ratings before and after Supreme Court rulings (gun control only)

On June 26, 2015, the U.S. Supreme Court issued an opinion in the case *Obergefell v. Hodges* that forbade states from banning same-sex marriage. This decision legalized same-sex marriage across the United States and brought a pro-gay ending to the national fight for marriage equality that began in Massachusetts and Iowa. In addition to being a historic capstone to the fight for marriage equality, *Obergefell* provides us perhaps the ideal opportunity to detect backlash following the expansion of gay rights. Once more we fielded a survey using Amazon Mechanical Turk shortly before the *Obergefell* decision was announced. However, this time we reinterviewed a subset of this sample and reassessed their attitudes on gay rights after the decision. The backlash perspective predicts that individuals will become more opposed to gay rights and feel less warmly toward gays and lesbians following this rapid and sweeping expansion of gay rights. We find no evidence that this is the case and ultimately find no evidence to support the backlash perspective.

We fielded the first wave of our panel study from May 20, 2015, until May 24, 2015, and the second wave from June 27, 2015, until June 30, 2015. In all, we received two completed survey waves from 2,051 respondents. As the purpose of this test is to assess opinion change following a historic expansion of same-sex marriage rights while holding any time-invariant individual characteristics constant, we restrict our analysis to respondents who completed both survey waves. Respondents did not demonstrate any meaningful panel attrition, so the results presented in the next section are unlikely to be a product of anyone's willingness (or unwillingness) to complete both waves of our survey.

How Did the Public React to the Nationwide Recognition of Same-Sex Marriage?

We first look for backlash among members of the general public—that is, our full sample. Recall that some popular notions of backlash argue that public opinion backlash will be present among the general public as a whole following a major policy change expanding same-sex marriage. Once more we look at backlash in the forms of policy support, warmth toward gays and lesbians, and the importance of the issue to respondents.

We present results for the general public (and subgroups we have identified as likely to exhibit backlash) in figure 4.4, which displays the average change in opinion from wave 1 (before the Supreme Court opinion) to wave 2 (after the Supreme Court opinion).[7] The general public is plotted in the left-most position in each panel. Negative opinion change indicates backlash.

The results in figure 4.4 do not support the backlash perspective, even using a within-subjects design following a powerful, definitive, and real-world stimulus that is expected to provoke a backlash around same-sex marriage. Support for same-sex marriage increased very slightly from a mean of 3.30 to 3.32. This increase of 0.02 on a five-point scale is very small and does not attain statistical significance under a paired t-test, which (in conjunction with our sample size of about two thousand respondents) typically allows for the detection of small effects as statistically significant. Warmth toward gays and lesbians increases from a pre-ruling average of 64.0 to a post-ruling average of 64.8. This positive opinion change is weakly statistically significant at the 90 percent threshold, but the fact that sentiment toward gays and lesbians becomes *more* positive following the *Obergefell* decision entirely contradicts the backlash hypothesis. Average reported importance of same-sex marriage increases slightly following the ruling, from a mean of 6.61 to a mean of 6.69, but this difference of just 0.08 is not statistically significant. We do not see evidence of backlash among the general public.

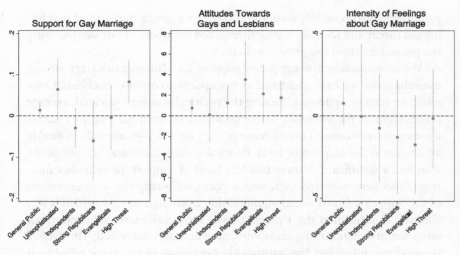

Error bars represent 95% confidence intervals

Figure 4.4. Average change in opinion between waves 1 and 2 (before and after Supreme Court ruling)

Backlash among Susceptible Groups

While we remain unable to detect opinion backlash among the general public—even in the presence of a powerful test—it is possible that we have merely ruled out backlash as a general phenomenon and left open the possibility that backlash still exists among groups particularly susceptible to it. To that end, we turn to the groups we have identified in previous tests as susceptible to backlash: those with poorly formed opinions (independents and the politically unsophisticated) and those who may feel a particular shock following the expansion of same-sex marriage rights (white evangelicals, strong Republican identifiers, and the psychologically threatened). For each of these subgroups, we use measures in the first wave of the survey (before the *Obergefell* decision) to identify group members and then examine how their opinions change following the historic Supreme Court decision.

We identify subgroups that are likely to be prone to backlash following the same procedure from the previous chapter, with one exception. Because of the limited nature of our panel survey, we ask fewer questions meant to measure psychological threat. Still, we are able to measure symbolic threat and stereotype threat, which are two of the threat measures we used in the previous chapter and correlate strongly with other measures of psychological threat. We combine these into a single measure of psychological threat and identify highly threatened members of our sample using the procedure from the previous chapter.

We first examine average policy support for same-sex marriage among the subgroups we have identified as susceptible to opinion backlash. Once more we turn to figure 4.3. Among the politically unsophisticated, average policy support for same-sex marriage increases from 3.25 to 3.32 across the two survey waves. This increase of 0.07 on a five-point scale is weakly significant at the 90 percent level. Psychologically threatened respondents, who had a significantly lower baseline level of support for same-sex marriage, also demonstrated increased support following the announcement of the Supreme Court decision, increasing from 2.49 to 2.85, which is statistically significant at the 1 percent level. However, increased support for same-sex marriage among unsophisticated and psychologically threatened respondents following the nationwide expansion of marriage equality is certainly evidence *against* public opinion backlash. None of the other subgroups demonstrate statistically significant opinion change on support for same-sex marriage. Support among moderates declines slightly from 3.41 to 3.38, while support among evangelicals drops even more slightly from 2.00 to 1.99. Strong Republican identifiers demonstrate a slightly more negative shift in support for same-sex marriage, from an average of 1.80 to 1.74, but this decline is again not statistically significant. Across all subgroups, we fail to detect the sharp and negative opinion change that would be consistent with a backlash against same-sex marriage.

Turning now to warmth toward gays and lesbians, we observe a pattern that is even less consistent with public opinion backlash. We plot the average changes in warmth following the *Obergefell* decision in the second panel of figure 4.4. Politically unsophisticated respondents become slightly warmer toward gays and lesbians, but this difference of less than one point (out of 100) is minuscule and not statistically significant. Political moderates' average warmth increases from 64.7 to 65.9, but this difference is also nonsignificant. Interestingly, white evangelicals and strong Republicans grew warmer toward gays and lesbians following the national expansion of marriage equality. Evangelicals increased by 2.1 points, from 46.0 to 48.1 (a difference that is not significant). Meanwhile, strong Republican identifiers' average warmth toward gays and lesbians weakly significantly increased from 42.3 to 45.9. Highly threatened respondents increased as well, from 49.3 to 51.1, which is statistically significant at the 5 percent level. This unexpected shift should, once more, be taken as strong evidence against backlash in the form of sentiment toward the group that most directly benefited from the expansion of same-sex marriage following *Obergefell*—that is, gays and lesbians.

Backlash against the national expansion of same-sex marriage is not evident in either policy support or warmth toward gays and lesbians, but it could have a psychologically mobilizing effect by increasing the perceived importance of same-sex marriage among groups potentially prone to backlash. We examine the changes in reported importance of the issue in the right-most panel of figure 4.4.

As is clear from the data presented in figure 4.4, the politically unsophisticated demonstrate no meaningful change in issue importance. This result is also true for independents, who decline from 6.75 to 6.68, a nonsignificant change of just 0.08 points on a ten-point scale. Interestingly, evangelicals, strong Republicans, and the psychologically threatened demonstrate declined intensity following the Supreme Court decision. Evangelicals declined from 6.60 to 6.43, Republicans declined from 6.57 to 6.44, and high-threat respondents declined from 5.98 to 5.97. In all cases, these differences are not statistically significant.

In sum, we see no significant opinion change consistent with backlash, despite the powerful within-subjects analyses we run using a panel survey designed specifically to measure opinion change following a real, salient, and historic expansion of same-sex marriage rights. Where we do see even weakly significant change, it is in the direction that is entirely inconsistent with backlash.

Measuring Backlash Using Self-Reported Behavior

Having thoroughly demonstrated that real, salient, and historic expansions of gay rights do not lead to mass opinion backlash, we now explore the possibility that backlash can be detected through one final channel: expressed willingness to engage in various political acts. We know that opinion change is rare, but it could still be the case that individuals demonstrate backlash through their actions and not their responses to opinion questions. In both waves of our *Obergefell* panel study, we include measures of respondents' willingness to engage in six political acts: voting, contributing to a campaign, writing a letter to an elected official, posting about politics on social media, attending a meeting about an issue, and participating in a march or rally related to politics. For all of these acts, we ask respondents to rate their willingness to perform them on a five-point scale, with higher values indicating greater willingness.

We graph the *change* in willingness to participate in the six political acts

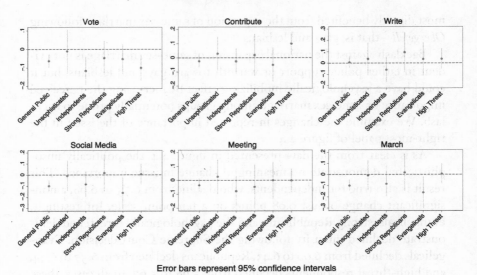

Error bars represent 95% confidence intervals

Figure 4.5. Change in willingness to participate

in figure 4.5 for the general public and for the groups we have identified as potentially prone to backlash. For each group, an *increase* in the stated willingness to participate in politics can be interpreted as mobilization that is potentially consistent with backlash.

We will consider each political act on its own. Turning first to voting, we observe significant but negative changes in respondents' stated propensity to vote in an upcoming election among the general public, political independents, and the psychologically threatened. In some cases (namely, independents), this negative effect is larger than a tenth of a point on our five-point scale. However, it is important to note that this is not consistent with backlash but instead demonstrates demobilization. Respondents offer a decreased willingness to vote following the *Obergefell* decision. Among the politically unsophisticated, strong Republicans, and evangelicals, we observe no significant changes in their stated propensity to vote.

We also asked respondents to offer their willingness to contribute to a political campaign. Only one key subgroup demonstrates a significant change in their stated willingness to contribute to a political campaign following the *Obergefell* decision. The sole exception to this is the psychologically threatened. Highly threatened respondents demonstrated an increased willingness to contribute of nearly a tenth of a point along a five-point scale. This increase is significant at a 5 percent level. Taken on its own, this increase could be viewed as evidence consistent with backlash. However, recall that high-threat respondents demonstrated significantly *higher* support for same-sex marriage and *increased* warmth toward gays and lesbians following the *Obergefell* decision, evidence that is wholly contradictory with the backlash narrative. This means we have either very mixed evidence with respect to backlash among the psychologically threatened or that high-threat respondents may actually be more willing to donate to a political cause that favors expansions of gay rights.[8] It is also important to note that this is the only positive change in respondents' willingness to participate in politics that we observe across all of the comparisons we conduct.

Respondents demonstrate no significant changes in their willingness to write to their elected officials following the *Obergefell* decision. More interestingly, two key groups offered a decreased willingness to post about politics or current events on social media platforms following the release of the historic opinion. Both the general public and white evangelicals indicated that they were significantly less likely to post about politics online and share their thoughts through social media. This indicates a decreased willingness to discuss backlash with one's peers (and no change in one's willingness to write to elected officials) following the Supreme Court decision and it is, once more, inconsistent with the backlash hypothesis.

Attending public meetings, marches, or rallies requires substantial investments of time and energy, so we should interpret an increased willingness to participate in these demanding ways as potential evidence of backlash. However, we see no such evidence. Respondents failed to demonstrate any significant changes in their willingness to attend a public meeting related to politics, and, again, the general public and white evangelicals offered a decreased willingness to attend a march or a rally following the *Obergefell* announcement.

While self-reports of behavior may fail to accurately predict citizens' actions, they may serve as markers of opinion change consistent with backlash. However, we see next to no increase in respondents' expressed desires to participate in politics following the historic *Obergefell* opinion.

Conclusion

In this chapter we have studied three highly visible, controversial, and important cases in the political debate surrounding gay rights. In each of these cases, there were challenges issued to the status quo at multiple different points during the issue cycle. By challenging the status quo at multiple points, each of these salient events serves as a potential catalyst to lead to opinion backlash. Our analyses employed a wide variety of data sources from nationally representative samples, examined whether opinion change occurred at a time when attitudes toward gays and lesbians were much more negative, examined major real-world and salient events that might provoke backlash, and examined data that tell us whether the same individuals changed their opinion at multiple points in time. Yet in each instance we reached the same conclusion: there is no evidence of mass opinion backlash. These cases are valuable because in addition to their substantive importance in the fight for marriage equality, they also overcome the limitations of the experiments conducted in chapter 3.

While it is difficult to establish the absence of a phenomenon, we have made every attempt to demonstrate or uncover backlash both using survey experiments and following three high profile, real world, events that seem very likely to trigger backlash. Our attempts include not only attempting to induce backlash through an original survey experiment, thereby ensuring that respondents would have to consider the possibility of a historic expansion of gay rights, but also examining opinion change surrounding actual historic expansions of gay rights. We have allowed for backlash to manifest as policy opinion on same-sex marriage, as warmth toward gays and lesbians, as perceived importance of same-sex marriage, and as expressed willingness to engage in numerous political behaviors and could not uncover any manifestation.

Given the absence of evidence demonstrating Mass Opinion Backlash, it's worth considering what explains journalistic, scholarly, and publicly held beliefs about the persistently looming threat of backlash. One possibility is that the opinion change central to backlash varies depending on the political institution that takes action. The next chapter takes a fresh look at our experimental data and examines whether some political institutions are more likely to cause opinion change than others.

FIVE

Institutions and Attitudes

On the morning of May 6, 2012, then Vice President, and now President, Joe Biden sat down for an interview with David Gregory on NBC's *Meet the Press*. After questions about the state of the economy and the presidential campaign, the discussion turned to social policy. For months, President Obama had skirted the issue of taking a strong stance in support of gay marriage, stating only that his views were "evolving" but he still opposed same-sex marriage. So Gregory asked Biden, had his views evolved? Biden at first responded somewhat coyly, saying that a majority of Americans were coming to the view that the issue was one about who one loves, regardless of whether those relationships were same-sex or not. Gregory pushed further asking the vice president if this was what he now believed and whether he was comfortable with gay marriage. Biden then took a clear position in support as he said:

> Look, I am vice president of the United States of America. The president sets the policy. I am absolutely comfortable with the fact that men marrying men, women marrying women, and heterosexual men and women marrying another are entitled to the same exact rights, all the civil rights, all the civil liberties. And quite frankly, I don't see much of a distinction—beyond that. (NBC News 2012)

Gregory then asked whether the administration would come out strongly in favor of marriage equality in a second term, to which Biden demurred, saying he didn't know the answer. But then, after discussing executive actions taken by President Obama aimed at preventing discrimination based on sexual orientation, Biden talked about a recent event in Los Angeles where he had met with a gay couple and their children:

> I was with—speaking to a group of gay leaders in—in Los Angeles— la—two, two weeks ago. And one gentleman looked at me in the question period and said, "Let me ask you, how do you feel about us?" And I had just walked into the back door of this gay couple and they're with their two adopted children. And I turned to the man who owned the house. I said, "What did I do when I walked in?" He said, "You walked right to my children. They were seven and five, giving you flowers." And I said, "I wish every American could see the look of love those kids had in their eyes for you guys. And they wouldn't have any doubt about what this is about." (NBC News 2012)

Some media outlets speculated this was perhaps a plan drawn up by the White House, yet insider accounts suggest Biden's action was far from planned. Instead, his comments during the interview sent the administration scrambling (Dovere 2014). Many aides grumbled that by coming out in support before the president, Biden had just launched his 2016 campaign for president and put the White House in an awkward position. Many accounts suggest that for some time Obama was privately a supporter of gay rights but opposed the issue publicly for political reasons. Internal debates within the administration of whether Obama should announce support for marriage equality before or after the 2012 election had led to a stalemate, as First Lady Michelle Obama argued in favor of coming out in support before the election, while longtime advisor David Axelrod counseled the president to publicly oppose such measures, despite the candidate's private belief in marriage equality (Miller 2015). But Biden's remarks had cornered the administration and forced the president's hand. Only three days later, President Obama gave an interview with ABCs Robin Roberts and pledged his support for marriage equality (Socrides 2014). The announcement by the most visible leader of the most prominent institution in the American political system was a major moment for the gay rights movement as Obama became the first president to support marriage equality. Events such as these lead us to ask the question, What role did the actions of institutions and key institutional actors such as the president serve in shaping public opinion?

Just as the findings of the preceding chapters raise significant questions about the existence of mass opinion backlash, so too does even a cursory glance at recent historical events. Between 2000 and 2015, at least forty-one state and federal supreme courts issued rulings effectively legalizing gay marriage, and public support for legalizing gay marriage increased from 42 to 60 percent (Wolf 2015; Gallup 2020). Despite a series of highly visible rulings with far-reaching consequences, courts legalizing gay marriage neither seem to cause opinion to shift against legalizing gay marriage nor lead people to hold gays and lesbians in lower esteem. The findings in the preceding chapters thus raise a host of questions about what role political and social institutions play in helping to shape public opinion toward gays and lesbians and whether the results observed in the previous chapters arise from the intensive analysis of the effects of court rulings on public opinion.[1]

Answering these questions is essential to understanding the dynamics of public opinion that might drive change. Like most research on the topic to this point, analyses in the preceding chapters focus primarily on the role of the court in influencing public opinion. Consequently, we know little about whether judicial institutions differ from other institutions in their ability to influence opinion on gay rights. If they do, then it is possible that the findings we report in previous chapters may be driven not by the insensitivity of the public to advances in gay rights but to the public's acceptance of rulings by the court. To what extent do attempts to obtain policy through legislatures, executives, or referenda affect how the public perceives an issue or the group that advocates it? The answer to these questions has important implications for understanding backlash and public opinion toward gays and lesbians: What role do political institutions play in shaping political attitudes toward gays and lesbians? In this chapter we investigate how different institutions influence public opinion in order to answer that question.

In general, the evolution of attitudes toward gays and lesbians can be explained by the changing of attitudes over time and gradual population replacement of older citizens who are more opposed to gay rights with younger ones who are more supportive (Barclay and Flores 2015; A. Flores 2014). Conversion has partly been facilitated by positive portrayals of gays and lesbians on television (e.g., Garretson 2018). Largely overlooked, however, is the role that formal political institutions play in shaping attitudes. When government institutions make policy decisions, they legitimize groups and policy in the eyes of the public. Governmental actions may force citizens to question their previously held beliefs by legitimizing policy and thereby galvanizing support. Less well recognized is the possibility that different institutions may influence public opinion in different ways. Decisions made by democratically elected bodies such as the U.S. Congress or a state legislature might influence public opinion differently than institutions run by appointees, such as the U.S. Supreme Court.

A variety of perspectives might explain the process by which institutions can influence public opinion. The *republican schoolmaster perspective* holds that because of their imprimatur of objectivity and legitimacy, citizens gradually come to accept court decisions with which they initially disagree (Franklin and Kosaki 1989). Alternatively, the public may be more likely to accept decisions by institutions over which they have more direct influence through the democratic process. Still another explanation is that opinion convergence occurs as the well-informed align their opinions with those of their partisan elites, and that the degree to which these cues are salient varies across institutions. Finally, institutions might have little influence on public attitudes (e.g., Zaller 1992).

In order to better understand the opinion dynamics at play regarding gay rights and to assess whether the absence of backlash observed in our studies is driven by our focus on judicial rulings, this chapter examines whether citizens respond differently to policy made by different institutions. To do so, we identify, develop, and test prominent explanations for how institutions might affect public opinion on gay rights. The results show that the lack of support we find in the preceding chapters for the theory of mass opinion backlash is not likely driven by the fact that most of the studies conducted herein focus on challenges to the status quo instigated by the judiciary.

Institutional Decision Making and Public Opinion

Perhaps the most prominent source for political information are the elites who provide cues that help shape mass opinion (Zaller 1992). The public, especially those citizens who are attentive, look to elites with whom they share partisan attachments as credible sources of information. When elites are unified in the cues they provide, a "mainstreaming" effect occurs in which public opinion tends to converge. When elites are divided, however, the public receives conflicting cues, and (among those who have awareness of the issue) they become more polarized in their views as well.

The influence of elite cues on public opinion is well understood, but the manner by which the public reacts to institutional decisions as cue givers is less well established. While the study of institutional actions other than court rulings is limited, an important exception focuses on the role of presidential rhetoric. As the most visible elected official in American government, no politician is better positioned than the president to shape public opinion (Kernell 2006). Presidents, for instance, have substantial influence in selecting which issues are placed before the public (Druckman and Jacobs 2009), moving public opinion on specific issues in the short term (Rottinghaus 2010; Kernell 2006), and are able to shift the standards by which the public evaluates their performance (e.g. Cohen 1997; Jacobs and Shapiro 1994; Druckman and Jacobs 2006, 2009, 2011). While presidents target their speeches to influence public policy by giving legislators and bureaucrats specific cues (Eshbaugh-Soha 2006), they rarely cater to public opinion unless their positions are in line with majority opinion (Canes-Wrone 2010). Others conclude that presidents often fail to shape opinion (e.g., Edwards 2003) and find that presidents are able to move public opinion only on some specific issues or in the short term (Rottinghaus 2010; Kernell 2006). Thus, while a variety of mechanisms by which presidents may influence opinion are offered, research as a whole seems to suggest that presidents are able to influence opinion, even if just in the short term.

Serving as Republican Schoolmaster? The Supreme Court and Public Opinion Change

In contrast to the presidency, research on the court's influence on public opinion is more mixed. Compared to the modern presidency and Congress, the U.S. Supreme Court may be less likely to influence public opinion because justices are appointed rather than elected. Theoretically, a lack of accountability might make voters less likely to pay attention to or become knowledgeable about their decisions. In fact, some find opinions to shift in a negative direction following Supreme Court rulings. Gregory Caldiera (1986), for example, finds that during periods in which the Supreme Court invalidates a large number of laws passed by Congress, public opinion can turn against the Court.

On the other hand, surveys show that citizens hold the court in high esteem, most especially when compared to the legislature or executive (Mate and Wright 2008). Justices work to protect the court's legitimacy, and their fear of being overturned by Congress may cause them to tread carefully and avoid taking extreme or unpopular positions (Lerner 1967). Further, scholars often find that opinion influences court decisions (Mischler and Sheehan 1993). Many studies find that court decisions can have a legitimizing impact on public opinion (e.g., Marshall 1987; Blake 1977; Canon and Johnson 1984; Marshall 1987; Uslaner and Weber 1979). The most oft-cited case in this regard is *Roe v. Wade*. In this instance, while some find more favorable opinion following the decision (e.g., Blake 1977; Rosenberg 1991; Uslaner and Weber 1979), others find more mixed results (Adamany 1973; Marshall 1987). Because citizens hold the Supreme Court in higher regard than other institutions, public opinion is generally in agreement with court decisions (Franklin and Kosaki 1989). The republican schoolmaster perspective holds that justices are aware of their roles as civic educators and use their position to influence the citizenry (e.g., Lerner 1967; Hanley et al. 2012). Prominent examples include some of the court's most important rulings, such as *Brown v. Board of Education* (1954), when Chief Justice Earl Warren waited years to get a unanimous decision and worked to limit the length of the decision so that newspapers could print the entire ruling (Abraham 1977). Moreover, the court works hard to maintain the perception that it is above partisan politics.

Given these conflicting theoretical perspectives, it is perhaps unsurprising that evidence on the republican schoolmaster perspective is mixed. Some contend that the court exerts little or no influence on public opinion (Marshall 1987; Rosenberg 1991). Others, however, find that under some circumstances the court can influence opinion, especially for those who regard the court positively (Hoekstra 1995).

Power to the People: Democratic Institutions and Public Opinion

While the president and the Supreme Court can influence public opinion under at least some circumstances, there is little research examining whether some institutions do so more effectively than others. One possibility is that policies that are passed by institutions viewed as more responsive are more likely to influence public opinion. In this view, public acceptance emanates from citizens ascribing greater legitimacy to various institutions in which they feel they have greater voice. Decisions made by institutions over which the people have the most direct control are more likely to be accepted. From this perspective, because justices are unelected, the Supreme Court might be the institution least likely to move public opinion. This view, which we refer to as the *power to the people perspective*, holds that the U.S. Congress or one's state legislature would be more likely than the Supreme Court to move opinion, as legislators are democratically elected.

In contrast, decisions by an executive (like the president) might be seen as more legitimate than those of the legislature, because executives are voted on directly by all citizens. Finally, when the people themselves vote on an issue, such a decision might be the most likely to influence public opinion, as decisions made by public referenda are made directly by the people.

Anecdotal evidence supports the notion that the public seems accepting of referenda, especially in the area of gay rights. The use of citizen initiative is widespread, with twenty-four states allowing citizens to vote directly on issues as of 2018. Giving citizens direct power over policy making in the form of direct democracy might lead them to participate and be more interested in the political process (Schmidt 1989; Jost 1990). For the question under examination here, public referenda may provide an opportunity for opinion to change as a consequence of salient policy changes (D. Lewis 2011, 2013). In fact, there have been many instances of anti–gay marriage amendments appearing on state ballots in the past fifteen years. In 2004 alone eleven states had an initiative on the issue of gay marriage (Tesler 2015). While some find little evidence that state initiatives move policy closer to the median voter (Lascher et al. 1996), recent research demonstrates that initiatives in the states can spread as citizens become more favorable of policy when they see neighboring states adopt new policy, such as antismoking legislation (Pacheco 2012). This suggests that the institutional action closest to the people might be most favorable with majority will.

The Opinion Convergence Perspective

One possibility is that our inability to detect opinion change is driven by people following elite cues rather than perceptions of institutional credibility. In contrast to the republican schoolmaster and power to the people theses, evidence suggests that if opinion change is driven primarily by elite cues, then what may appear to be the influence of institutional behavior may actually be a function of the cues that partisan elites are giving about the policy made by the institution. Specifically, while individuals' unwillingness to accept new information often impedes opinion change, events that make an issue salient can serve to highlight discrepancies between an individual's opinions and those held by their social (or reference) groups (Zaller 1992; McGuire 1968). As decades of research in psychology show (e.g., Festinger 1954), individuals have a strong desire to conform to the views of their peers. Consequently, we argue that individuals change their opinions to conform with their reference group when salient events make attitude discrepancies apparent. A variety of disparate empirical studies are consistent with this conjecture (e.g., Uslaner and Weber 1979; Franklin and Kosaki 1989). We describe these insights from psychology to develop the *opinion convergence perspective*.

While research on opinion formation finds that mass opinion change is rare, a variety of studies find opinion change among subgroups. Scholars studying law and courts, for instance, have long been interested in the idea that court rulings can legitimize policies and, in doing so, motivate the public to embrace positions they previously opposed (Franklin and Kosaki 1989). While research on this legitimation (i.e., republican schoolmaster) theory finds little aggregate change, opinions appear to become more consistent with that of the court, depending on an individual's social interactions or context (e.g., Uslaner and Weber 1979; Franklin and Kosaki 1989). Specifically, as an individual's social environment becomes more homogeneous, pressure to conform to the norms of their surroundings on an issue seems to increase (Franklin and Kosaki 1989). In the case of abortion, for instance, Americans seemed to grasp previously held opinions even more tightly in response to the court's ruling (Uslaner and Weber 1979). Similarly, Rebecca J. Kreitzer, Allison J. Hamilton, and Caroline J. Tolbert (2014) find that opinion change in favor of gay marriage in Iowa was most common among those whose views before the ruling were at odds with the dominant view of their political party. Overall, these findings appear consistent with Michael Tesler's (2015) observation that lasting opinion change (rather than priming) occurs with issues on which people hold less well crystallized views.[2]

The opinion convergence perspective builds on the long-held finding in the psychology literature that individuals strive to reduce disagreement with members of reference groups (Asch 1958). Irrespective of the extent to which they instill a sense of threat, salient events can also serve to make apparent one's opinion differences with friends, respected opinion leaders, or fellow group members. Building on Leon Festinger's theory of social comparison (1954), we argue that when events make differences in opinion between individuals and their social groups salient, and the social group exhibits a high degree of opinion agreement, individuals will seek to reduce disagreement by adopting the position of their group. Consequently, rapid opinion change is most likely to occur among those whose views are inconsistent with the social groups in which they are embedded. Specifically, to the extent that events make differences with fellow group members salient, individuals with incongruent opinions are more likely to converge toward the opinions of these fellow group members.

This theory of opinion convergence helps provide order to previous empirical findings in the backlash and legitimation literatures. It explains why opinion can change in both positive and negative directions, since those who change their opinions may be moving toward groups that either favor or oppose the policy. Moreover, opinion convergence appears to explain results observed by Kreitzer and her colleagues (2014) and Charles H. Franklin and Liane C. Kosaki (1989), who find that opinion change is rare but that it occurs primarily among those who hold opinions inconsistent with the strong majority of their fellow group members.

Bringing It All Together: Theory, Implications, and Hypotheses

To what extent do policies made by different institutions have different effects on attitudes toward gays and lesbians? Are changes in opinion better explained by psychological rather than institutional theories? The power to the people perspective argues that the more control that citizens have over an institution, the more likely they are to accept their policies or decisions. In short it holds that decisions made by public referendum lead to greater movement of public opinion than those made by other institutions. The republican schoolmaster perspective holds that the court has a legitimizing effect on opinion and predicts that public opinion will become more positively associated with the court's ruling following salient decisions. Moreover, opinion change should be large and sustained following a ruling.

Recall that there is reason to believe opinion may be unlikely to change. As attitude change is a function of a multistep process that requires that an individual "receive" and then "accept" information, the likelihood that a person comes to agree with a policy depends on whether the policy is congruent with existing beliefs (e.g., McGuire 1968; Zaller 1992). Moreover, rather than change their position, those with firmly held views tend to seek out information that reinforces those already strong views (e.g., Redlawsk 2002). Conversely, while those lacking well-formed attitudes are more likely to accept new information and therefore change their (poorly formed) views, they are unlikely to receive new information in the first place (McGuire 1968; Zaller 1992). Consequently, neither those with well nor poorly formed views are likely to lash back.

Alternatively, a variety of explanations might explain opinion change as a result of institutional action. The opinion convergence perspective holds that opinion change should occur among those who, prior to the salient event, held positions contrary to those they identify with as their peer or reference groups when elite opinion among the group is largely unified. In essence, they converge to the opinion of the group with whom they most strongly identify. Since the view held by any group can be positive or negative, opinion can change in either direction depending on the positions held by the individual and the group. In contrast to backlash, convergence occurs when salient events make individuals aware that their opinions are at odds with those of their relevant social reference group. Individuals then begin to shift their opinions toward the dominant position held by the group.

To identify those who should change opinions, we seek social groups with strong and cohesive opinions on the issue of gay marriage. Upon the issue being made salient, the dominant opinion among the group should become stronger in the direction held by the group. With respect to the issue of gay marriage, two obvious groups are those who identify as strong Democrats or strong Republicans. Specifically, we expect subjects who identify as strong Democrats who hold less favorable positions on gay marriage to moderate their views and come to support gay marriage; conversely, we expect strong Republicans who hold favorable views on gay marriage to begin to hold more negative views. One logical implication is that as a consequence of incongruent members of the group changing their opinion, holding all else constant, average group opinion should become slightly more extreme among those strong partisans exposed to non-gay related issues like the immigration policy conditions.

Each of these theoretical perspectives leads to differing predictions in terms of whether and under what conditions public opinion might change. We summarize each in table 5.1. In the next section, we test these theoretical perspectives using the multiple actions taken by President Obama on the issue of gay rights.

TABLE 5.1. How institutions affect opinions according to each theory

Theoretical Perspective	Opinion Change	Who Changes?
Republican schoolmaster	Large change toward court decision	General public
Power to the people	Large change toward democratic institutional decision (e.g., referenda or legislature)	General public
Opinion convergence perspective	Positive or negative	Individuals whose views are incongruent with the group with whom they identify (strong Democrats and Republicans)

Testing Opinion Change following Presidential Action

To this point, our analysis of the effects of different institutions on support for gay rights has focused on the court, legislature, and public referendum. The reason for this is practical. Many respondents would surely detect a contrived scenario involving the U.S. president, Congress, or Supreme Court. As a consequence, our analysis so far has been somewhat limited in the institutions we examine and has come at the cost of potentially making any threat that policy change poses somewhat less relevant to the subjects and ensuring that they have consumed the information necessary to instigate opinion change.

In particular, the president is uniquely visible, receiving far more press attention than any other institution in the American political system, and voted on, if only indirectly, by all citizens. By setting the agenda, lobbying his allies, wielding his veto pen, and directing the administration and the bureaucracy, the president is also the single most important policy maker. The president's unique position thus provides an incredibly useful case for study and raises an important question for our analysis: What effect does the presidency have on public acceptance of gay rights?

To explore this question, we examine public opinion on attitudes toward marriage and gay rights at three points between 2010 and 2014. This time period is important because it precedes and then follows President Barack Obama's 2012 announcement of support for legalizing same-sex marriage. In May 2012, a prominent position change by such a visible and powerful politician is precisely the type of action held to both trigger opinion backlash and provide the elite cues that are central to the opinion convergence perspective. Moreover, the presidency's nationwide electoral base makes it the ideal institution for examining the power to the people thesis. Finally, this test adds an important layer to our analysis beyond experimental evidence by using real-world events.

The case of Obama's public shift also presents a threat to those who are opposed to gay marriage and thus had the possibility of activating backlash among those opponents. Obama's support for gay rights contrasted sharply with his predecessor George W. Bush, who remained staunchly opposed to gay marriage during his presidency. Thus, this presidential announcement allows us to examine whether our findings are limited to court rulings, which might be less likely to activate backlash than public announcements by the president.

In 2008 candidate Barack Obama was asked his opinion of California's Proposition 8, which would ban marriage between same-sex couples.

While Obama said he felt a change in the law was unnecessary, he made clear his position that marriage was a right available only to heterosexual couples. As he told MTV News, "I believe marriage is between a man and a woman. I am not in favor of gay marriage" (C. Harris 2008). As public opinion shifted, however, his opinion changed. In May 2012 President Obama declared in a national television interview that he had gone through an evolution on the issue and "just concluded that for me personally it is important for me to go ahead and affirm that I think same-sex couples should be able to get married" (Bowers 2012). In addition to publicly favoring gay marriage, the Obama administration also pushed equal treatment in policy that same year. In December 2010 President Obama signed a bill with the intention of ending the seventeen-year practice of "Don't Ask, Don't Tell" (DADT), which prevented gays and lesbians from openly serving in the military. While the policy did not take effect until September 2011, Obama had pushed the issue early in his presidency, as the public was largely supportive of ending the policy (Bumiller 2011). Importantly, the repeal of DADT represents a powerful and visible cue that is somewhat distinct from the opinion change on gay marriage, as it reflects the action of both the president and Congress.[3]

As we have seen in previous chapters, extensive research shows that elites like the president provide important cues that influence how people orient themselves in the political world. Mass opinion is influenced by exposure to elite discourse on salient issues (e.g., Zaller 1992). The president's public announcement on gay marriage and an end to DADT, as well as the media coverage that followed, presents us with the possibility of examining the public's response at different points in time, before and after a key political elite brings attention to the issue. This also presents the opportunity to see how opinion was changing later in the issue cycle than when our survey experiments were conducted while examining a nationally representative sample on a salient issue.

The president's announcement and shift in stance on gay marriage thus presents an important case that allows us to examine whether key institutional actors can influence opinion. These events and the public's reaction to them serve as a different kind of stimuli that speaks to the generalizability of the findings from our previous chapter in which we largely rely on experimental evidence. Importantly, opinion data surrounding Obama's policy shift also allow us to more precisely examine opinion change, as we measure opinions by the same set of individuals both before and after the president's announcement. Moreover, the data allow us to examine the persistence of any potential opinion change, since we use a panel study that occurred every two years for a six-year period. This time frame should allow us to detect any lasting changes that occurred as a result of the president's announcement.

In order to study the possibility of backlash following the president's shift on the issue of gay marriage, we use data from a panel study conducted by the Cooperative Congressional Election Study (CCES) (Ansolabehere and Schaffner 2015). The 2010–2014 panel study includes a subset of 9,500 (of the 55,400) adults interviewed in 2010 who were reinterviewed before and after the 2012 presidential election and again during the 2014 congressional elections.[4] The CCES includes two measures that directly allow us to test whether opinions change on gay rights following presidential action. Each survey contains questions that ask respondents whether they support or oppose both a constitutional amendment banning same-sex marriage (SSM) (yes or no) as well as the policy of "Don't Ask, Don't Tell." Each question is asked in a simple "support" or "oppose" format.

As these data were collected before and after each action by the president, we are able to test competing explanations of opinion change as predicted by the republican schoolmaster, opinion convergence, and power to the people perspectives. While the republican schoolmaster thesis has generally been applied to the Supreme Court, its general prediction is that following an institutional decision, opinion should change in a positive direction due to legitimation of that decision. While the court might be more well-regarded and seen as independent among the public, the public now looks to the executive branch as a first actor and to solve problems (Rudalevige 2005). Thus, the republican schoolmaster perspective predicts that the general public is likely to come to support an issue following a shift in stance by the president. The power to the people perspective predicts that opinion by the general public will be most accepting of decisions made by institutions for which they have the most control. While the president is indirectly elected through the Electoral College, the president is more democratically elected than the appointed Supreme Court and Congress as a whole. Thus, the power to the people perspective suggests that the general public will be more favorable following Obama's changing positions.[5] The opinion convergence perspective would predict that partisan cues will drive opinion changes, as individuals will shift their opinions to conform with their reference group when salient events, such as major announcements by the president, make attitude discrepancies apparent. Thus, President Obama's very public changing of positions on both DADT and marriage equality should lead to strong Republicans shifting against the president's position, while strong Democrats should shift with the president.

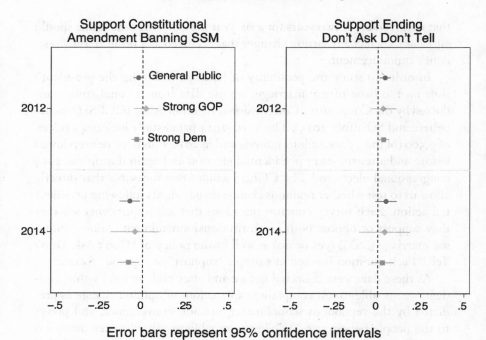

Error bars represent 95% confidence intervals

Figure 5.1. Differences (from 2010) in gay rights opinion (CCES panel)

In order to test the effect that Obama's announcement might have on public opinion, we conducted a panel regression with individual fixed effects for two questions that measure support for gay rights. While the full results can be found in the appendix to this chapter, the main results are shown in figure 5.1. The figure shows the coefficient plot for the panel regression for the groups of interest.[6]

The left panel displays average change (from 2010) in an individual's support for a constitutional amendment banning same-sex marriage. The right panel shows changes in an individual's support for ending the policy of "Don't Ask, Don't Tell," which allowed gays to serve openly in the military. Each figure displays the regression represented by a dot along with the 95 percent confidence intervals of the estimate of change from the 2010 survey. Error bars that do not cross zero indicate a statistically significant change in opinion from 2010, which would demonstrate a change not due to chance alone.

Beginning with the left-most panel, we see that strong Democrats are significantly less likely to support a constitutional amendment banning same-sex marriage in both 2012 and 2014 (after Obama's announcement) compared to 2010 (before Obama's announcement). The general public has a negative and statistically significant change in support for a constitutional amendment banning same-sex marriage in 2014 (compared to 2010). Overall, most groups do not change significantly, and when they do, the differences are tiny.

In terms of the theoretical perspectives outlined earlier, these results provide mixed support for opinion convergence, as strong Democrats shift opinion on same-sex marriage although strong Republicans do not. Neither group exhibits a statistically significant shift in opinion following Obama's changing stance on DADT. The republican schoolmaster and power to the people perspectives also receive mixed support, as the results are consistent with these perspectives for same-sex marriage though not following the president's changing position on DADT. The general public is more likely to oppose an amendment banning same-sex marriage following Obama's embrace of gay marriage but is not significantly more likely to support ending DADT. The most consistent finding is that overall opinion remains quite stable, and when there is a small change, each group becomes *less* supportive of a ban on same-sex marriage following Obama's announcement.

We find similar results when respondents are asked whether they support ending the Don't Ask, Don't Tell policy that originated in the Clinton era. Both the general public and strong Democrats are slightly *more* favorable to ending the policy in 2012 than in 2010. And while there is no significant opinion change in 2014 (compared to 2010), every group, including those most opposed to gay rights, shows positive movement for ending a policy that prevents gays and lesbians from serving openly in the military. Moreover, if the mechanism at work as detailed by the republican schoolmaster perspective is correct, we should observe stronger changes in opinion with time as the decision recedes. In fact, we find this to be the case, at least for same-sex marriage. When comparing attitudes between 2010 and 2014, we observe a shift in opinion for both strong Democrats and the general public. Thus, while we find limited support for opinion convergence, we find some support for the republican schoolmaster perspective.

Testing Whether Opinions Change following Institutional Decisions

In order to test the extent to which the institution making policy drives public attitudes toward gays and lesbians, we examine whether opinion changes when the institution granting rights to gays and lesbians varies. We test the republican schoolmaster perspective by examining whether opinion becomes more favorable toward gays and lesbians following court rulings that grant them equal rights. We test the opinion convergence perspective by examining whether the general public, or specific groups, reconcile opinion differences that are incongruent with those with those held by leader of groups with whom they identify, following advances in gay rights. And by comparing attitude change across institutional rulings that vary in the extent to which they are democratically elected, we test the power to the people perspective.

Our first strategy for assessing whether different institutions affect people's attitudes is to conduct an experiment in which different actors are responsible for the creation or legalization of policy. The basic idea is this: If two institutions promulgate the exact same policy, will people react differently to one rather than the other? Building on the experiments used to detect opinion change in previous chapters, we assess the effects of exposure to information about gays and lesbians (a short excerpt from a news article) on attitudes about same-sex marriage and LGBT Americans relative to a baseline condition that includes no information about gays and lesbians. After exposing subjects to one of five randomly assigned experimental conditions, we then assess their attitudes using a questionnaire. Here the conditions vary the institution making the policy, which allows for a test of the power to the people thesis and the republican schoolmaster perspective as well. We can compare how and whether attitudes change across groups using the demographic data collected prior to exposure to the news articles. Table 5.2 describes the experimental conditions.

These conditions alter whether a subject is exposed to gay rights issues in the context of the legislature passing a law, the court making the same

TABLE 5.2. Summary of experimental conditions

Condition	LGBT Content	Policy–Related	Institution	Article Headline
1	No	Yes	Courts	"Court Overturns Concealed Carry Policy"
2	Yes	No	n/a	"Thousands Attend Gay Pride Parade"
3	Yes	Yes	Legislature	"Legislature Overturns Gay Marriage Ban"
4	Yes	Yes	Courts	"Court Overturns Gay Marriage Ban"
5	Yes	Yes	Referendum	"Referendum Overturns Gay Marriage Ban"

issue legal, a public referendum passing the law, or a news story that high-lights gays and lesbians that is unrelated to policy (or institutions). In con-dition 2 there is no institutional action or policy change (i.e., court rul-ing, referendum, or legislative action), but a gay rights issue is presented. This condition allows us to assess change in attitudes based solely on non-policy information about gays and lesbians. For this condition, respondents viewed a short paragraph about a gay pride parade in Oregon. In condi-tion 3, we inform subjects that a legislature passed a pro–gay marriage bill. Similarly, conditions 4 and 5 present this same issue (framed in the same way) but instead attribute gay marriage becoming legal to the action of the court and a public referendum, respectively.

We assess opinion change by comparing the differences between atti-tudes in each treatment condition with the baseline and intensity of posi-tions on gay marriage and toward gays and lesbians across the conditions. While this experiment does not allow us to assess whether opinion change endures, it does allow us to identify large attitude shifts, opinions that are sharply more negative, and levels of intensity that are more positive than those observed in the baseline condition, which are all consistent with opinion change (e.g., in the direction of backlash).[7] Attitudes and intensity are assessed through the instruments administered following the experi-ment. We measure opinion change through an online survey experiment using AMT as a subject recruitment program.[8]

Public Opinion and Institutional Policy: Evidence from Experiments

In order to evaluate the effects different institutions have on public opin-ion, it is important to identify which groups are expected to change their views under each of the theories. To examine opinion convergence theory, we identify two groups with strong and cohesive opinions on the issue of gay marriage: "strong Republicans," who are least supportive of gay rights, and "strong Democrats," who are most supportive. The republican school-master thesis predicts that among the masses, public opinion will be more positive toward gay rights following a ruling expanding gay rights. The power to the people perspective suggests that the greater the influence citizens have on an institution, the more supportive they will be of policies the institution makes. Thus, we expect laws passed by public referendum to increase public support more than bills passed by the legislature, and both to be greater than rulings made by the Supreme Court.

The results of experiments conducted in chapter 3 indicated little evidence of opinion change, even among groups (such as white evangelicals) that might be most likely to be predisposed to view gays and lesbians negatively. Thus, in the next section, we focus on whether the type of institution making a pro–gay rights ruling leads to differential responses by the general public as well as strong Democrats and strong Republicans, groups who are, respectively, positively and negatively disposed toward gays and lesbians.

Building on our work in the preceding chapter, we measure policy opinion backlash by asking respondents to rate their support for gay marriage on a scale ranging from "strongly oppose" (1) to "strongly favor" (4). We also examine issue intensity by asking respondents to indicate how strongly they feel about gay marriage on a scale from 0 ("don't care at all") to 10 ("most important issue").[9] Finally, we examine whether opinion backlash may "spill over" and negatively affect attitudes toward gays and lesbians by using a feeling thermometer, which asks respondents to rate gays and lesbians on a scale from 1 to 100.

Our first test examines whether opinion changes following a ruling by a court, which primarily allows for a test of the republican schoolmaster thesis. We are also able to test the opinion convergence perspective, as we can examine whether opinion changes among either specific groups or the general public. Recall that opinion convergence predicts that people's views will converge toward that of the social groups with which they identify. Specifically, opinion among strong Democrats should become more supportive (i.e., have positive differences) and opinion among strong Republicans should become less supportive (i.e., have negative differences). Finally, the power to the people thesis holds that the public should be most accepting of decisions made through institutions over which they have greatest influence or control.

We measure opinion change by subtracting the mean opinion in the parade (noninstitutional) condition from mean opinion in the treatment (institutional) condition. By comparing these two differences, we obtain an estimate of how much larger the shift in attitudes stemming from political institutions is than the shift stemming from non-policy events. Positive scores indicate that those exposed to the court rather than the parade vignette rated gays and lesbians more highly. The plots in figure 5.2 show the difference in mean support for gay marriage, intensity about gay marriage, and thermometer ratings of gays and lesbians by comparing court decisions to the parade condition. The differences in means are indicated by dots, while the lines above and below are the 95 percent confidence interval around this estimate.

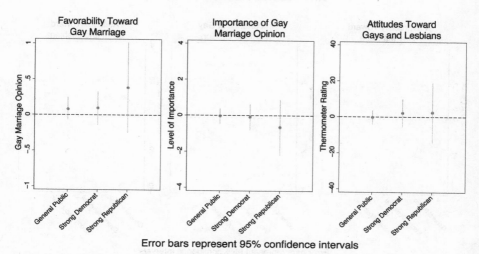

Error bars represent 95% confidence intervals

Figure 5.2. Differences in attitudes toward gays and lesbians between political (court) and noninstitutional actors (parade conditions)

Beginning with the left-most panel, we see that, relative to the parade condition, opinion toward gay marriage becomes slightly more positive for all groups who learned of the court's ruling (as the republican schoolmaster perspective would predict). Similarly, in terms of importance (middle panel) and attitudes about gays and lesbians (right-most panel), the results for each group hover right around zero, which indicates almost no change in opinion. On the whole, then, these results provide little evidence for the republican schoolmaster perspective. Moreover, we also find no differences for either the general public or strong partisans on any of the measures. Consequently, while the results provide no evidence for the opinion convergence perspective, the lack of opinion change is consistent with the results from our previous chapters.

Finding little evidence for the republican schoolmaster perspective, we examine whether a law passed by the legislature might influence opinion. Doing so allows for additional tests of the opinion convergence perspective. Figure 5.3 shows the difference in means between the legislative and parade conditions. Positive scores indicate opinion shifting to be more favorable toward gays and lesbians following the legislature granting gays and lesbians equal marriage rights.

In the left-most panel of the figure, we see that for each group, opinion is more positive following a legislative decision. While these differences in opinion are tiny (only a .3 shift on a five-point scale), only the gen-

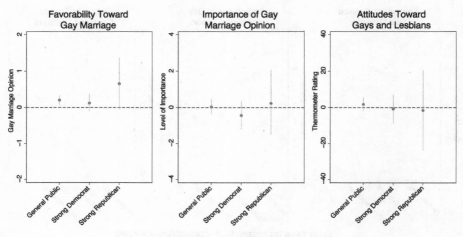

Figure 5.3. Differences in attitudes toward gays and lesbians between political and noninstitutional actors (legislature vs. parade conditions)

eral public is statistically significantly more favorable toward gay marriage when the decision comes from the legislature. The results of the other measures, however, are more mixed, as we observe rather small differences between conditions. Neither the general public nor strong partisans view the issue as more (or less) important, and views about gays and lesbians do not change. Once again, we see little evidence for the opinion convergence perspective.

We can test the power to the people thesis by examining the effect of the passage of gay rights via referendum versus the parade condition, where levels of acceptance should be highest. Figure 5.4 shows the difference in mean support between the referenda to the parade condition for gay marriage, intensity about gay marriage, and thermometer ratings.

The results in the left-most panel of figure 5.4 show that the general public becomes statistically significantly more favorably disposed toward gay marriage when the issue is passed by public referendum. The magnitude of the shift in opinion, however, is extremely small. Nor are the differences in attitudes toward gays and lesbians as a group significant or large. While attitudes toward gays and lesbians are more positive for the general public, these results are not statistically different from zero and are small.[10] Taken together, the evidence for the power to the people thesis is somewhat mixed, as it seems while attitudes become more positive, the change is very small.

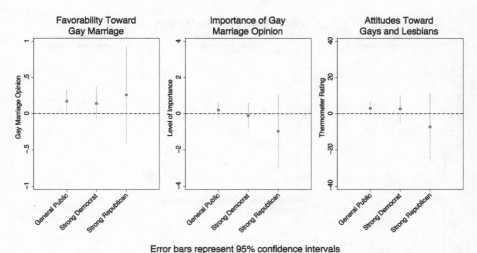

Error bars represent 95% confidence intervals

Figure 5.4. Differences in attitudes toward gays and lesbians between direct democracy and noninstitutional actors (referenda vs. parade conditions)

One way we can more deeply investigate the power to the people thesis is by comparing the extent to which opinion is likely to change in the referenda relative to other venues. Recall that power to the people holds that individuals will become increasingly acceptant of decisions made by institutions or processes based on the influence or say that they have on them. Specifically, as an institution becomes democratically accountable, the more favorable the public will become toward that decision. As the theory makes no prediction about importance, we examine only policy opinion on gay marriage and attitudes toward gays and lesbians as a group. According to this thesis, opinion should be most favorable toward decision by referendum, followed by the legislature, with a court decision being the least favorable when compared to the others. Consequently, the difference in opinion change between the court and the parade condition should be smaller than the difference between the legislature and the parade, which should in turn be smaller than the difference between the referendum and the parade. We test this hypothesis by comparing the opinion changes that result across institutions (referendum minus parade vs. court minus parade; referendum minus parade vs. legislature minus parade; court minus parade vs. legislature minus parade). Figure 5.5 shows the plots of these comparisons, where the rows indicate the two different measures and the columns present the comparisons across conditions for the general public.

Beginning with the left-most column, we compare the overall change

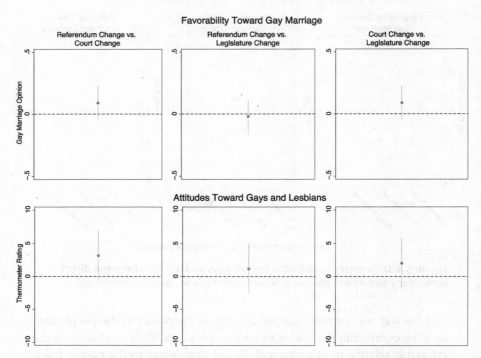

Figure 5.5. Differences in attitudes toward gays and lesbians between direct democracy and institutional actors (referenda vs. court conditions) and comparing institutional change (e.g., court vs. legislature)

between referendum versus court change for gay marriage opinion and attitudes toward gays and lesbians. Positive values indicate more favorable reactions to decisions passed by referendum as opposed to the court. These results show that there is a very small but positive difference between referendum and court change—though it is not significant. The center column compares the referendum to the legislature and shows no change. The right-most column compares court versus legislature. Once again, all differences are small and none statistically indistinguishable from zero. Considered as a whole, the results in figure 5.5. lend no evidence to the power to the people thesis.

Taken in combination, several conclusions become apparent. First, these results suggest that the findings of the previous chapters are not likely a product of simply studying the court. Opinion change is quite rare, and when it occurs it is quite small in magnitude. Contrary to the republican schoolmaster perspective, we find no evidence that the court moves public opinion. Nor is there much evidence that the public becomes more supportive of rulings on gay marriage with increases in the democratic accountability of institutions, such as a legislature passing a law or a public referendum as the power to the people perspective predicts. While we do find that opinion becomes more favorable following the referendum, the opinion shift is tiny and not validated by our comparison of that shift to those in less accountable institutions, like the legislature. That is, we do not see a similar increase in acceptance when institutions more directly controlled by the people who make decisions. Similarly, the issue convergence theory received no support, as the opinions of strong Democrats and Republicans did not change under any institutional condition.

Conclusion

To what extent does the institution making policy affect public attitudes toward gays and lesbians? Is the absence of backlash and support for elite mobilization driven by our focus on court rulings? The results of this chapter suggest that the courts are no more likely than other institutions to incite anti-gay backlash. We find no evidence that courts are any more effective at convincing the public to accept their policies than are other institutions. Moreover, alternative perspectives that explain opinion change once an institution grants equal rights to gays and lesbians found little consistent support. The republican schoolmaster perspective holds that the public is likely to come to accept the court's (or president's) decision with time. The power to the people thesis argues that citizens will be most accepting of decisions over which they have the most direct control, such as the result of public referenda or presidential position taking. Another perspective (convergence theory) suggests that the well-informed align their opinions with those of their partisan elites and that the degree to which these cues are salient varies across institutions.

Our studies using an online experiment and observational evidence during Obama's presidency demonstrated little support for mass opinion backlash, fleeting evidence for the opinion convergence perspective, and more mixed support for the republican schoolmaster and power to the people perspectives. The court was not shown to move public opinion in any of our tests. Strong partisans were no more likely to change positions than the general public. Moreover, our experiments found no evidence for the idea that people are more supportive of decisions made by an institution over which they have more influence. We were unable to detect differences in opinion whether a decision was issued by the court, legislature, or public referendum. We do find some evidence that opinion changes following major decisions by the president, though in a positive direction and not one consistent with backlash. Even as the individual occupying the most powerful and prominent position in the American political system changed positions on same-sex marriage and signed an end to DADT that was passed by Congress, we find no evidence of mass opinion backlash against these decisions. While opinion did shift to become more supportive of gay rights following the president's changing positions on same-sex marriage, our data did not allow us to test whether this was due to its being a more democratically elected position or one that led to a legitimation process among the public.

Overall, the evidence presented in this chapter echoes earlier findings, in which there is little evidence of opinion change about gays and lesbians regardless of which institution holds the decision-making power. While we find some evidence of opinion change following action by the president, this opinion change is positive, and when opinion changes, it is small and lasts only for a short time. The results from this chapter demonstrate that the lack of evidence for mass opinion backlash from previous chapters is not a function of focusing on court decisions or on specific institutions. Looking across a variety of institutional settings at the state and national levels, we again find no evidence of mass opinion backlash. Our focus now turns to the development and testing of elite theories of reaction to advances in gay rights. We do so by first examining salient historical events and how they each speak to theories of opinion backlash and elite mobilization (chapter 6). Then we examine a difficult test for the theory of elite mobilization by examining the 2010 Iowa judicial retention election (chapter 7).

SIX

The History of Gay Rights

Backlash or Elite-Led Mobilization?

In this chapter we begin to assess the extent to which Elite-Led Mobilization explains opposition to gay rights. By tracing the history of advances in gay rights, we develop a better sense of how the politics of gay rights has evolved and can assess how the challenges to the recognition, public acceptance, and incorporation of gays and lesbians across American history is more consistent with Elite-Led Mobilization Theory or Backlash. To do so, we develop and evaluate predictions for when and how anti-gay elites mobilize against gay rights.

The analysis makes two important contributions: First, it allows us to better understand how opposition to acceptance of gays and lesbians as members of society has developed over time. Second, it allows us to evaluate how well the theories of Mass Opinion Backlash (MOB) and Elite-Led Mobilization (ELM) explain historic opposition to gay rights. The results show that ELM provides a more compelling explanation of how organized opposition to gay rights evolved.

In the preceding chapters we have presented two competing approaches to understanding the opposition to gay rights that is so often termed "backlash." The conventional wisdom, Mass Opinion Backlash, holds that in response to some salient challenge to the status quo, a negative, enduring, and large opinion shift against a policy or against gays and lesbians more broadly occurs. MOB represents a grassroots, bottom-up phenomenon reflecting people's visceral reaction to challenges to the status quo.

Recall that Elite Led Mobilization Theory argues that opposition to policies supported by gays and lesbians is the product of well-organized and well-resourced elites who maintain an ongoing campaign against the public acceptance of gays and lesbians, bisexuals, and transgender persons as legitimate members of society. Pursuit of policy goals represents just one set of objectives in this campaign. Anti-gay elites use a variety of tactics to advance their goals of opposing the public acceptance of gays and lesbians as legitimate members of society, enhancing the acceptability and legitimacy of their organizations, and mobilizing their like-minded supporters to help generate resources.

According to Elite Led Mobilization Theory, one tactic elites employ in response to challenges to the status quo on issues of LGBT politics is mobilization. However, mobilization is necessary only when gay rights are contested. Absent challenges to the status quo, anti-gay elites need not act to mobilize their like-minded supporters, because the prevailing policy reflects their preferences. Historically, the status quo has been one in which gays are closeted and without recognition, acceptance, or rights (e.g., Wald, Button, and Rienzo 1996). Only in the last few decades have we seen a measured but increasing retrenchment in this regard, as gays have gradually but increasingly come out of the closet, sought and gained public acceptance, and publicly begun to advocate their interests (e.g., C. Smith 2011; Pew 2013).

The hegemony of anti-gay policy—that is, the extent to which current policy is hostile to the LGBT community—affects the extent to which we observe conflict over gay rights at different points in American history. Specifically, throughout most of American history, individuals and groups did not organize to advocate *for* gay rights and thereby challenge the status quo. As a result, the stimulus necessary to incite Mass Opinion Backlash did not occur. Similarly, the elites at the heart of Elite Led Mobilization Theory did not need to mobilize to oppose gays and lesbians or gay rights as there was no threat sufficient to challenge or disrupt the anti-gay status quo. Consequently, we expect neither backlash nor elite mobilization to occur until gays and lesbians mobilize, or are perceived to be capable of mobilizing, to challenge this anti-gay hegemony that characterizes most of American political history. There are, however, examples of elite-led scapegoating of the LGBT community. From the Harvard University purge of gays in the 1920s to the Lavender Scare in the 1950s (discussed below), elites have not shied away from attacking the gay community when convenient. However, because backlash is a concept tied to public opinion and mass behavior, we need to differentiate the mobilization, orchestration, or manipulation of public opposition to gay rights by elites from the organic reaction by the public to contemporary events.

Understanding the development of public opposition to gay rights requires explaining how gay rights became publicly contested. To do so, we describe the political environment in which gay and anti-gay advocacy organizations began to emerge. Specifically, we identify the important events that framed the modern movements both for and against gay rights. Our focus is on events in which gay rights activists challenged the status quo in pursuit of acceptance, legitimacy, or policy, and in which those opposing gay rights worked to oppose policy advances or increased social acceptance of or legitimacy for gays and lesbians. As we will see, while the roots of the gay rights movement date back to the late 1940s, public contestation over those rights began only in the 1970s after gays and lesbians started making advances that posed a threat to those who opposed their public acceptance.

Before the development and organization of the gay rights movement, policy was overtly discriminatory and hence there was little need for those who opposed societal acceptance of gays and lesbians to organize. Consequently, we can think of American history as divided in two eras, the first being one of pre–public contestation, which predates the development of a public gay rights movement. The second is an era of public contestation in which both pro-gay and anti-gay movements regularly have worked to advance their causes.

As we will see in the pages that follow, while gay rights advocates began to mobilize with the Stonewall Inn riots, those opposed to gay rights began mobilizing in response to the Miami-Dade Non-Discrimination Ordinance (Kenney 1998; Fetner 2001). We therefore mark the period of contestation as beginning with the referendum to overturn that ordinance in 1978.

The pre-contestation era is one in which small idiosyncratic steps were taken, often at the local or state level that were disconnected from larger national movements, both by those who supported and those who opposed public acceptance of gays and lesbians. During this era, challenges to the status quo were typically limited to local issues, motivated by local political power dynamics, and seldom gained national visibility. This stands in contrast to the post-contestation era, where actors on both sides strategically have coordinated to advance particular policies or fulfill political and social goals central to their broader organizations or campaigns. Consequently, during the era of contestation, once the status quo was challenged, groups on both sides organized, mobilized, and regularly fought over society's acceptance of gays and lesbians.

Both eras provide important evidence that speaks to the efficacy of Elite-Led Mobilization Theory. Elite Led Mobilization Theory predicts a lack of coherent organization and opposition to gay rights during the pre-contestation era because those advocating gay rights posed little threat. Specifically, we expect the opposition to acceptance of gays and lesbians to appear somewhat idiosyncratic and often conducted for purposes other than impeding the public acceptance of gays and lesbians in society or advancing anti-gay organizations. Similarly, we expect the mobilization and organization of gays and lesbians to be directed less toward promulgating policy through government or opposing attempts to set back or vilify gays and lesbians than to achieve other, more immediate objectives.

The era of contestation describes a period when the anti-gay hegemony is challenged and elites mobilize to defend it. Elite-Led Mobilization Theory predicts much more coherent, strategic, and purposive behavior by anti-gay elites. In particular, we should see elites working to oppose acceptance of gay rights and, contrary to mass opinion backlash, to do so proactively—where they can advance their agenda—in addition to doing so in response to challenges to the status quo by gays and lesbians. In contrast, we should see gays and lesbians, as well as their advocacy groups, challenging the discriminatory status quo in a variety of contexts in which it affects their lives.

Evaluating the Historical Evidence

When examining history to describe and evaluate explanations for contemporary events, it is important at the outset to identify criteria used to determine which events should be studied. This is especially the case when examining the development of social movements where, particularly at the early stages, actors work largely independent of any broader national movement to advance their own or their local or personal interests. The criteria we use are guided by the fundamental question of this book: What explains the public opposition to gay rights in the United States? The cases we examine include all significant federal political developments, as well as significant state and local political events.[1] In some cases we provide background to these events when the context is important for understanding or interpreting their significance. By "significant" events, we refer to those widely recognized as representing some important claim, advance, or conflict. Political events refer not just to acts of policy but also include both expressions of and attempts to gain power. In particular, we are interested in how people respond to particular events, and how, when, and why they organize into groups and movements.

TABLE 6.1. Predictions of opposition to gay rights during eras of contestation

	Era	
Theory	Pre–Contestation	Contestation
Mass opinion backlash	Yes	Yes
	(Reaction)	(Reaction)
Elite–led mobilization	No	Yes
		(Proactive or Reaction)

In order to assess the extent to which the history of the movements for and against the acceptance of gays and lesbians is consistent with ELM, we develop a simple framework for assessing our expectations. We examine major events in both eras to evaluate the theories by describing the key events that occurred during these periods. Simply put, we seek to identify salient elite or governmental attempts to oppose public acceptance, legitimacy, or policies that are publicly advocated by gays and lesbians and their advocates. Building on the logic described in the preceding section, we summarize the expectations of each theory in table 6.1.

In the pre-contestation era, we should see little effort by anti-gay elites to develop coherent opposition to the widespread acceptance and legitimation of gays and lesbians, as such conditions already prevail. With respect to MOB, irrespective of the era, whether or not backlash occurs depends on whether gay rights advocates make salient challenges to the status quo. In both eras, salient challenges to the status quo lead to MOB.

In the era of contestation, we expect to see attempts by anti-gay elites to oppose public acceptance of gays and lesbians whenever possible, and efforts by LGBT organizations to advocate policies that more fully incorporate them into the polity. As we will see, challenges to the status quo necessary for backlash occur only during the era of contestation. Consequently, during the contestation era we are best able to assess the extent to which opposition to gay rights is led by a cadre of organized elites, or whether the events lead to a sharp, negative, and enduring opinion shift consistent with Mass Opinion Backlash.

The Pre-Contestation Era:
The Origins of the Gay Rights Movement

In the United States, the gay and lesbian rights movement began in earnest in 1950, following Senator Joseph McCarthy's (R-WI) infamous Wheeling, West Virginia, speech, in which he claimed that more than two hundred "card-carrying Communists" were embedded in the State Department. This inflammatory speech marked a new phase in the era of the "Red Scare" and the era of McCarthyism and led to a broad congressional inquiry.[2] As part of the investigation sparked by McCarthy's speech, Deputy Undersecretary of State John Peurifoy testified in front of a congressional committee that, although there were no communists employed by the State Department, ninety-one gays and lesbians had been purged as security risks. These firings did little to satisfy the politicians in Washington, the press, or apparently the public and ushered in what came to be known as the Lavender Scare (Griffith 1987; D. Johnson 2004).

Between 1947 and 1955, President Harry Truman and President Dwight Eisenhower implemented the National Security Loyalty Program, which purged over 1,200 gays and lesbians from the federal government over concerns that their sexuality made them susceptible to blackmail (Caute 1978; Theoharis 1971). Although there was little public awareness of this targeting of gays and lesbians, the Loyalty Program laid the foundation for the very public Red Scare and less public Lavender Scare by confirming the existence of gays and lesbians in government (Freeland 1971).

While McCarthy rode the Truman Doctrine to notoriety and instigated the larger witch hunt, the Lavender Scare was the creation of Undersecretary Peurifoy and others in the Senate, such as senators Styles Bridges (R-NH), Kenneth Wherry (R-NE), and Clyde Hoey (D-NC), all of whom pressed the issue of sexuality as a security risk in their committees.[3]

As the fervor of McCarthyism spread, Senator Hoey chaired an investigatory subcommittee within the Committee on Expenditures in Executive Departments, which produced the Hoey Report. The report argued that "sex perverts" employed in the federal government posed a national security risk (D. Johnson 2004, 114–15). Senator Hoey's disinterest in the investigation and Senator McCarthy's publicity tactics allowed for the chief counsel of the subcommittee, Francis Flanagan, to investigate far more broadly than the executive branch preferred (D. Johnson 2004, 103–105). While the Truman administration advocated classifying homosexuality as a medical condition, which justified the aggressive purge of gays and lesbians from positions dealing with classified material, Flanagan wanted to go even further (D. Johnson 2004, 106). He argued that homosexuals were highly vulnerable to blackmail. The media echoed this point, affecting public opinion and deafening the testimony of the Truman administration's medical experts (D. Johnson 2004, 113–14). Beyond suggesting that gays and lesbians were a national security risk via blackmail, however, the Hoey Report further branded them as unsuitable for government employment owing to their weak moral code and violation of sodomy laws (116–17).

While the Hoey Report claimed all government agencies consulted for the report agreed with the conclusions contained therein—in particular that gays in the federal government posed a serious and imminent security risk—this was not true. The U.S. Navy's Crittenden Report revealed that the Navy had disagreed strongly with the analysis and the conclusions of the Hoey Report. The Crittenden Report was released too late to impact policy, however, and was not made public until 1967.

The Hoey Report came about just as the McCarran Internal Security Act, also known as the Subversive Activities Control Act of 1950, sailed through Congress, which also overrode President Truman's veto. The act had four major provisions: barring the immigration of communists and homosexuals into the United States, establishing the ability to expel subversive immigrants, mandating that communists register with the Subversive Activities Control Board (SACB), and ruling that persons registered with SACB could be denied employment with the government or with any business that worked on defense facilities. The immigration ban was upheld in 1954 in *Galvan v. Press*. While categorical immigration restrictions dated to the Chinese Exclusion Act of 1882, the McCarran Act was the first to hold sweeping restrictions for an identity.

Suspected gays and lesbians were routinely purged from government service throughout President Eisenhower's first term (1953–1957). In an attempt to contrast himself from alleged corruption in the Truman administration, Eisenhower campaigned on the belief that "even the suspicion of wrongdoing warranted a removal from public office" ("Eisenhower" 1958, 18). This included not only the ousting of a Federal Communications commissioner for potential corruption but also policing the mere perception of "immorality." This preoccupation with moral rectitude was also driven by a desire many held to venerate those seen as above reproach as the Cold War began.

In the wake of the Hoey Report, in 1953, Eisenhower issued Executive Order 10450, which significantly expanded Truman's loyalty program from his 1947 Executive Order 9835. This compelled the Office of Personnel Management to work in conjunction with J. Edgar Hoover's FBI to investigate the loyalty and potential security risks of all federal employees. Truman's 1947 order established a program that sought to verify State Department employees' loyalty, largely to placate Republicans, who thought that the Democrats were not aggressive enough in stopping communist and Soviet threats. And while Eisenhower's executive order did not explicitly preclude homosexuals from federal employment, the notion that a homo-sexual could be a national security risk because of their susceptibility to blackmail made their sexuality a sufficient condition for termination of their employment.

In effect, this order became a categorical ban for homosexuals in the federal government, which lasted until it was partially reformed in the 1970s. Eisenhower's gay purge ultimately resulted in 381 suspected homo-sexuals being fired from the State Department, more than twice the number of suspected communists (Kaiser 1997, 80). By 1955 the combined effect of Truman's programs and Eisenhower's rules cost 1,200 men and women their federal jobs.

Perhaps the most direct result of the Lavender Scare purge was the politicization of the Mattachine Society. Conceptualized by Harry Hay in 1948 and built out between 1950 and 1953, the Mattachine Society is one of the earliest gay rights organizations in the United States (Roscoe 2013). It was initially founded to create a support group for gay men who had lost their jobs because of their sexuality (Meeker 2001). The Mattachine Society held a few scattered meetings before 1950, but thereafter it swiftly became a large and vocal pro-gay activist group as well as a social network. Fueled by a judicial victory for one of its founding members and inflamed by the mass firing of gays in the State Department, the Mattachine Society promoted the idea that gays should not hide their sexuality and become open members of society.

Hay and the Mattachine Society were radical for the time. Their central philosophy was assimilation, which held that familiarity with gays would lead to acceptance and rights by the straight world (Vaid 1985; Howard 2005). Specifically, they believed that the most effective method of com-bating homophobia was to normalize gays as average everyday Americans who simply had different sexual partners.[4] After quickly shedding its early structural similarities to communist groups, the Mattachine Society began establishing regional branches throughout the country and embarked on civil and political rights campaigns like those of the fledgling black civil rights organizations.

Two major events presented serious challenges to the assimilationist strategy of the Mattachine Society and their allies. First, Eisenhower's sweeping layoffs of gay federal employees meant that no matter how much they were on par with their straight colleagues, they could never become straight enough to no longer be branded a national security risk. Accord-ingly, assimilation had a structural barrier—overt employment discrimi-nation by the federal government—which meant the consequences for coming out (losing your job) far exceeded the benefits of the aspirational goals of acceptance of gays. Second, Alfred Kinsey's reports on his studies of human sexual behavior received national and controversial publicity shortly after their initial publication in 1948 and 1953. The two tomes, which studied male and female sexuality respectively, both sold exceptionally well, and the findings received immense public attention and caused a public uproar.

One of the Kinsey Reports' major contributions came to be known as the Kinsey Scale, which, based on thousands of interviews, argued that human sexuality was nonbinary. The other broad set of findings was that Americans generally prefer a wider array of sexual activities than those they would be comfortable admitting publicly. Taken together, the Kinsey Reports sent empirically grounded shockwaves that catalyzed the sexual revolution. They also served as a basis for challenging the narratives and "scientific" claims of the unreliability and untrustworthiness of gays that came out of the Hoey Report and Eisenhower administration. If the majority of people—even those who identify as "straight"—are deviant to some degree, then vulnerability to blackmail because of deviance would approach ubiquity.

While at first blush it might seem that the Kinsey Reports would have helped advance the cause of acceptance, the truth was much more complicated. Instead, political elites, social commentators, and media leaders argued that the Kinsey Reports were wrong and fraudulent (Terry 1999). The aspects of the Kinsey Reports that were interpreted as controversial ranged from a demonstration of the prevalence of same-sex sexual contact among men and women to the sexual lives of women having comparable importance to them as that of men (Terry 1999, ch. 9). The traditionalists who rejected these propositions used the claims to further entrench their beliefs and insist that things like homosexuality were no more than the perversions of a marginal few (Reumann 2005). So the mission of the Mattachine Society—normalization of gays for straight people leading to general assimilation— ran into a wall of opposition stoked by elite mistrust of gays and the perceived threat to the status quo represented by the advancement of the science of sex through the Kinsey Reports (Terry 1999, ch. 9).

Movement Expansion: The 1960s

In the 1960s gay rights activists began broadening their portfolio of strategies to achieve change. Following the lead of Black civil rights groups, gay rights groups began to pursue litigation and lobbying efforts to achieve change. The goals of these activities initially focused on employment non-discrimination like the right to be a public school teacher, access to public facilities like public pools and beaches, and general commercial rights like landlord tenant issues or the right to open a bar. During this time Frank Kameny, an astronomer assigned to the U.S. Army's Map Service, was fired because of his homosexuality. He sued for reinstatement and, while ultimately unsuccessful, his appeals made it all the way to the U.S. Supreme Court. In 1965 the growing media coverage and activism resulted in the first protests outside the White House for gay rights since the Lavender Scare days (Pierceson 2016, 26–28; Bullough 2002).

In 1969 the Civil Service Commission, the primary agency tasked with assessing the meritocratic procedures in hiring, firing, and promoting employees in the federal government, suffered its first loss as a result of a firing over sexuality in the case *Norton v. Macy*. Clifford Norton was a budget analyst for NASA who admitted, under intense interrogation from law enforcement after a mere traffic violation, that he may have had homosexual experiences in the past. Norton's suit was supported both by Kameny and the ACLU (Faderman 2015). Although neither the traffic violation nor any of the sexual experiences he referred to happened while working, NASA terminated his employment. The Civil Service Commission upheld his firing, resting on the precedent that NASA and the federal government as a whole could fire an employee for being gay even if being so did not affect job performance or pose a clear security threat. Ultimately, the U.S. Court of Appeals for the D.C. Circuit found that NASA and the Civil Service Commission wrongly terminated Norton. The court ruled that an individual cannot be fired solely for being a homosexual and that the government had to demonstrate that an individual's homosexuality negatively affected their job performance or served as a clear security risk in order to fire them. Fearful of the U.S. Supreme Court's sympathy for civil rights, the Civil Service Commission chose not to appeal in order to preserve their employment authority (Siniscalco 1976).

These cases represent the first steps in what would gradually become a larger movement (Marcus 1992). They were of mixed success and of limited importance and visibility to the broader public. While borrowing strategies from other social movement organizations helped advance civil rights for homosexuals, gay rights activists garnered nowhere near the notoriety or publicity that Black civil rights leaders or anti–Vietnam war protesters did. Public awareness remained comparatively low.

The Era of Contestation:
Stonewall, Harvey Milk, and the 1970s

Awareness about gay rights activism changed dramatically following the Stonewall Inn riots in the summer of 1969. The Stonewall Inn was a gay dive bar on Christopher Street in Greenwich Village in New York City. With no liquor license or even running water but a fully stocked bar, it was a local hangout for an eclectic crowd of gays, transgender individuals, and lesbians as well as other outcasts (Armstrong and Crage 2006, 736). Although the Stonewall Inn paid protection money to the Mafia, it was subject to frequent aggressive police raids (Carter 2004, 140–43). These bars were important centers of social interaction, as gays and lesbians could not generally be themselves in public. Moreover, police across the nation had taken to harassing gay bar patrons (see D'Emilio 1983; D'Emilio 1992, 74–95).

Tired of being subject to police abuse, the patrons of the Stonewall Inn fought back, and the physical altercations with police that night quickly evolved into several days of riots in the streets. The spontaneous push back from the diverse crowd, which included gays and lesbians and members of the trans community, created a lasting media narrative (Armstrong and Crage 2006).

Despite the publicity of the Stonewall Inn riots, they were met with little reaction from the broader public. While hostility toward gays could have been the driver of the harassment and the raids and arrests, other vulnerable populations, such as African Americans and immigrant enclaves, faced similar harassment (Fogelson 1968; Tuch 2006). In other words, the police harassment may have been driven not only by animus but also because the group was politically powerless and publicly invisible (D. Johnson 2004).

The Stonewall Inn riots did not lead to a new wave of anti-gay activity by the police but rather may have actually pushed gay activists to organize around the country (Armstrong and Crage 2006, Kuhn 2011, 65–80). The riots seemed to signal the gay community the importance of standing together to fight violence and exploitation. In the months following the march, several new groups organized and gay newspapers were started.

While the Stonewall Inn riots were not met with conservative opposition, they did serve to galvanize supporters of gay rights. For instance, many same-sex couples around the country sought to obtain marriage licenses, and after they were denied the right to get married, some went to court (Pierceson 2016, 93). In Minnesota, Jack Baker and Michael McConnell claimed (correctly) in their suit that no statute actually specifically prohibited them from obtaining a marriage license and that marriage was a fundamental right (Brandzel 2005, 181–82). The court was unsympathetic. Eschewing the basic premise that statutes must be narrowly read, the court observed:

> The institution of marriage as a union of man and woman, uniquely involving the procreation and rearing of children within a family, is as old as the book of Genesis. . . . This historic institution manifestly is more deeply founded than the asserted contemporary concept of marriage and societal interests for which petitioners contend. The due process clause of the Fourteenth Amendment is not a charter for restructuring it [marriage] by judicial legislation. (*Baker v. Nelson* 191 N.W. 2d 185 at 186 [Minn. 1971], appeal dismissed *Baker v. Nelson* 409 US 810 [1972]).

Whereas the Mattachine Society focused on assimilation, the Stonewall Inn riots catalyzed a push toward an egalitarian ideology that helped to connect a cluster of gay rights issues that had previously seemed unrelated (Duberman 1993). The movement shifted from emphasizing radical assimilation to emphasizing equality as issues ranging from employment protections to criminal procedural law became more obviously connected under a general notion of equity under the law (Pierceson 2016, 31–32).

The Stonewall Inn riots also resulted in the reconsideration of the tactics that might be used to achieve these goals so that litigation, legislation, and protest were all possible avenues of advocacy for change. Rather than limiting the battles over gay rights to the courtrooms, the movement advanced a broader agenda by pursuing a wide range of policies that adversely affected gays and lesbians. This increasingly diversified approach led to important nonlegal gains.

In response to the activism of Frank Kameny and Barbara Gittings, a New York based LGBT activist, as well as the scholarship of psychologist Evelyn Hooker, in 1973 the American Psychiatric Association delisted homosexuality as a mental disorder from the *Diagnostic and Statistical Manual of Mental Disorders* (*DSM*) (Pierceson 2016, 27–28). In 1975 the U.S. Civil Service Commission eliminated its rule precluding homosexuals from serving in government jobs (G. Lewis 1997).

More broadly, the activism spurred on by Stonewall led to a variety of legal gains and an expansion of local efforts to recognize and combat discrimination against gays and lesbians in progressive cities across the nation (Fejes 2008). Between 1972 and 1976, for instance, twenty-nine local governments enacted ordinances protecting gays and lesbians from some forms of discrimination (Fejes 2008, 53). These laws generally, but not always, passed as part of a broader package of liberal reforms and faced little opposition because of the omnibus nature of the reform packages, the relatively progressive political climates of the cities where they were considered, and the lack of organized opposition in the cities where they were proposed (Fejes 2008, 53–57).

The now notorious Miami-Dade nondiscrimination ordinance, and its subsequent repeal by popular initiative, at first appeared to be just the next in a growing line of antidiscrimination ordinances passed by cities. Like many of the other cities, the Miami-Dade ordinance grew out of activism by a small group of representatives from local gay and lesbian groups. In the run up to the 1976 elections, activists formed the Dade County Coalition for the Humanistic Rights of Gays (DCCHRG) to identify and support candidates who supported gay rights. The coalition then circulated endorsements and provided donations and volunteers for their preferred candidates (Clendinen and Nagourney 1999). Perhaps aided by turnout for Jimmy Carter, the first presidential candidate to publicly support gay rights, Election Day saw forty-four of the forty-nine endorsed candidates get elected, including five of the nine seats on the county commission (Clendinen and Nagourney 1999; Fejes 2008).

Almost immediately after the election, Commissioner Ruth Shack proposed the nondiscrimination ordinance supported by the DCCHRG. The commission acted quickly after the election, holding a unanimous vote on December 7 to schedule a public hearing on the ordinance in January, where it would become law with that second reading (Clendinen and Nagourney 1999).

In the interim, however, opponents became activated. A celebrity spokesperson and former Oklahoma beauty pageant winner named Anita Bryant was informed by her pastor that the ordinance would require the school her children attended to "hire practicing homosexuals" (Clendinen and Nagourney 1999, 296). Bryant had been a staple in Republican political circles in Florida and was vocal about her evangelical worldview. Bryant's sense of outrage about the nondiscrimination ordinance was heightened because she felt betrayed, since the ordinance had been authored by her agent's wife. Although Bryant had contributed money and recorded a radio commercial endorsing Ruth Shack in the previous campaign, she was determined to defeat the ordinance. The ordinance became the focus of substantial local attention as talk radio shows presented both proponents and opponents. Along with Bryant, local conservative religious leaders mobilized opponents to attend the January meeting. In contrast, the gay community failed to present even a single civil rights leader to speak, and only one religious leader, a Reform rabbi, spoke on its behalf (Fejes 2008).

At the same time, former commissioner Robert Brake, who had been working with the Catholic Church, which was upset because of the lack of an exception for religious schools, planned to circulate a petition to hold a special election to overturn the ordinance after it passed (Fejes 2008). After spirited debate the commission passed the measure by a vote of five to three (Clendinen and Nagourney 1999). Having seen her speak at the meeting, Brake asked Bryant if she would head a petition drive to overturn the ruling (Clendinen and Nagourney 1999). Bryant enthusiastically agreed. The countermovement against the ordinance was swift. Bryant and Brake immediately called a meeting of key supporters, and Republican leaders interested in cultivating supporters on the issue, to begin laying out a plan and subsequently developed a basic strategy to overturn the ordinance via a referendum at a special election (Fejes 2008). On January 28 Bryant hosted a meeting with more than thirty religious and civic leaders to formally create the organization that would be called Save Our Children (Fejes 2008; Clendinen and Nagourney 1999).

Tapping into conservative church networks and support from national religious leaders like Jerry Falwell, the ensuing campaign mobilized hundreds of demonstrators at government meetings and collected tens of thousands of signatures to repeal the ordinance using a referendum during a special June election. Voters overwhelmingly sided against the ordinance. While the county Democratic Party publicly opposed repeal, internally they were divided over this new issue.[5] Gay rights activists and members of the gay community in Dade County were completely unprepared for such a massive and coordinated opposition.

The politics surrounding repeal of the Miami-Dade nondiscrimination ordinance were important because this was the first time organized political opposition, led by religious leaders, developed against gay rights. It would foreshadow the movement of conservative religious leaders toward the GOP nationwide (e.g., Fejes 2006; Fetner 2008). By building an organization and strategy to oppose civil rights for gays and lesbians, the campaign to repeal the nondiscrimination ordinance in Miami-Dade activated religious conservatives, especially evangelical churches. Many of these church leaders were already looking for an opportunity to galvanize their supporters to translate their large memberships and their members' devotion into political power (Pierceson 2016, 31–32).

Save Our Children mobilized a wide range of groups, including Cubans and Jewish leaders, to support repeal (Young 1982). Elites opposed to gay rights tapped into the organization and its opposition to gay rights and fear mongering about predation on children to build their own organizations to challenge the legitimacy of gay rights and oppose equality for gays and lesbians more generally.

Moreover, once the success of the anti-gay campaign became apparent, political elites exploited their constituents' homophobia in order to gain financial and political support. In short, the movement not only resulted in the repeal of nondiscrimination ordinances in Miami-Dade and other cities, but perhaps more importantly, it also set the foundation for the battles over gay rights that were to follow.

While the anti–gay rights efforts that were sparked in response to the Dade County nondiscrimination ordinance led to the repeal of similar statutes in cities like Minneapolis, Eugene, and Wichita, their political successes were relatively limited. In Seattle the attempt to repeal the gay rights ordinance at the ballot box failed. The success of the Save Our Children campaign was in large part due to a confluence of Bryant's celebrity; the mobilization of previously untapped voters, like Cuban Americans; cleavages among some liberal groups, like Jewish religious leaders who opposed the ordinance; the activation of latent public opinion by using fear of sexual predation; and especially the use of preexisting conservative religious organizations (i.e., churches). The repeal campaign was also indirectly helped by the political inexperience and shallow support base of the gay rights advocates (Clendinen and Nagourney 1999). Together, various elements of this coalition were able to rapidly mobilize against gay rights in a range of cities across the country (Young 1982; Rich and Arguelles 1985).

Gay rights advocates had not previously experienced countermovements of such scale, however, and faced strategic and operational challenges mounting the campaign. Locally, the movement lacked leaders with the experience and resources needed to run an effective campaign, and they faced a variety of challenges developing and disseminating a clear and effective message (Fejes 2008). The *Miami Herald*, for instance, refused to print some of their ads and required extensive revisions to others.

Despite these problems, the loss also galvanized gay rights advocates both locally and nationally. Shortly after the Save Our Children defeat, gay rights activists and celebrities began to organize and to develop a national campaign. They raised hundreds of thousands of dollars and led huge rallies attended by thousands of people from coast to coast. In October 1979 hundreds of thousands participated in the National March on Washington for Lesbian and Gay Rights, an event that signaled the beginning of a nationalized movement for gay rights (Smith 2016). Moreover, the active role played by prominent Republicans in supporting repeal, and by the Miami–Dade County Democratic Party presaged the partisan issue attachments and group incorporation that would gradually begin to accelerate on the issue (e.g., Karol 2012).

The year after reversing the Dade County ordinance, Anita Bryant and Save Our Children backed California's Proposition 6, also known as the Briggs Initiative, which aimed to ban gays from working in public schools. At first the proposal garnered strong public support due in large part to the use of appeals to people's fear of gays as child molesters (Potter 2012). Efforts to defeat the Briggs Initiative led to an emphasis on urging closeted gays to come out to their families, friends, and social networks (Kneupper 1981). The goal was to make gays and lesbians more relatable to the public, as people's ignorance of the unknown and largely unseen community stoked their fears (Potter 2012).

Opposition to the Briggs Initiative was led by Harvey Milk, the first openly gay man to hold elected office in the state of California, when he was elected to the San Francisco Board of Supervisors in 1977 (Kneupper 1981; Shilts 1987). Milk was a skilled organizer and a gifted speaker. He formed a coalition of union workers, racial minorities, and supporters from his district to oppose the initiative.

The Briggs Initiative was politically controversial among elites across parties as the national impact of the anti-gay movement was just beginning to take hold. Republican Gerald Ford and Democratic president Jimmy Carter, a Southern Baptist, spoke out against it, as did California's former Republican governor Ronald Reagan, who by then was the leader of the conservative wing of the Republican Party. The Briggs Initiative cross-pressured gay conservatives, who in response founded the Log Cabin Republicans in large measure to counter the growing prominence of the anti-gay campaigns led by Falwell and members of the Christian Right. Within a few short months, public opinion largely flipped from support to opposition. Proposition 6 ultimately lost by seventeen points (58.4 to 41.6 percent).

The failure of the Briggs Initiative was a major setback for Save Our Children. The Supreme Court's 1985 ruling in the case of *National Gay Task Force v. Board of Education* found that Oklahoma's version of the Briggs Initiative was unconstitutional because it violated free speech rights. This ruling hindered efforts to enact the Briggs Initiative in other, more conservative states. However, the court denied that sexual orientation was a suspect class, meaning the government did not have to demonstrate a compelling state interest in order to regulate it.

The 1970s saw the first organized and significant nationwide counter to gains made by gay rights activists. The events surrounding the Miami–Dade County ordinance and Save Our Children, in particular, provide a crucial inflection point in the politics of gay rights. Gay rights advocates organized and passed a nondiscrimination law. The passage of that law led to the activation of anti-gay elites. Those elites tapped into religious organizations and employed tropes about gays as pedophiles in order to mount a campaign to repeal the ordinance in Miami. They used the same strategies and approaches in other cities and areas. The goal was to expand opposition to public acceptance of gays and lesbians to other areas like they did with the Briggs Initiative. In contrast to previous attacks on gays and lesbians, in the 1970s opposition to gay rights and social acceptance of gays and lesbians was not used as a tool to achieve other ends, but was an end largely in and of itself.

Reagan and the Christian Right: The 1980s

In the 1980s the gay rights movement faced unparalleled opposition from the national Republican Party and its affiliated groups. The period saw the politicization of the religious right through the rise of groups like the Moral Majority, organized around religious conservatism, that sought to protect so-called traditional morality in large part by opposing gay rights and the acceptance of gays and lesbians as legitimate members of society (e.g., A. Lewis 2017; Fitzgerald 2017).

Ronald Reagan's 1980 presidential primary and general election campaigns were aided by the backing of leaders of the Christian Right who were reaching a new apex of influence (Harley 1980). Although Reagan had earlier opposed the Briggs Initiative, he was no friend of the gay community. His coordination with the Christian Right pushed his policies far to the right on the social issues that Christian conservatives cared about most deeply (Green and Guth 1988).

The Christian Right, led by figures such as Jerry Falwell, Pat Robertson, and James Dobson, had begun their rise to national political prominence in the 1970s. With growing influence of televangelism and other media, and having recently created ultraconservative universities, the leaders of the Christian Right had a growing conservative but politically inactive audience (Lienesch 1982). In part, this inactivity was by design, as many evangelical churches sought to stay out of politics (Fitzgerald 2017). Increasingly, however, the Christian Right sought ways to translate their extensive resources—that is, their large memberships, wealth, and media reach—into political power. After Miami's repeal of the nondiscrimination ordinance, the base quickly became energized, and members of the Christian Right were placed on the 1980 Republican National Committee's (RNC) platform committee, resulting in the GOP's formally dropping its support for an equal rights amendment to the Constitution, among other socially conservative moves (Green and Guth 1988). This, in conjunction with Reagan's advocacy of supply-side economics, further linked social and economic conservatism to complete the Republican Party's conservative Southern realignment that had started with Richard Nixon (Lienesch 1982; Green and Guth 1988).

Months before President Reagan began his first term in office, the Centers for Disease Control (CDC) found unusual clusters of pneumocystis pneumonia in gay men in Los Angeles. The CDC released the first report about the cluster of pneumonia cases on June 5, 1981, marking the beginning of the AIDS epidemic in the United States. The Christian Right and the Republican Party saw the AIDS epidemic as an opportunity to mobilize their followers through demonization of gays (Rimmerman 2008). AIDS (acquired immune deficiency syndrome) is a manifestation of the human immunodeficiency virus, or HIV. The virus is spread through contact with some bodily fluids—in particular, semen and blood. Although at the outset of the epidemic in the United States, HIV/AIDS was framed as a disease that primarily afflicted gay men and Haitians, in other parts of the world straight people were the primary population who suffered from the infection (Pierceson 2016, 119–20). Jerry Falwell, the leader of the Moral Majority, declared HIV/AIDS to be the judgment of God, and Patrick Buchanan, a former speechwriter for Richard Nixon, advisor to Ronald Reagan, and subsequent presidential candidate with a culture war platform observed: "The poor homosexual. They have declared war on nature and now nature is exacting an awful retribution" (Rimmerman 2008, 37). HIV/AIDS continues to be a central dimension of the propaganda of the Christian Right to justify discrimination against gays and lesbians (Pierceson 2016, 120).

Widespread fearmongering about this new disease by the leaders of the Christian Right and other conservative elites resulted in schoolchildren barred from classes, athletes barred from competition, those diagnosed with AIDS fired or evicted, and, of course, religious zealots using the epidemic as an opportunity to evangelize about the evils of homosexuality (Dunlap 1989).

The lack of public understanding about HIV and AIDS in the early 1980s was compounded by the lack of federal research dollars to help understand, diagnose, treat, and prevent its spread (Pierceson 2016, 120–21). More than one thousand Americans died from HIV- and AIDS-related illnesses in Reagan's first year alone. Reagan refused to speak publicly about AIDS until halfway through his second term in office and actively pressured Surgeon General C. Everett Koop to not speak or publish any reports about AIDS (Brier 2009, 78–120). The death from AIDS of Rock Hudson, the famous actor and a close friend of the Reagans, sparked a burst of activism and philanthropic work to fight the spread of AIDS in part because he had famous and rich friends like Elizabeth Taylor and because the public could now put a familiar face to the epidemic (Krim 2011). By the time President Reagan began commenting in some fashion in 1986, more than twenty thousand Americans had died from an AIDS-related illness (Shilts 1987, 596). In 1987 Reagan issued Executive Order 12061 to create the Watkins Commission, which reported on the HIV/AIDS epidemic and strategies to combat the illness (Kirp 1989).

The failure by federal and state officials to adequately respond to the new disease of HIV/AIDS led Larry Kramer and a small group of friends in New York to organize the Gay Men's Health Crisis activist group in 1982 (Chambre 2006, 15). Kramer envisioned an advocacy group that also provided education and support services and relied on volunteers to conceptualize and implement the services available (Chambre 2006, 16–19). The anemic response of the Reagan administration to the epidemic, coupled with the continuous demonization of the gay and lesbian community by Christian conservatives and Republican leaders, also led to the creation of ACT UP (AIDS Coalition to Unleash Power) (Pierceson 2016, 120). ACT UP modeled its activism strategies on emotional appeals and radical approaches that included public demonstrations, public shaming of politicians and policy makers, and relentless efforts to educate the public (Gould 2009). ACT UP persistently protested Cardinal John O'Connor—a vocal anti-gay leader of the Catholic Church in New York—despite the claims by the press and public that they were courting public backlash by, among other actions, protesting inside St. Patrick's Cathedral (Chambre 2006). Their slogan "Silence = Death" powerfully communicated the severity of the epidemic (Pierceson 2016, 120).

The AIDS crisis, combined with the neglect from the Reagan administration and the overt hostility toward gays and lesbians from Republican elites, acted as a catalyst for organizing the LGBT community and creating an activist infrastructure that would prove critical for mobilizing on other issues as the LGBT rights movement matured (Gould 2009). ACT UP and the Gay Men's Health Crisis brought the LGBT community together and gave gays and lesbians more direct political experience (Siplon 2002). The experience in organizing and advocacy gained through the early era of AIDS demonstrated successful ways to utilize the newly found structure of social activism in the coming fights over gay and lesbian rights (Siplon 1999).

Gay Rights as a Wedge Issue: The 1990s

In the 1986 election, the Democrats took back a majority in the Senate and in the House. On paper this promised to provide Bill Clinton, who in 1992 ran on the most pro-gay platform of any major party nominee in history, enough support to push through some pro-gay achievements (Sherrill 1996). Fred Hochberg became the first openly gay person to hold a cabinet-level position as the acting administrator of the Small Business Administration. Roberta Achtenberg became the first openly gay person to obtain Senate confirmation when she was confirmed as the Assistant Secretary of the Department of Housing and Urban Development. Clinton also issued an executive order that ended screening for sexual orientation in national security clearance checks and secured large funding increases to combat HIV/AIDS. Most prominently, Clinton sought to reverse the ban on openly gay and lesbian people serving in the armed forces (Neff and Edgell 2013).

In 1988 activists formed the Military Freedom Project to protest campaigns to oust gays from the military, most notably at the Paris Island Depot. In 1989 Joseph Steffan challenged the legality of his dismissal from the U.S. Naval Academy for violating the ban on homosexuals serving in the military. During discovery for the case, the Crittenden Report (long since buried by the authors of the Hoey Report) was uncovered. It showed that the arguments against gays serving in the military as enumerated in the Hoey Report, particularly the claim that homosexuals constituted a security risk, had been refuted by the Navy itself. With the unearthing of the Navy report and increased activism, in 1991 senators Brock Adams (D-WA) and Barbara Boxer (D-CA) introduced the Military Freedom Act to fully repeal the ban, which had existed in the military since the Revolutionary War (Neff and Edgell 2013). Still, the leaders of the Republican Party were uniformly opposed to the removal of the ban, and there was no possibility the bill would become law until a Democrat was in the White House (Frank 2009).

Bill Clinton's 1992 victory over George H. W. Bush and Ross Perot promised additional momentum for repealing the military service ban, which the public no longer supported (Saad 2017). Clinton was the first major presidential nominee to explicitly campaign to the gay community and during the Democratic primary became an outspoken advocate for equal rights, including a promise to allow gays to serve in the military. Once elected, Clinton pushed for legislation repealing the military ban, but opposition in Congress and segments of the public pushed to codify the ban instead. Although Clinton and many Democrats wanted an outright repeal, other Democrats like Senator Sam Nunn from Georgia aligned with elites like Colin Powell—Clinton's chairman of the Joint Chiefs of Staff, who was a holdover from the two previous Republican administrations and openly a Republican after 1995—to oppose the repeal (Frank 2009). Ultimately, Clinton agreed to a compromise in which Democrats in Congress joined with Republicans to create "Don't Ask, Don't Tell," a policy that allowed gays and lesbians to serve, so long as they stayed in the closet (Pierceson 2016, 118–19; Sinclair 2009).

While the ban on military service was being contested in Washington D.C., the plaintiffs in *Baehr v. Lewin*, a 1993 marriage equality case in Hawaii, argued that the state constitutional right to privacy dictated that same-sex marriage should be legal (Jaffe 1996). The Hawaii Supreme Court ultimately remanded the case to the trial court in a split decision. The majority found that a ban on same-sex marriage was not consistent with the equal protection provision of the state's constitution. The Supreme Court asked the trial court whether the state effort to violate the equal protection clause of the state constitution by precluding gay marriage met the heightened standard of "strict scrutiny." More specifically, because restricting who can marry impinges on a constitutional provision of a fundamental right, the court required a showing of a compelling governmental interest and clear evidence of social harm. In response to the remand order, the trial court asked the State to study whether the ban on same-sex marriage furthered a compelling state interest (Farrell 1995).

Recognizing that the court ruling threatened the marriage ban, conservative religious elites mobilized to place a constitutional amendment on the ballot that would remove the issue from the court's domain and ban marriage equality. In 1998, before the case could be fully resolved in the lower courts, the voters approved the constitutional amendment. The amendment reserved to the Hawaiian state legislature the power to define "marriage." This ballot initiative later served as the basis for which the legislature removed the issue of marriage equality from the courts and explicitly defined "marriage" as being between a man and woman (Gerstman 2017, 5–6).

Like the Miami-Dade repeal, the *Baehr* case drew national attention. In response to the same-sex marriage battle in Hawaii, congressional conservatives and the elites of the Christian Right claimed they feared "activist judges" who might, as a result of the robust privacy rights institutionalized in federal jurisprudence, force marriage equality on the country (B. Adam 2003). The battle over same-sex marriage in Hawaii had two important consequences. First, marriage equality was front and center on the national agenda. Second, the case spurred conservative religious groups to mobilize against the issue in Hawaii, across states, and at the federal level. State and national anti-gay groups coalesced and worked to write and pass legislation and amend constitutions to prevent gay marriage from becoming law.

Almost immediately, religious conservatives began working to pass legislation in state legislatures across the country (Haider-Markel 2001). Facing little organized opposition, their campaign was extraordinarily successful. Starting with the state of Utah, between 1995 and 2003, thirty-seven states prohibited something that did not exist in any place in the United States: same-sex marriage (B. Adam 2003).

State laws, however, had an important limitation. They were unable to ensure that states would not be required to recognize marriages performed in other states. To address this problem, conservatives in the U.S. Congress proposed the Defense of Marriage Act (DOMA) and made it part of the 1996 Republican platform. It quickly became law (Koppelman 1997). DOMA was approved in the House of Representatives on a 342–67 vote and in the Senate on an 84–14 vote, as Republicans were unified and just a handful of Democrats opposed it. Only one Republican, Steve Gunderson—a gay man outed involuntarily on the floor of the House by Republican Representative Bob Dornan—voted against it. It was then quietly signed into law by President Clinton around 1:00 in the morning on September 21, 1996 (Koppelman 1997).

The resulting bill prohibited something that did not exist. DOMA's stated aim was to prevent the legalization of marriage in one state from being binding in another. Perhaps more importantly, however, DOMA provided an issue for religious conservatives to mobilize their supporters in order to build their political organizations. By prohibiting the federal government from recognizing same-sex marriage, DOMA prevented gays and lesbians from receiving any government benefits or protections afforded on the basis on marriage (e.g., joint tax returns, social security, preferential immigration status).

The fact that many gay rights groups and activists did not support the quest for marriage equality also inhibited the effort (Bernstein and Taylor 2013). The Lambda Legal Defense fund, for instance, refused to assist on the initial *Baehr* case, and the national gay rights advocacy group the Human Rights Campaign did not see marriage legalization as a priority (Stone 2013).

The Briggs Initiative ushered in an era in which religious conservatives sought to use the ballot box to lever public opinion against gay rights by making policy that opposed gay rights. In response, gay rights advocates increasingly turned to the courts. The litigation that resulted after Colorado voters approved Amendment 2, which stripped local antidiscrimination ordinances of protections based on sexual orientation, reached the Supreme Court (Pierceson 2016, 87). In *Romer v. Evans* (1996), the Court struck down the discriminatory amendment after it determined that the only rationale for the amendment was moral disapproval of gays and lesbians (Flagg 1997). While the case was a courtroom success for the LGBT movement, it also provided fodder for the conservative Christians, and to this day the Republican Party continues to portray the LGBT community as a social and political threat.

The final conflict of the decade was fought over hate crimes. In 1998 Matthew Shepard was picked up in a bar in Laramie, Wyoming, by two men who then took him to a remote area outside of town and savagely tortured him (Petersen 2011). He was found the next day unconscious and tied to fence posts, his arms out Christlike, with tear tracks frozen in the blood on his cheeks. He eventually died from his injuries, and his assailants were convicted and sent to prison (Ott and Aoki 2002). Shortly after Matthew Shepard's murder, an African American in Texas named James Byrd was assaulted and then dragged to death with one end of a chain around his neck and the other end tied to the bumper of a pickup truck (Pierceson 2016, 112). The media covered these crimes in excruciating detail, and this media focus put the issue of hate crimes into the public policy debates (Trout 2015).

In March 1999 Senator Edward Kennedy introduced S.622, the Hate Crime Prevention Act of 1999 in response to the murders. The bill promised to expand existing hate crime protections to include crimes committed based on sexuality and removed the limits on existing law that applied only to federal activities, like voting. Although the public was horrified by the crimes, Republicans stalled as Christian conservatives led by James Dobson opposed it (Stout 2007). Democratic majorities were elected to both the House and the Senate in 2006, allowing the bill, which had been attached to the defense budget, to pass (Pierceson 2016, 112). However, Republican president George W. Bush threatened a veto of the entire defense budget if the hate crime rider remained, so it was stripped from the bill. The election of President Barack Obama along with a Democratic majority in both the House and Senate removed the final obstacle (Pierceson 2016, 112). Eleven years after their brutal murders, the law that became known as the Matthew Shepard and James Byrd Hate Crimes Prevention Act was enacted.

The Reemergence of Old Issues: The 2000s

The new millennium brought increased confrontation between religious conservatives and gay rights advocates. As the GOP increasingly aligned with religious conservatives, Democrats accelerated their embrace of gay rights. Suffering from decline in support and stinging from policy defeats following eight years of the Clinton presidency, religious elites saw the public opposition to gay rights as an opportunity to invigorate their movement and activate their followers (Fitzgerald 2017). While major national issues like civil unions, marriage, and military service were emerging and becoming more intense, the battle over gay rights broadened to include issues ranging from the ongoing debate about whether gays and lesbians could march in a St. Patrick's Day parade to whether the Boy Scouts could exclude gays and whether states could enforce prohibitions on consenting adult sexual behavior (Pierceson 2016, 87–88).

The first of these conflicts came to a head during President Bush's first year in office when the Supreme Court issued an opinion that was a high-profile defeat for the gay rights movement. In *Boy Scouts of America v. Dale* (2000), Eagle Scout James Dale was expelled from the organization for publicly announcing he was gay (Pierceson 2016, 87–88). In the 5–4 decision, the Supreme Court supported the claim that the First Amendment's freedom of association meant a group could deny membership to a gay person (Koppelman and Wolf 2009). In short, the court was saying that the First Amendment rights of those who wish to discriminate trump the equal protection rights of those who are discriminated against (Pierceson 2016, 86). This strategy would help lay the foundation for the increased use of rights-based arguments by religious conservatives on issues of sexuality (e.g., A. Lewis 2017).

Beginning in late 2001, religious leaders came together under the banner of the Arlington Group to develop a plan to politicize gay marriage and draw the Bush administration into the fray (Fleischmann and Moyer 2009; Fitzgerald 2017). The leaders of the Christian Right recognized that their followers were perhaps *the* core Republican constituency that gave conservative religious activists like James Dobson and Jerry Falwell lever-age over the administration. As we saw in chapter 2, these anti-gay elites worked hand in hand with the Bush administration and campaigned to pass marriage laws in key states, primarily through referenda (Fleischmann and Moyer 2009). The states were selected primarily to help boost GOP turnout in the 2004 and 2006 elections (Pinello 2007). In the key battle-ground state of Ohio, for instance, a marriage ban had already been passed by the legislature and signed by the governor in early in 2004, making the amendment largely redundant (Fitzgerald 2017). During Bush's two terms in office, twenty-five states passed bans, even in somewhat liberal states such as Oregon. Gay rights organizations did, however, move quickly in state and federal courts to stem the tide.

Research suggests that the success of Bush's alliance with anti-gay elites of the Christian Right was somewhat mixed (e.g., Campbell and Monson 2008; Garretson 2014a). While Republican turnout increased and the state constitutional bans on same-sex marriage and civil unions passed, it seems unlikely that the increased turnout for Republicans swung many states toward Bush, as the heaviest impact occurred in the most Republican states (Pinello 2006). The largest impact, however, may have been in Ohio, a key swing state that saw massive mobilization by religious conservatives and that Bush only narrowly won (e.g., Fitzgerald 2017).

In the 2003 case of *Goodridge v. Dept. of Public Health*, the Massachusetts Supreme Court found that denying civil marriage on the basis of sexual orientation violated the state constitution (Keck 2009). The court ordered the legislature to codify the new policy, and Massachusetts began issuing marriage certificates to gay couples in 2004 (Burge 2003). The Massachu-setts court ruling provided new fodder for religious conservatives to pres-sure the White House to publicly support a constitutional amendment that would ban gay marriage. Anti-gay groups led by members of the Arling-ton Group mobilized and pressured the president to act (Fitzgerald 2017). The group's leaders eventually gave him an ultimatum: if Bush wanted the support of religious conservatives in the November election, he would have to publicly support the Federal Marriage Amendment (Strode 2004; Grzymala-Busse 2015). Bush was reluctant at least in part because he had long emphasized the importance of states' rights, with the idea that laws about sexuality should be left to the states, and supporting a federal law would contradict that position (Strode 2004). In response, Bush increas-ingly publicized his opposition to gay marriage and began to hint that he would support a constitutional amendment.

Gavin Newsom, the newly sworn-in mayor of San Francisco, was stunned by Bush's use of the 2004 State of the Union speech to emphasize the issue (Pinello 2007). On February 6, 2004, Mayor Newsom began to issue marriage licenses to gay and lesbian couples (Mello 2015). Along with the issuance of marriage licenses in San Francisco in early February, the implementation of the Massachusetts law provided Bush the opening he needed. After years of demurring, on February 24 President Bush publicly announced his support for the Federal Marriage Amendment. Ultimately, the California courts issued a stay on March 11, 2004, as a result of California attorney general Bill Lockyer's petition but not before over four thousand licenses had been issued (Pinello 2007). Newsom's actions directly set into motion the advancement of marriage equality, although they also set the stage for California's Proposition 8, discussed below, which amended the state constitution to prohibit marriage between same-sex couples (Murray 2009).

Gay rights advocates were also victorious in 2003 in federal court. In *Lawrence v. Texas* the U.S. Supreme Court struck down anti-sodomy laws in thirteen states. In a 6–3 decision, the court determined that anti-sodomy laws violate the substantive due process rights conferred in the Fourteenth Amendment and that private consensual sex acts are not something that the government has the authority to regulate regardless of the sex(es) of the participants (Pinello 2007). The cases about sodomy were important to the leaders of the Republican Party and the Christian Right because focusing on the sexual aspect of gays and lesbians helped trigger disgust in their followers (Gadarian and Vort 2018; Nussbaum 2010; Eskridge 2005).

The *Lawrence* ruling was remarkable in that it overturned the 1986 case of *Bowers v. Hardwick*, which upheld a state's right to ban oral and anal sex among consenting adults in private (Pierceson 2016, 89–90).[6] The *Lawrence* ruling is also notable because it is one of the few cases where some scholars claim they can actually show backlash in public opinion, although those claims have been challenged (Keck 2009). Indeed, a growing body of literature questions the extent to which opinion changed against gay rights following the case, as the wording of the question asked in surveys changed around this same time (Bishin et al. 2016; Garretson 2018). More important, even if public opinion appears to have shifted against gay rights for a brief period of time, as we saw in chapter 2, it seems to have shifted back shortly thereafter, as the period between 2003 and 2010 saw massive increases in public support for gay rights on every issue surveyed (Garretson 2018).

The Christian Right began to shift their approach during the early contestation over marriage equality. Increasingly, facing losses on issues ranging from abortion to gay marriage, the religious right employed rights-based arguments in order to litigate on the basis of religious freedom rather than their desire to uphold community morals (A. Lewis 2017). In short, the Republicans and the Christian Right employed a rights discourse to construct a "victim" identity for those who opposed marriage equality while continuing to paint gays and lesbians as deviants and "others" (e.g., Mello 2015).

The Obama Administration

Given the anti-gay legislation that proliferated throughout the majority of states during the George W. Bush presidency, the course reversal that occurred after the election of President Obama in 2008 is remarkable. Whereas just ten years earlier, Democrats were split on a variety of questions of gay rights like DOMA, by 2008 the party had converged on broad support of a wide range of policies supported by the LGBT community. The polarization of the parties on the issues became especially clear in the general election. In 2008 the Democratic platform and the presidential primary candidates, including Barack Obama, Hillary Clinton, and John Edwards, all supported civil unions (but not marriage equality), ending Don't Ask, Don't Tell, inclusion of gays and lesbians in media coverage of hate crimes, and passing federal antidiscrimination laws, while the Republican platform and the presidential candidates uniformly took the opposite position on these issues (Jacobs 2008).

As we discussed in chapter 3, Proposition 8 in California—a state constitutional amendment that prohibited marriage between two people of the same sex—passed with over 57 percent of the vote (Murray 2009). The "Yes on 8" campaign was funded by the LDS Church (Mormons), the Catholic Church, and anti-gay individuals from across the country (Shin 2009). Importantly, the proposition process in California is elite driven, as resources and organization are needed both in qualifying an initiative to appear on the ballot and to cue voters how to vote in a low information and nonpartisan context (Lewkowicz 2006). Indeed, over $83 million was spent on the passage of Prop 8, with only the race for president costing more (Ewers 2008).

Barack Obama, a pro-gay if not pro–gay marriage presidential candidate, was elected at the same time Prop 8 was passed by California voters. Following Obama's election, Democrats held majorities in Congress, thirty-two governorships, and control of at least one chamber in thirty-five state legislatures. At the state level, strong partisan dominance enabled several state legislatures to either formally recognize same-sex marriage or repeal the bans that had been passed earlier by simple legislative action. Some of the states that moved to legalize same-sex marriage did so without popular support. Only a plurality of people in New Hampshire, for example, were in favor of same-sex marriage a year after it was passed, but support increased from 44 percent to 62 percent support in six months (Jensen 2011; WMUR/UNH Granite State Poll 2011).

Obama's promise to repeal Don't Ask, Don't Tell stalled in the face of a GOP filibuster. Following passage of comprehensive health care reform, Democrats lost their majorities in Congress during the 2010 midterm elections. In December 2010, however, shortly before the 111th Congress ended, Democrats and Republicans in Congress passed the Don't Ask, Don't Tell Repeal Act as part of a deal to forestall the expiration of the Bush tax cuts, and the repeal was signed into law by President Obama. Nonetheless, most Republican members of Congress continued to oppose the repeal of Don't Ask, Don't Tell. Still, despite the repeal, general anti-sodomy provisions remained in the Uniform Code of Military Justice, the legal statutes to which members of the military are subject, until Congress forced their removal through the National Defense Authorization Act three years later.

Dating back to the *Baehr* case in Hawaii, national gay rights advocacy groups refused to support court cases opposing marriage bans for fear of backlash (Keck 2009). Specifically, they were concerned that adverse court rulings would lead to not only negative precedent that might take decades to overcome but also to increased public opposition that might bleed over into opposition in other policy areas. Initially, advocacy groups like the Human Rights Campaign refused to assist in cases like *Windsor* and *Obergefell* as well. Once individuals decided to pursue these cases on their own, however, national groups joined the fight, as they recognized the importance of winning.

Around this time, a series of state and federal court decisions sprouted up throughout the country challenging the Defense of Marriage Act. Also, the Obama administration "evolved" to support same sex marriage in part because then vice-president and now President Joe Biden publicly came out in support (Steinmetz 2010; Bowers 2012). The marriage cases culminated in 2013 with *United States v. Windsor*, wherein the Supreme Court delivered a 5–4 defeat to DOMA's definition of "marriage" as only between a man and woman. Striking down DOMA meant that all federal benefits and privileges of marriage henceforth had to be afforded to married same-sex couples.

The *Windsor* case did not address the constitutionality of state-level bans on gay marriage. The court precedent from *Baker v. Nelson* allowing gay marriage bans remained law. Lawsuits against challenging various state bans had begun almost immediately after the bans were ratified. After mixed decisions through several federal appeals courts, the Supreme Court heard *Obergefell v. Hodges* in 2015. With the identical division of justices as the *Windsor* case, the Supreme Court found gay marriage bans to be unconstitutional two years to the day of the *Windsor* decision and twelve years to the day that *Lawrence v. Texas* was decided. All state bans, regardless of whether or not they were amendments to state constitutions, were struck down and same-sex marriage was made legal nationally (Pierceson 2015).

The Trump Era and the Trans Community

When Donald Trump was elected president in 2016, the LGBT community faced a new uncertainty because of a lack of clarity about his actual policy positions. In contrast to Trump's approach, former Vice President Mike Pence is stridently anti-gay, having, for example, served as an outspoken critic of gay rights dating back to his opposition to hate crimes legislation when it was first introduced in 1999 (Stout 2007; Girard 2017). That the administration would oppose LGBT rights was not a surprise given the critical role that anti-gay white evangelicals played in Trump's election (Blair 2016). Like many policy aspects of his administration, the approach to gay rights was disjointed, chaotic, and marked by lurching between overt hostility and benign neglect. Most directly, the administration placed record numbers of conservative justices, some of whom have expressed anti-gay views, on the federal courts. It has also worked to harm the LGBT community. Among the earliest anti-gay decisions, the Trump administration decided to stop gathering census data about same-sex households, which renders the population invisible in that context (Gossett 2018).

One consistency of the Trump administration was that it was relentlessly anti-trans, having eased nondiscrimination protections for health care, reversing rules allowing trans people to serve in the military under their identified or assigned gender identities, and reversed Title IX protections based on gender identity, among others (Fadulu 2019).

On June 15, 2020, the Supreme Court decided the cluster of cases termed *Bostock v. Clayton County* 590 U.S. (2020). Three employees were terminated from their jobs expressly for being transgender or gay and then sued under Title VII of the Civil Rights Act of 1964. Title VII makes it "unlawful . . . for an employer to fail or refuse to hire or to discharge any individual, or otherwise discriminate against any individual . . . because of such individual's race, color, religion, sex, or national origin" (42 U.S.C. 2000e-2(a)(1)). The appellate courts split decisions across the Eleventh, Second, and Sixth Circuits as to whether Title VII applied specifically to anti-gay or anti-trans animus. The Supreme Court ruled in favor of the employees in a split decision that determined this discrimination was indeed covered by Title VII. At first blush these cases seem to have handed the LGBT community a terrific victory. There are indications, though, that both Chief Justice John Roberts and Justice Neil Gorsuch would be amenable to a very broad religious exception to the antidiscriminatory structure. This follows the logic of the 2014 *Hobby Lobby* case, where a 5–4 Court decided the corporate entity could deny health insurance coverage of birth control because of the deeply held religious beliefs of its owners (*Burwell v. Hobby Lobby Stores* 573 U.S. 682(2014)). The specter of an incrementally expanding window of religious exemption for compliance with the constitutional mandates of equal protection and the myriad of legislative prohibitions on discrimination presents an ongoing and imminent threat to LGBT rights and the promise of equality.

In addition to the peril that these advances in rights may face in the federal political institutions, elites have a long and successful track record of anti-LGBT sloganeering that can move the public to act against the civil and political rights of the community. The Trump administration targeted the trans community specifically and the larger LGBT community generally with more than seventy specific alterations of rules and regulations to diminish their rights (NCTE 2020). Notably, in his first 24 hours in office, President Joe Biden reversed those anti-LGBT administrative actions that had been implemented through executive orders signed by former President Trump. The Trump focus on the trans community followed the strategies from other levels of government used by the elites of the religious right movement and their allies in politics (Castle 2019).

Two notable examples are the repeal of the HERO ordinance in Houston and the HB2 bathroom bill in North Carolina. On an 11–6 vote, Houston passed a broad nondiscrimination law called the Houston Equal Rights Ordinance on May 28, 2014 (Morris 2014). Shortly after the ordinance a was adopted, conservative religious elites and the Republican Party sought to force the ordinance onto the ballot for public confirmation. Although the lower court found a host of problems with the petitions, including fraudulent signatures, the Texas Supreme Court sided with those seeking to hold a vote, and HERO was placed on the ballot for the November 2015 election (Taylor et al. 2018, 213–14). The campaign to repeal the ordinance referred to HERO as the "Sexual Predator Protection Act" and used the slogan "No men in women's bathrooms" (Taylor et al. 2018, 214). HERO was repealed with 61 percent of the vote in a very light turnout despite the pro-HERO groups spending about three times as much as the repeal groups (Castle 2019). By successfully framing the question at hand as one of public safety and bathroom peril, the pro-discrimination forces were able to sully the notion of a broadly applicable antidiscrimination bill. The anti-HERO campaign was a high-profile example of the strategy of focusing on the threat to women and children that "men" using the bathroom could present.

Republican elites in North Carolina took note of the HERO campaign and, in the face a close gubernatorial election with an imperiled incumbent Republican, initiated a broadly anti-LGBT bill known as HB2 (House Bill 2) (Jones and Brewer 2020). The contestation over HB2 was framed by Republican members of the state legislature, who, seeking to increase conservative voter turnout, immediately dubbed it a "bathroom bill" because it required, among other things, that people use the public bathroom that aligned with their birth certificate and the sex assigned at birth (Jones and Brewer 2020, 71). Although ultimately the Republican governor lost his reelection bid, this elite effort at spurring conservative voter turnout pushed anti-trans sentiment to the front of public discourse and legitimated animus toward the trans community.

Assessing Elite Mobilization and Backlash

As the preceding pages show, the political history of gay rights in the United States occurs in fits and starts. Prior to the passage of the nondiscrimination ordinance in Miami–Dade County, there was no organized attempt to oppose gay rights, in large part because gay rights advocacy posed little threat to the status quo. Successful gay rights advocacy had largely been limited to smaller, more liberal cities with little religious opposition (Wald, Button, and Rienzo 1996). The opposition that developed out of the Miami-Dade nondiscrimination ordinance, however, signifies an important inflection point in this history. By creating a new organization (i.e., Save Our Children) and leveraging resources from existing, especially religious organizations, anti-gay elites mobilized in order to create a campaign to repeal the county ordinance.

To evaluate the extent to which the history of the gay rights movement is better explained by Mass Opinion Backlash, or Elite-Led Mobilization, we can compare the theories' expectations to the historical record. Recall that MOB is fundamentally a popular (i.e., mass) movement that arises out of a response to challenges to the status quo (e.g., Weaver 2007). It is evidenced by a sharply negative and enduring shift in opinion against the policy or group advocating it (Bishin et al. 2016). Elite-Led Mobilization, on the other hand, holds that opposition to gay rights, especially attempts to advance such rights, is driven by well-organized elites who use a variety of resources and institutions to oppose acceptance of gays and lesbians as full members of society. Most commonly they use campaigns that allow them to employ their most powerful resource: their millions of like-minded followers, who are primarily conservative Christians.

At first glance, using history to evaluate these theories poses a challenge. While both Mass Opinion Backlash and Elite-Led Mobilization explain opposition to challenges to the status quo on gay rights, during a long stretch of history there is no clear opposition to gay rights, led by either the elites or the masses. How, then, are we to assess the history of the movement from the prism of the two theories?

The direct answer is that we can examine the extent to which the expectations of each theory are met. With respect to Mass Opinion Backlash, theoretically we would expect to see this bottom-up response whenever gays make salient challenges to the status quo. In practice, however, we do not expect to observe backlash, because before gay rights were contested, salient challenges to the status quo did not occur. Similarly, with respect to Mass Opinion Backlash we would not expect to see elites organizing to oppose gay rights, because there was no need to organize. In short, the expectations of these two theories is that we should not expect to see either elite-led or mass responses to attempts to procure rights until gays and lesbians begin making visible attempts to challenge the status quo. Specifically, unlike the theoretical predictions described in table 6.1, we should not expect to see either elite-led or populistic reaction until the era of contestation begins, because there is no action for either elites or masses to react against. Once contestation occurs, however, we should see opposition to gay rights instigated by a bottom-up mass reaction if Mass Opinion Backlash is correct. If Elite-Led Mobilization Theory better describes events, the important historical examples of opposition to gay rights should be initiated by elites.

Assessment: Before Gay Rights Were Contested

At the outset of the gay rights movement, both the Lavender Scare and the emergence of the Mattachine Society appear consistent with the expectations of Elite-Led Mobilization Theory in the pre-contestation era. Anti-gay elites did not need to organize on the issue of gay rights, because gays and lesbians made few organized policy demands. Issues of sexuality were not the object of the action but a means toward achieving other stated goals, like increasing national security. The Lavender Scare was a product of elite zealots in Congress and was significant in shaping the narratives that came out of the news media. Opposition to gays and lesbians serving in government appears centered less on their behavior or sexuality than on the possibility that such behavior might lead them to be a security risk.

Elites did not need to organize to oppose gay rights or to mobilize voters, because anti-gay sentiment was the status quo. Specifically, there was no organized campaign in support of gays and lesbians, nor was there any organized attempt to reform the system more broadly because of the widespread homophobia of the time. Gays and lesbians in government, as in society more broadly, were overwhelmingly closeted and lived their lives in fear of discovery (D. Johnson 2004). In most places, gays and lesbians were not visible, so there was little fear of challenges to the status quo, as gays and lesbians posed little threat to those who did not see them (Burack 2008). Moreover, few organized groups advocating gay rights existed, and those who did were small and espoused a philosophy of assimilation that did little to challenge the status quo. Anti-gay elites did not need to act, because issues of gay rights were not meaningfully or openly contested at the time.

Rather than mobilizing to oppose the acceptance of gays and lesbians or gay rights, it appears more likely that those who claimed that gays and lesbians were a threat to national security were simply looking for a scapegoat or diversions from congressional oversight regarding other issues. Further, if the elites driving the Lavender Scare intended to mobilize the public against gays and lesbians based on preexisting animus, they would not have needed to work so hard to link being gay or lesbian with national security issues. Rather, tapping into previously held beliefs about homosexuality would have been sufficient to publicize the work of anti-gay elites. Instead, it seems members of Congress linked homosexuality with the highly salient communist threat (i.e., the Soviet Union, the Cold War) in order to justify the purges rather than pursuing the existence of gays and lesbians in government as a problem on its own merits.

While the absence of contestation over gay rights or attempts to oppose acceptance of gays and lesbians as inherently bad policy are consistent with the expectations of Elite-Led Mobilization Theory, there is also little evidence of Mass Opinion Backlash. Given that there was no concerted effort to advance acceptance of gays and lesbians or gay rights, there was no stimulus to lash back against. The few attempts to organize were limited and largely invisible to the broader public.

While the Mattachine Society was energized and increasingly politicized as a direct result of the politics of the purges occurring at the State Department, their actions were mostly organizational at this point and far away from the sight of the average voter. Moreover, their ability to challenge the status quo and effect political change was limited by the inherent tension between their adoption of an assimilationist philosophy, which would have required them to come out, and the knowledge that doing so would lead to even further sanctions against their members. As a consequence, the organization and politicization of the Mattachine Society did little to directly challenge the status quo in ways that would require those who oppose them to respond.

Simply put, Mass Opinion Backlash did not occur, because there was little to lash back against. Moreover, because of the vague nature of newspaper reporting at the time, the public writ large had no way of knowing that the purge had occurred as a result of sexual identity. Specifically, the press would not even put the word "homosexual" in print at the time, so, for instance, the purge of civil servants was reported as a campaign against the much broader and more vague concept of "moral turpitude," which included such sins as adultery, drug use, excessive drinking, and embezzlement, among others.

In sum, while the Lavender Scare was not by itself driven by organized attempts to oppose the public acceptance of gays and lesbians in a manner consistent with ELM theory and was not characterized by mass opinion backlash, it did play an important role in the development of the gay rights movement. The Lavender Scare triggered a series of attempts by gays and lesbians to gain public acceptance and among opponents to organize in order to stop them.

The early periods of gay rights contestation fail to demonstrate public opinion backlash in large part because the contestation was not in the public domain. Also, elites did not mobilize the public for the exact same reason, and they controlled the mechanisms of government and policy and could implement discrimination at will. Finally, there was no organized pro-gay movement. All of this amounts to an era devoid of organic, grassroots backlash.

Assessment: The Era of Contestation

To what extent do these theories explain events during the era of contestation? One of the challenges in assessing backlash lies in the unavailability of baseline public opinion data prior to the Dade County Commission passing the nondiscrimination ordinance. The overwhelming support for repeal of that ordinance and the placement of the Briggs Initiative on the ballot indicate substantial public opposition to gay rights. Nonetheless, it seems clear that to the extent that even these segments of the public lashed back, the reaction was instigated, organized, and promoted by elites and their strategic decision to frame the nondiscrimination ordinance as a threat to children.

The success Save Our Children had both in Miami and nationwide was in large part a product of the organization's ability to quickly mobilize into the political arena, thanks to its affiliation with the extant religious organizations and the absence of well-organized opposition. That success was stifled once Harvey Milk and other pro-gay elites organized and countermobilized. This era in gay rights suggests that elites believed they could mobilize voters, and there is at least some suggestion that Save Our Children was effective even if those electoral successes were short-lived. While the emergence of elite-led social movements created a long-term framework of contestation over gay rights that persists today, the brief success of those anti-gay efforts suggests there was no widespread and enduring public backlash about gay rights. In short, opposition to gay rights was less a product of people's visceral reaction to gays' and lesbians' challenges to the status quo than a product of elites mobilizing previously latent support. While it is true that the *Baehr* case ultimately led to a ballot initiative that resulted in a constitutional amendment allowing the legislature to pass a marriage ban, the referendum was a result of elites mobilizing around the issue.

Moving into the 1980s, the politics of DOMA are highly consistent with the theory of Elite-Led Mobilization. Anti-gay elites at the state and federal level organized nationwide to head off the possibility that gay rights might be legalized in their state. At the time, there was no push by gay rights advocates for marriage equality. After all, it had not previously been an issue for the public in the more than forty years of the gay rights movement that predated it. Moreover, it is important to recognize that the events that occurred in Hawaii did not directly change policy and consequently posed little direct threat to those who cared about the issue. There is no evidence of opinion shift indicative of backlash in response to the Hawaiian court's ruling, as opinion on marriage became increasingly supportive of gay rights over time. Nationally, the public supported allowing gays and lesbians to serve openly in the military by wide margins, but that element and dimension of equality was stymied by elites pandering to the white evangelical subconstituency.

The events of the 2000s provide a clear picture of the role played by elites. As we saw in chapter 4, there is little evidence of mass opinion backlash following the events of 2003 and 2004. Both federal- and state-level elites played a role in rallying public support for the ballot measures to create same-sex marriage bans in their states. Moreover, with respect to President Bush's support for the Federal Marriage Amendment, the absence of widespread popular support likely contributed to its stalling. Just like the state DOMA laws of the late 1990s, the ballot initiatives of 2004 and 2006 were part of a concerted campaign by anti-gay religious elites (Fitzgerald 2017). The bans were a strategic reaction to declining influence of religious elites and a joint attempt by religious conservatives and Republican politicians to harness the mobilizing power of the evangelical movement. This period is marked by the most dramatic shift in opinion on gay rights ever seen. As we saw in chapter 2, these data are highly suggestive that backlash as theorized does not occur, since had Mass Opinion Backlash occurred, we would have seen a shift in public opinion against gay rights. Consequently, the evidence supports Elite-Led Mobilization and fails to provide support for Mass Opinion Backlash.

With such monumental gains in gay rights, like marriage equality, one would think that this era would be the most fertile ground for backlash. Yet new widespread public opposition to same-sex marriage did not manifest. In fact, as we have seen in previous chapters, support for gay rights generally and same-sex marriage specifically dramatically accelerated during this period. The outcome is exactly the opposite of what MOB theory predicts. Moreover, to the extent it occurred, opposition to gay rights was led by elites who sponsored ballot initiatives to overturn court rulings prior to the Supreme Court rulings.

Conclusion

In this chapter we briefly outlined the history of modern gay rights contestation in the United States. Considering the history of major events throughout the timeline of the gay rights movement, we sought to determine whether Mass Opinion Backlash or Elite-Led Mobilization Theory better matches the empirics of the history. Recall that Mass Opinion Backlash suggests the public will mobilize against threats to the status quo with a sharp, negative, and enduring rebuke of the policies or advocates of change. The implication is that the promotion of rights for gays must go slowly lest the public turn against the movement. Elite-Led Mobilization

Theory suggests that elites employ their resources, particularly their ability to mobilize their like-minded supporters, to achieve their goals using a variety of public and political institutions. The history of the development of opposition to gay rights can generally be described as an era of pre-contestation and an era of contestation. During the pre-contestation era, two important features stand out. First, there is little opposition to gay rights or public acceptance of gays and lesbians, in large part because gays are closeted and hence do not threaten the status quo, so those who would oppose gay rights have no need to either organize or mobilize the public. Second, we also see little conflict during this period, as American society reflected a social context in which gays and lesbians were pressured to remain closeted both because laws actively discriminated against them and because society imposed large personal costs on those who came out. Consequently, anti-gay elites controlled the mechanisms of policy implementation and there was no organized opposition, so anti-gay policies were easily implemented. Moreover, disapproval of homosexuality was so pervasive in the early periods of the movement that the politics of the time is rooted in the *assumption* that the public would not accept such behavior as legitimate.

The era of public contestation for gay rights began to mature in Miami in 1976 when gay rights activists elected allies to the county commission and then lobbied them to pass the nondiscrimination legislation. Failing to prevent the law's passage, religious conservatives, especially white evangelical Protestants, organized and mobilized to successfully overturn the Miami–Dade County Commission's nondiscrimination ordinance by passing a ballot initiative in the special election. Without the elite-led mobilization from religious conservatives and Republicans, the ordinance seemingly would have gone unchallenged as similar legislation had in several other cities. Resources from conservative religious organizations employing the strategies used to fight the Miami-Dade ordinance—in particular the cynical and demonizing emphasis on the threat posed by gays and lesbians to children—are exported to other cities both to oppose nondiscrimination laws and to justify other policies nationwide. The elite-led opposition is entirely consistent with Elite-Led Mobilization Theory, as the public becomes widely aware of the issue only after elites mobilize around it.

Once the political arguments over gay rights become public and two-sided, in every era, the contestation over gay rights seems more consistent with Elite-Led Mobilization than with Mass Opinion Backlash. There is simply no evidence of politics or policy being led by an organic and enduring mass reaction consistent with Mass Opinion Backlash at any critical juncture in the gay rights movement. Even with the case of the ballot initiatives, the political institution that most directly reflects public opinion attempts to ban same-sex marriage look like Elite-Led Mobilization. So, while we cannot yet be entirely certain there was no mass opinion backlash, as we lack opinion data on many of these events, the evidence is far more consistent with elite-led mobilization, as elite action preceded public behavior.

Despite what appears to be an absence of evidence to support the notion of backlash, judges and social movement leaders have routinely considered the fear of potential backlash when they craft opinions and strategies. The preoccupation with backlash spans political ideologies and modes of jurisprudential interpretation. In *The Hollow Hope*, Gerald N. Rosenberg (2008) made the claim that the Supreme Court has generally been unhelpful in promoting social change because of the backlash its progressive opinions have sparked.[7] Cass R. Sunstein, the most often cited contemporary legal scholar, has argued that jurists should, to one of four degrees, consider potential social backlash as they craft their opinions (2007). The historian and gay rights leader John D'Emilio (2006), who was cited in Justice Kennedy's majority opinion in *Lawrence v. Texas*, once argued that the gay rights gained through the courts have largely been thwarted by state legislative responses to public opinion backlash at both the state and federal level. Gay rights advocacy groups have often taken a similar position. As just one significant example, the Human Rights Campaign, the largest and most powerful gay rights advocacy organization in the country initially took the position that it would not help plaintiffs fight for gay marriage for fear of backlash (Fuchs 2013). If scholars, judges, and activists take the threat of public opinion backlash seriously and adjust their strategies and behaviors in anticipation of backlash, they may delay the advancement of rights despite a clear absence of evidence to support the backlash thesis.

SEVEN

Iowa's Judicial Retention Elections

Backlash or Elite-Led Mobilization?

The description of the gay rights movement and its opposition by anti-gay elites offered in the previous chapter provides important context for understanding and evaluating explanations for the emergence of opposition to gay rights. One challenge of the historical analysis is that data and evidence necessary to directly evaluate differences in how Mass Opinion Backlash and Elite-led Mobilization Theory explain the emergence of opposition to gay rights over time are limited. In this chapter we examine the differences between these two theories in order to answer the questions posed in the introduction by examining the most prominent case of backlash to occur in recent years: the 2010 Iowa judicial retention elections. Importantly, these elections provide a case not only where data are available but also where the differences in the processes by which gay rights are opposed can be examined and evaluated for each theory.

Why Study Iowa?

From one perspective the attention we direct to the Iowa judicial retention election is curious. After all, Iowa is a small, homogeneous, Midwestern state that is politically consequential almost exclusively for its role as a first mover in presidential nomination contests. Moreover, judicial retention elections are usually unremarkable, because they are typically low visibility and uncompetitive and the judges are almost always retained. Together these characteristics raise the question: Why study Iowa?

The case of the 2010 Iowa judicial retention election fulfills four important criteria for evaluating Backlash and Elite-led Mobilization. First, as these theories seek to explain opposition to gay rights, assessing them requires finding a political contest in which those opposed to gay rights seek to stop, roll back, or oppose gay rights. Second, assessing the internal logic of the theories requires a case where they generate different predictions about the events that should occur and allow us to evaluate the extent to which the actual events conform to those predictions. Third, a case should have data available for simultaneously evaluating the competing theories. Finally, an ideal case would be one that poses a difficult test for Elite-led Mobilization Theory, thereby making evidence consistent with it less likely to occur but, once found, more compelling.

The Iowa judicial retention election meets all of these criteria. By working to remove the judges who legalized gay marriage, the campaign was a clear attempt to oppose gay rights and prevent future rulings that might advance them. As we will see, these races provided an election in which the theories generate differing predictions and for which data are available allowing for assessment of these predictions. Finally, as we showed in chapter 1, the election was widely viewed as a classic case of backlash.

Perhaps the central challenge in testing competing theories explaining opposition to gay rights is that both MOB and ELM predict similar if not identical outcomes: that people will act to oppose gay rights. Recall that the central actors in Mass Opinion Backlash are individuals who, in response to a challenge to the status quo, react by shifting their opinions sharply against the policy or group that violates it. Elite-Led Mobilization, in contrast, focuses on the role of elites who work to advance their policy and organizational goals. Achieving their goals often requires mobilizing their like-minded supporters.

The key question then is, in which contexts might we expect both elites and masses to act in ways that allow us to differentiate between the theories? Elites work constantly to achieve their goals in a variety of settings that include influencing electoral, judicial, legislative, and executive institutions (Hume 2013). In contrast, mass opinion backlash is evidenced both by the shift in attitudes that follow challenges to the status quo and the behavior that results as a consequence of these attitude changes. One context in which the implications for these mass- and elite-driven theories both occur and conflict is during campaigns and elections.

Elections and the campaigns that precede them provide numerous opportunities for individuals to oppose the policies, candidates, or groups they hold responsible for violating the status quo. Elites also use campaigns and elections to advance their policy and organizational goals. The challenge, then, is to identify campaigns and elections that should reflect the different patterns of behavior the theories predict. Ideally, the cases we examine might allow for examining variation both across states and elections to get the largest amount of leverage possible for assessing the theories. With respect to evaluating anti-gay backlash, the recent history of referenda campaigns on issues of gay rights provides a potentially rich source of elections for study.

While there are a number of campaigns and elections that might seem appropriate for examination, data necessary to evaluate many of the most prominent campaigns are not available. Perhaps the most interesting case historically, for instance, might be the special election referendum to overturn the nondiscrimination law in Miami–Dade County in 1977. Similarly, a detailed examination of how opinion changed and the role elites played in the *Baehr* case in Hawaii could be highly informative. While excellent analyses and descriptions of these events already exist, it is unfortunate that the data necessary to evaluate the theories using these cases are unavailable.

Other problems also limit our ability to test the theories. Perhaps the most salient recent campaigns around gay rights were the referenda placed before voters to ban gay marriage in eleven states during the November 2004 elections. These referenda were ostensibly motivated by backlash to the legalization of gay marriage in Massachusetts and the decision by San Francisco mayor Gavin Newsom to issue marriage licenses in the spring of 2004. As we have seen in chapter 2, however, these initiatives were developed and placed on state ballots as the result of strategic coordination between the Bush/Cheney campaign and white evangelical religious groups who came together under the banner of the Arlington Group (Fitzgerald 2017).

These referenda were just one part of a broad campaign to increase turnout among Republicans and white evangelical voters to ensure President Bush's reelection and hence were selected for strategic political reasons. In Ohio, for instance, a constitutional amendment was placed on the November ballot even though gay marriage had already been outlawed by the state's legislature earlier in the year (Fitzgerald 2017). Moreover, attempts to mobilize voters were limited neither by the choice to campaign in these states nor by the use of the gay rights issue. The collaboration with the Bush/Cheney campaign complicates our ability to evaluate the effects of MOB and ELM. It is not clear, for instance what other efforts by the campaigns to mobilize, demobilize, or persuade potential voters might have on the behavior of people in these states. Indeed, research on the effects of such referenda on voter turnout suggests their effects are far more nuanced than widely appreciated (e.g., Campbell and Monson 2008; Garretson 2014a).

A Strategy for Evaluating Elite-Led Mobilization

Despite clear differences between Elite-Led Mobilization and Mass Opinion Backlash, definitive tests between the two theories are hard to identify, as evidence of the strategic choices that lead to the elite behavior at the core of ELM is difficult to obtain. Many prominent cases of opposition to gay rights do not provide clear observations needed to distinguish between and evaluate the theories. Identifying the universe of potential cases of anti-gay backlash is particularly difficult given that our goal is to identify a "difficult" case for which data are available—one widely accepted to be a hallmark example of Mass Opinion Backlash (MOB) and see whether it or Elite-Led Mobilization Theory (ELM) better explains the outcome. The 2010 Iowa judicial retention elections that followed the Iowa Supreme Court's 2009 ruling that overturned the ban on gay marriage is the best recent example that meets these criteria.

Perhaps more than any other recent event, the 2010 defeat of three Iowa jurists who ruled to legalize gay marriage is hailed as a classic case of anti-gay backlash. Television ads opposing retention excoriated the judicial activism of the same-sex marriage ruling that overturned the will of the people (Pettys 2011). Validating this view, scholars show that the justices lost *because* of their ruling on gay marriage (A. Harris 2019). Consequently, it is unsurprising that the press described the election as one characterized by backlash. The *Des Moines Register* described the race as "backlash fueled," while the *New York Times*, *Time* magazine, CNN, *USA Today*, and numerous other media described the events in Iowa as examples of backlash, generally describing a context in which the public rose up to defeat judges who contravened its will (e.g., Gramlich 2010; Jackson 2014).

On the other hand, as we noted in chapter 1, news reports describing the campaign to oppose the judges raise questions about whether the events were consistent with mass opinion backlash. In particular, gay marriage became *more* rather than less popular following the campaign and election. Moreover, descriptions of the politics behind the election were ambiguous; while some reported on the significant role outside religious groups played, others saw it as a simple example of majoritarian democracy.

Judicial retention elections provide an almost ideal setting for testing MOB, as those individuals who are angered by a ruling or a series of rulings can relatively easily hold a judge accountable by opposing their retention. Similarly, the Iowa elections also provide a relatively low salience context in which elite cues should be influential, for which data are available, and on which both masses and elites might be active in response to an issue that provides sufficient threat to trigger opinion change. After all, legalizing gay marriage is precisely the type of challenge that should evoke a sense of symbolic threat—an act that violates one's morals, beliefs, or sense of how society should work (e.g., Kinder and Sears 1981). Taken in combination, the availability of campaign finance records, election outcome and turnout data, as well as public opinion data allows for evaluating the elite- and individual-level implications of the two theories.

Iowa's 2010 Judicial Retention Elections

In 2010 three Iowa State Supreme Court justices were voted out of office after their 2009 ruling to overturn the state's gay marriage ban. Not only did the Iowa Supreme Court create a new policy—gay marriage was not legal prior to the court's ruling—but they did so on an issue on which only about 27 percent of the public agreed with them.[1] The supreme court justices were the first in Iowa's forty-eight-year history of retention elections not to be retained (Sulzberger 2010a).

The campaign to unseat the judges centered on their role in overturning the state's marriage ban. The group Iowa for Freedom coordinated the campaign against retention, emphasizing the judicial activism that the ruling on same-sex marriage represented. The justices themselves did not raise any money or mount campaigns, though an outside group organized relatively late as a 501(c)3 to support them. Retention opponents spent almost $1 million to defeat the justices, running hundreds of television ads in Iowa's largest media markets (Sample et al. 2010). Web commercials also micro-targeted those most likely to be sympathetic (Pettys 2011).

While it did not see the heaviest spending or receive the most attention, the retention election was the most closely contested statewide race. Although there was a gubernatorial race, it was not competitive, as Terry Branstad defeated unpopular incumbent Democrat Chet Culver by 9.7 points. Similarly, the U.S. Senate election saw five-term incumbent Chuck Grassley defeat his Democratic opponent, Roxanne Conlin, by nearly 31 points.

The Role of Anti-Gay Elites in Iowa's 2010 Judicial Retention Election

To this point we have seen that there is good reason to question whether the opinion change central to backlash in fact occurred. Our alternative explanation, Elite-Led Mobilization Theory, however, requires that anti-gay elites organize and work to oppose the justices by mobilizing their like-minded supporters. What evidence is there that elites did this? An examination of the events leading up to the election documents how the white evangelical elites initiated the recall effort.[2]

Perhaps somewhat surprisingly, examination of the effort to oust the judges shows that the campaign to remove them did not come as an immediate response to the ruling. While marriage opponents immediately pressed for a constitutional amendment following the ruling, the issue of gay marriage was not publicly tied to the judicial retention election until August 6, 2010, well over a year after the April 2009 ruling in the case of *Varnum v. Brien*. Moreover, even after the ruling, the public as a whole (i.e., non-evangelicals) were somewhat mixed in terms of their support for a constitutional amendment.

The campaign against retention was launched in the summer of 2010 by Bob Vander Plaats after he lost the Republican gubernatorial primary (Buller 2011, 8). A religious and social Tea Party conservative, Vander Plaats formed an organization called Iowa for Freedom, which was a coalition of marriage opponents largely funded by two prominent national white evangelical groups: American Family Action and the National Organization for Marriage (Kingkade 2010; Belin 2010a and 2010b).

Newspaper reporting shows that Vander Plaats coordinated the anti-retention campaign with white evangelical elites. Television ads run during the campaign focused on the gay marriage ruling, especially the judicial activism it represented, and were paid for by the National Organization for Marriage and American Family Action among others (Belin 2010c; Brennan Center 2011; Pettys 2011).

The campaign coordinated by white evangelical elites was multifaceted. One tactic was to mobilize pastors against retention (e.g., Pettys 2011). Some pastors directed parishioners to websites with materials produced by the Iowa state arm of Ralph Reed's (national) Faith and Freedom Coalition (Kingkade 2010). Activists organized pastors against retention, encouraged them to emphasize the issue to their parishioners, arranged a campaign of over 100 pastors to speak against retention on three Sundays preceding the election, got 834 of them to sign a petition opposing the retention of the justices, and provided voter guides to churches (Eckholm 2011; Schulte 2010). At least one web ad targeted Iowa pastors and emphasized the importance of both preaching from the pulpit and informing parishioners of the importance of turning the ballot over to vote because the retention elections were printed on the back of the ballot (Mullen 2010).

Evidence of elite coordination is perhaps best seen by the ability of the coalition to emphasize a common theme throughout the campaign. While some web advertisements presented variations of the attack on gay marriage and judicial activism, as when a web ad presented a story suggesting that the ruling opened the way for a brother and sister to marry, television ads regularly referenced the ruling legalizing same-sex marriage as an example of the judicial activism that countermanded the people's will (Pettys 2011).

The ability to coordinate the message is also clear, since the messages conveyed in the major media ads were very similar in content to themes expressed in letters to the editor published in Iowa newspapers. Tyler Buller (2011) conducted a content analysis examining a sample of 331 letters to the editor randomly selected from those published in the twenty-five Iowa newspapers with the largest circulation. He found that 88 percent of those writing in opposition to retention cited the gay marriage ruling as the reason to oppose the judges, while only 14.5 percent of letters supporting retention mentioned the case (Buller 2011, 1776). Moreover, as compared to those writing in support, those writing in opposition were both more likely to write multiple letters (57 percent) than those writing in favor (43 percent); they were also much more likely to emphasize the themes of judicial activism and the ruling on gay marriage to advocate removal of the justices (88 percent) than were those who wrote only once (69 percent) (Buller 2011, 1776).[3] Documenting the use of these themes is important because they were also emphasized in the media advertisements coordinated by Iowa for Freedom. Taken together, these results along with the evidence examining public opinion and voter participation provide substantial evidence of elite coordination.

Implications and Expectations

The judges' defeat and the widespread claims of backlash, combined with the active role played by elites, make Iowa's judicial retention elections a fertile context for testing our two theories. Recall that as a bottom-up movement, Mass Opinion Backlash predicts a sharp, negative, and enduring opinion shift in response to the legalization of gay marriage. These conditions should be evident both in the behavior of citizens during the election and in the contributions made by supporters during the campaign.

The first implication with respect to public opinion is that we should see a shift in opinion against gay rights or against gays and lesbians as a group immediately following the court's ruling. Second, we should expect that the challenge to the status quo causes increased participation among the citizens who are incited by the court's ruling. Third, we should see widespread opposition to the justices who supported the ruling. Specifically, as the ruling was unanimous but only three justices were up for retention, we should see increased opposition to the justices.

Increased opposition to the justices should also be evident in examination of campaign contributions. Mass Opinion Backlash suggests that patterns of campaign contributions should reflect the fact that backlash is a broad-based phenomenon that occurs among those whose sense of the status quo is triggered by the policy threat. Specifically, MOB theory predicts that contributions to the campaign opposing retention should consist of a large number of small contributions that come primarily from citizens within the state of Iowa, as they are most directly threatened by the policy.

The central thesis of Elite-Led Mobilization Theory, on the other hand, is that elites act to further their own organizational and policy goals. With respect to mass participation, ELM suggests that we should see little in the way of opinion change, because members of the like-minded groups to whom elites appeal already opposed gay rights prior to the judges' ruling. Moreover, when necessary to build electoral support, elites will work to mobilize their like-minded supporters rather than the public as a whole. In the case of gay marriage, these supporters come primarily from the ranks of religious conservatives, especially white evangelical Christians. Consequently, we should see increased participation among white evangelicals. Finally, ELM theory also provides clear predictions about the pattern of campaign contributions. Contributions to oppose the justices should come primarily from elites and, reflecting their greater financial resources, be smaller in number but greater in amount, and a larger proportion of them should be made by large interest groups, which tend to be located outside of Iowa.

Public Opinion after *Varnum*

The central implication of Mass Opinion Backlash is that opinion should change sharply and negatively following a challenge to the status quo like the one that occurred when the Iowa Supreme Court issued its ruling. Typically, public opinion data about judicial retention races are scarce. In 2010, however, Rebecca Kreitzer and her colleagues in Iowa fielded a panel study under the auspices of the Hawkeye Poll assessing how individuals' opinions on gay marriage changed from the week before to the week after the *Varnum* ruling. Their central finding is that support for gay marriage *increased* from 26.8 to 28.7 percent in the week after the ruling (Kreitzer et al. 2014). Moreover, by the time the next Hawkeye Poll with an Iowa sample was fielded, in March 2011, four months after the election, support for gay marriage had further increased to about 36 percent (Kreitzer et al. 2014).

Unfortunately, these data do not allow us to compare the amount of opposition before and after elites attempted to mobilize their like-minded supporters (i.e., during the campaign). Hence, we cannot directly test Elite-Led Mobilization Theory on public opinion data. These data do, however, allow for the examination of two important conditions the theory requires. First, recall that since elites try to mobilize those who are predisposed to agree with them, we expect little change in negative attitudes about gay marriage before versus after the ruling. Indeed, comparison of support for gay marriage among whites who describe themselves as evangelical went from 12.6 percent to 13.2 percent among those who responded to both panels (Boehmke 2013).[4]

These data also allow us to assess the extent to which Iowa's white evangelicals were sympathetic to mobilization efforts. Recall that a central premise of Elite-Led Mobilization Theory is the attempt to appeal to the like-minded because they are susceptible to mobilization efforts. If true, then white evangelicals should exhibit that sympathy by viewing gay marriage as a particularly important issue. Specifically, we can examine differences between how important white evangelicals versus non-evangelicals saw the issue of gay marriage and what action should be taken in response to its legalization.[5] Indeed, the data show that 55.2 percent of evangelicals but only 24.6 percent of non-evangelicals saw gay marriage as "the most" important issue or "very important." Respondents were also asked if they would accept the ruling, or if a constitutional amendment should be passed to overturn it, or if they didn't know what should happen. Among white evangelicals, just 18 percent said they would accept the ruling, while a staggering 75.6 percent thought there should be a constitutional amendment to overturn it. Among non-evangelicals, 43.2 percent supported a constitutional amendment. Moreover, neither these differences nor the gay marriage opinion data appear to be a product of white evangelicals being better informed, as 63 percent of white evangelicals and 63.4 percent of non-evangelicals reported that they had heard "a lot" about the ruling in the last week.

In summary, we have seen the absence of shifts in opinion among the mass public consistent with mass backlash after the *Varnum* ruling. We have also seen that white evangelicals were both more likely to describe gay marriage as the most important issue and were more supportive of action to overturn the court ruling than were non-evangelicals, consistent with the premise of the ELM (Kreitzer 2014).

Voter Participation: Roll-Off and Vote Choice

One of the most difficult challenges in testing Elite-Led Mobilization Theory is showing that elites' cues affected the behavior of their like-minded supporters. Finding such evidence is difficult partly because the cues elites provide through the mass media reach everyone and because advocates on both sides of an election may seek to mobilize their supporters using similar instructions. The 2010 Iowa judicial retention election provides a unique opportunity to assess the effectiveness of these cues on their targets.

Religious conservatives under the banner Iowans for Freedom mounted an extensive advertising campaign that clearly targeted conservative Christians and their pastors. One important part of this campaign was an emphasis on the need for voters to turn their ballots over to the back, where the judicial races were listed. An example of this advertising is seen in figure 7.1.

We created the storyboard presented in figure 7.1, which is typical of the ads aired during the campaign in mid to late October (Pettys 2011).[6] Importantly, it references both the key arguments made by religious conservatives and the importance of turning the ballot over.[7] These messages were not limited to the general public, as videos targeted at pastors circulated the same message.[8]

In theory, pro-retention advocates might have used similar messages to ensure their supporters cast votes in the retention elections. Recall, however, that the justices themselves refused to campaign, and a key pro-retention group, Iowans for Fair and Impartial Courts, registered as a 501(c)3 organization. That designation legally precluded their making direct electoral appeals and, consequently, from urging people to vote for retention or to turn their ballots over. A second organization, Iowa for Fair Courts, did run radio spots and sent direct mail (but not television) ads urging retention supporters to turn over their ballots, but these did not air until October 14, less than three weeks before the election (Belin 2010b).[9]

Narrator: "Some in the ruling class say its wrong for voters to hold Supreme Court judges accountable for their decisions."

Former Supreme Court Justice Mark McCormick: "There is no such thing as an activist judge"

Narrator: "When activist judges on Iowa's Supreme Court imposed gay marriage, they were the only judges within 1200 miles to reach such a radical conclusion."

Narrator: "If they can redefine marriage, none of the freedoms we hold dear are safe from judicial activism."

Narrator: To hold activist judges accountable. Flip your ballot over and vote NO on retention of Supreme Court Justices.

Figure 7.1. Storyboard of an advertisement run by the National Organization for Marriage

This advertising campaign, combined with the ballot design, provides a unique opportunity to assess MOB and ELM. Specifically, to measure voter interest we examine *voter roll-off*, the rate at which people choose not to vote in the down-ballot retention races. Studying voter roll-off also provides a particularly valuable test of Elite-Led Mobilization Theory, because advertising opposing retention emphasized the importance of voters turning their ballots over. As we can see in figure 7.2, which presents a sample ballot from Cherokee County, the judicial race was listed on the back of the ballot. Importantly, Iowa employs a fairly standard ballot across counties, as state law requires use of paper ballots and optical-scan voting technology.

The sample ballot in figure 7.2 shows that in order to vote "No" on retention, voters had to flip the ballot over to mark the correct box. Consequently, examining roll-off, or the rate at which people who turned out to vote actually turned their ballot over and cast a vote in the judicial races, provides one of the few direct tests of the extent to which voters followed elite cues that are available.

The competitive retention election appears to have had a large impact on ballot roll-off. To get a sense of the changing electoral landscape, we

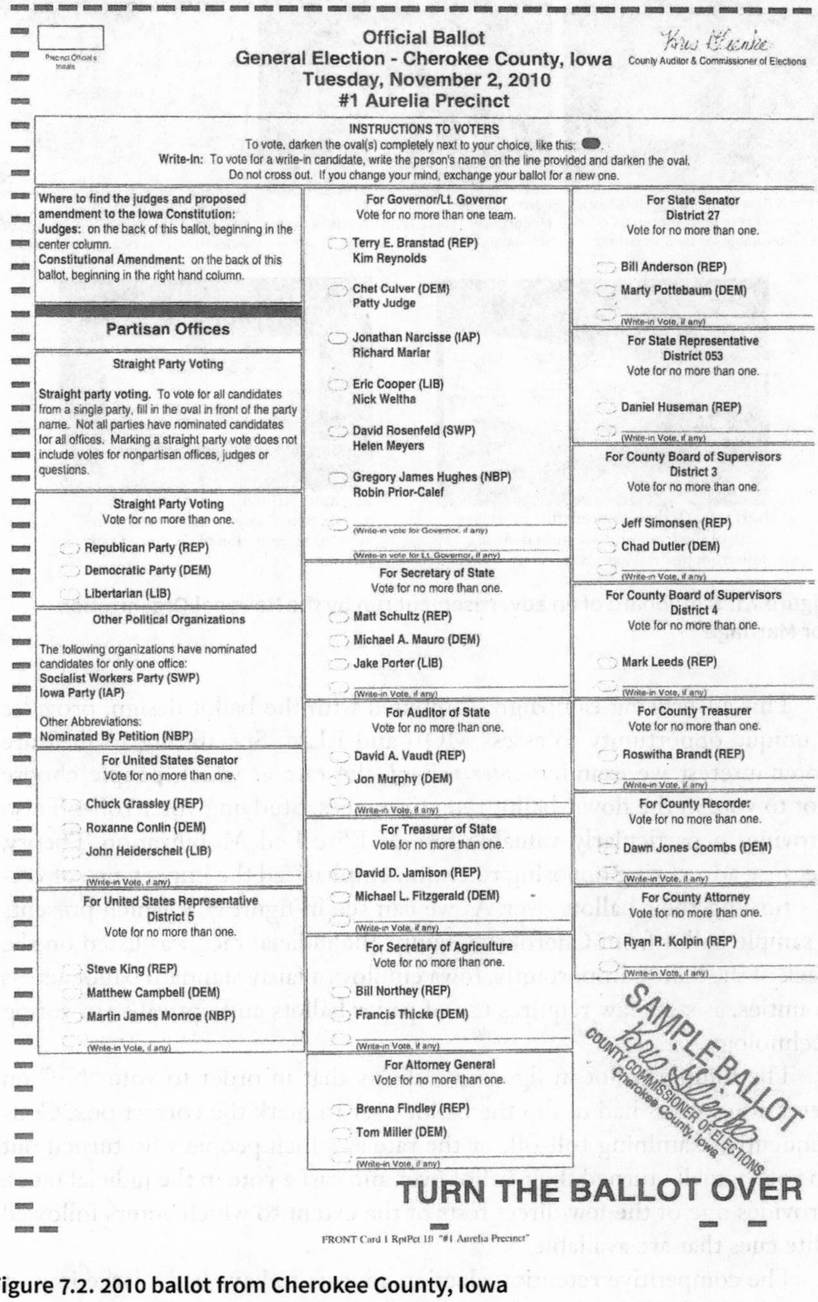

Official Ballot
General Election - Cherokee County, Iowa
County Auditor & Commissioner of Elections
Tuesday, November 2, 2010
#1 Aurelia Precinct

Precinct Officials Initials

Kris Glienke

INSTRUCTIONS TO VOTERS
To vote, darken the oval(s) completely next to your choice, like this: ●.
Write-In: To vote for a write-in candidate, write the person's name on the line provided and darken the oval.
Do not cross out. If you change your mind, exchange your ballot for a new one.

Where to find the judges and proposed amendment to the Iowa Constitution:
Judges: on the back of this ballot, beginning in the center column.
Constitutional Amendment: on the back of this ballot, beginning in the right hand column.

Partisan Offices

Straight Party Voting

Straight party voting. To vote for all candidates from a single party, fill in the oval in front of the party name. Not all parties have nominated candidates for all offices. Marking a straight party vote does not include votes for nonpartisan offices, judges or questions.

Straight Party Voting
Vote for no more than one.

○ Republican Party (REP)
○ Democratic Party (DEM)
○ Libertarian (LIB)

Other Political Organizations

The following organizations have nominated candidates for only one office:
Socialist Workers Party (SWP)
Iowa Party (IAP)

Other Abbreviations:
Nominated By Petition (NBP)

For United States Senator
Vote for no more than one.

○ Chuck Grassley (REP)
○ Roxanne Conlin (DEM)
○ John Heiderscheit (LIB)
_____
(Write-in Vote, if any)

For United States Representative
District 5
Vote for no more than one.

○ Steve King (REP)
○ Matthew Campbell (DEM)
○ Martin James Monroe (NBP)
_____
(Write-in Vote, if any)

For Governor/Lt. Governor
Vote for no more than one team.

○ Terry E. Branstad (REP)
Kim Reynolds

○ Chet Culver (DEM)
Patty Judge

○ Jonathan Narcisse (IAP)
Richard Mariar

○ Eric Cooper (LIB)
Nick Weltha

○ David Rosenfeld (SWP)
Helen Meyers

○ Gregory James Hughes (NBP)
Robin Prior-Calef

_____
(Write-in vote for Governor, if any)
_____
(Write-in vote for Lt. Governor, if any)

For Secretary of State
Vote for no more than one.

○ Matt Schultz (REP)
○ Michael A. Mauro (DEM)
○ Jake Porter (LIB)
_____
(Write-in Vote, if any)

For Auditor of State
Vote for no more than one.

○ David A. Vaudt (REP)
○ Jon Murphy (DEM)
_____
(Write-in Vote, if any)

For Treasurer of State
Vote for no more than one.

○ David D. Jamison (REP)
○ Michael L. Fitzgerald (DEM)
_____
(Write-in Vote, if any)

For Secretary of Agriculture
Vote for no more than one.

○ Bill Northey (REP)
○ Francis Thicke (DEM)
_____
(Write-in Vote, if any)

For Attorney General
Vote for no more than one.

○ Brenna Findley (REP)
○ Tom Miller (DEM)
_____
(Write-in Vote, if any)

For State Senator
District 27
Vote for no more than one.

○ Bill Anderson (REP)
○ Marty Pottebaum (DEM)
_____
(Write-in Vote, if any)

For State Representative
District 053
Vote for no more than one.

○ Daniel Huseman (REP)
_____
(Write-in Vote, if any)

For County Board of Supervisors
District 3
Vote for no more than one.

○ Jeff Simonsen (REP)
○ Chad Dutler (DEM)
_____
(Write-in Vote, if any)

For County Board of Supervisors
District 4
Vote for no more than one.

○ Mark Leeds (REP)
_____
(Write-in Vote, if any)

For County Treasurer
Vote for no more than one.

○ Roswitha Brandt (REP)
_____
(Write-in Vote, if any)

For County Recorder
Vote for no more than one.

○ Dawn Jones Coombs (DEM)
_____
(Write-in Vote, if any)

For County Attorney
Vote for no more than one.

○ Ryan R. Kolpin (REP)
_____
(Write-in Vote, if any)

SAMPLE BALLOT
Kris Glienke
COUNTY COMMISSIONER OF ELECTIONS
Cherokee County, Iowa

TURN THE BALLOT OVER

FRONT Card 1 RptPct 18 "#1 Aurelia Precinct"

Figure 7.2. 2010 ballot from Cherokee County, Iowa

Non Partisan Offices	Judicial Ballot	Public Measures
	Notice to voters: Vote on all names by filling in the appropriate oval below each name.	

Non Partisan Offices	Judicial Ballot	Public Measures
For Soil & Water Conservation District Commissioner Vote for no more than two.	**Shall the following Judges be retained in office?**	Notice to voters: To vote to approve any question on this ballot, fill in the oval in front of the word "Yes". To vote against a question, fill in the oval in front of the word "No".
○ Nathan Anderson	**Supreme Court**	
○ Russell Winterhof	Marsha Ternus	**1**
○ _____ (Write-in Vote, if any)	○ Yes	Shall the following amendment to the Constitution be adopted?
○ _____ (Write-in Vote, if any)	○ No	Summary: Adopts Iowa's Water and Land Legacy Amendment which creates a dedicated
For County Agricultural Extension Council Vote for no more than five.	David L. Baker	trust fund for the purposes of protecting and enhancing water quality and natural areas in the State including parks, trails, and fish and
○ Christopher H. Johnson	○ Yes	wildlife habitat, and conserving agricultural soils in this State.
○ Nathan Foresman	○ No	Full Text: Article VII of the Constitution of the
○ Eric Ogren	Michael J. Streit	State of Iowa is amended by adding the following new section:
○ Bryan K. Dirks	○ Yes	NATURAL RESOURCES. SEC. 10: A natural resources and outdoor recreation trust fund is
○ Donna Amundson	○ No	created within the treasury for the purposes of protecting and enhancing water quality and
○ Gina Rassel	**Court of Appeals**	natural areas in this State including parks, trails, and fish and wildlife habitat, and
○ Tom Kellen	Ed Mansfield	conserving agricultural soils in this State.
○ Guy Fishman	○ Yes	Moneys in the fund shall be exclusively appropriated by law for these purposes.
○ _____ (Write-in Vote, if any)	○ No	The general assembly shall provide by law for the implementation of this section, including by
○ _____ (Write-in Vote, if any)	Amanda Potterfield	providing for the administration of the fund and at least annual audits of the fund.
○ _____ (Write-in Vote, if any)	○ Yes	Except as otherwise provided in this section, the fund shall be annually credited with an
○ _____ (Write-in Vote, if any)	○ No	amount equal to the amount generated by a sales tax rate of three-eighths of one percent
	Gayle Vogel	as may be imposed upon the retail sales price of tangible personal property and the furnishing
	○ Yes	of enumerated services sold in this State. No revenue shall be credited to the fund until
	○ No	the tax rate for the sales tax imposed upon the retail sales price of tangible personal property
	David R. Danilson	and the furnishing of enumerated services sold in this State in effect on the effective date of
	○ Yes	this section is increased. After such an increased tax rate becomes effective, an
	○ No	amount equal to the amount generated by the increase in the tax rate shall be annually
	Rick Doyle	credited to the fund, not to exceed an amount equal to the amount generated by a tax rate of
	○ Yes	three-eighths of one percent imposed upon the retail sales price of tangible personal property
	○ No	and the furnishing of enumerated services sold in this State.
	District Court 3A Associate	
	David C. Larson	○ Yes
	○ Yes	○ No
	○ No	
	Charles K. Borth	**2**
	○ Yes	Shall there be a convention to revise the Constitution, and propose amendment or
	○ No	amendments to same?
	District 3A Associate Juvenile	
	Mary L. Timko	○ Yes
	○ Yes	○ No
	○ No	

TURN THE BALLOT OVER

BACK A

note that overall turnout in the gubernatorial race increased by about 110,355 votes between 2002—the last time this judicial class was up for election—and 2010. In 2002, however, while there were 1,025,802 votes cast for governor, there were only 620,642 votes cast for Michael Streit, for example, in the judicial retention election, reflecting roll-off of 405,160 missing votes.[10] In 2010 roll-off between the gubernatorial and retention race for Michael Streit declined to 149,115, indicating substantially more interest in the judicial races. Importantly, this shift is not likely due to differences in ballot design or election administration, because in both years the judicial retention elections were listed on the back of the ballot.

To assess whether patterns of voter participation are more consistent with MOB or ELM, we examine roll-off and retention support to test both hypotheses. Recall that the opinion change that underlies Mass Opinion Backlash reflects a broad-based reaction to the issue or group. This reaction should be reflected by increased interest in and opposition to the justices by a broad range of citizens. Hence, our insight is that if MOB occurs and people are motivated to participate because of the justices' ruling, then increased voter participation should be negatively associated with changes in both roll-off and support for retaining each justice between 2002 and 2010.[11] That is, roll-off and support for retention should decrease. In contrast, if anti-gay elites are effectively mobilizing their like-minded supporters through advertisements telling them to both vote against retention and turn their ballots to the back side, the size of the evangelical population should be negatively associated with both roll-off and retention.

Data from the 2002 judicial retention election provides an opportunity to examine whether the gay marriage ruling led to changes in county-level support for the justices between 2002 and 2010. As two of the three justices stood for retention in 2002, results from that election allow for an assessment of their popularity before the ruling.[12] Importantly, examining county change over time adds tremendous leverage to our analyses by controlling for all unobserved time-invariant explanations (e.g., race, income, education, gender, partisanship). For these reasons, our dependent variables in these analyses are the change in roll-off and the vote share in favor of retaining Justice Marsha Ternus and Justice Michael Streit.

The primary targets of mobilization are religious conservatives. To account for religious conservatism and opposition to gay rights, we employ county evangelical church membership as a proxy for those with strong anti-marriage attitudes (e.g., Burack 2008). Specifically, we employ county-level estimates from the Association of Religion Data Archives from 2000 and 2010 (Association of Statisticians of American Religious Bodies 2002, 2012).

We begin by examining voter roll-off. Our expectations are as follows: Mass Opinion Backlash implies that ballot roll-off should decrease as county voter turnout increases; alternatively, if Elite-Led Mobilization occurs, roll-off should decrease as the size of a county's white evangelical population increases. To test these hypotheses, we regress the difference in roll-off percentage by county from 2010 to 2002 on the change in voter turnout between 2002 and 2010 and white evangelical percentage (in 2010).[13] Next, to examine whether the effect of turnout or the evangelical population significantly changed between the two elections, as we would expect if the court case led to mobilization or backlash, we pool the data from 2002 and 2010 and examine roll-off in each county as the dependent variable. We create interactions between election year (2010) and turnout and between election year and evangelical % population to assess these hypotheses. Recall that our design accounts for county-level variables that do not change over time. The results of this regression are shown in table 7.1.

The results presented in table 7.1 depict a large and significant role for the variable *Evangelical %* across all models. Counties with large evangelical populations roll off at much lower rates in the 2010 judicial retention election, a result consistent with ELM theory. In contrast, we find no evidence that turnout is negatively associated with roll-off. Importantly, the

TABLE 7.1. Regression of difference in voter roll–off on group membership

	Streit Roll–Off Difference	Ternus Roll–Off Difference	Pooled Streit	Pooled Ternus
Constant	−.183***	−.173***	.407***	.445***
	(.028)	(.026)	(.116)	(.108)
Turnout	.169	.05		
	(.245)	(.233)		
Turnout %			−.138	−.229
			(.208)	(.193)
Evangelical %	−.641***	−.719***	.544***	.624***
	(.173)	(.165)	(.128)	(.119)
Year (2002)			−.198	−.246*
			(.156)	(.145)
Evangelical % x 2010			−.672***	−.75***
			(.183)	(.171)
Turnout % x 2010			.01	.119
			(.284)	(.264)
N	99	99	198	198
Adj. R2	.11	.15	.71	.74

Standard errors in parentheses. * $p < .10$, ** $p < .05$, *** $p < .01$.

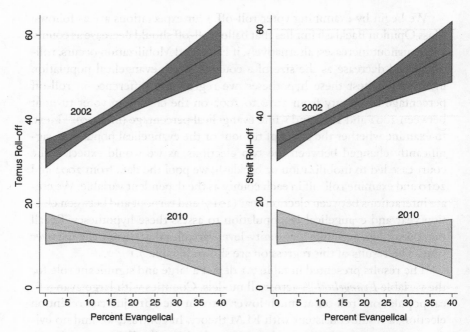

Figure 7.3. Percent of voters abstaining for Ternus and Streit by evangelical population

interaction terms for the *Evangelical* % and the 2010 election are large, negative, and statistically significant, while the interactions between *Turnout* % and the 2010 election are not significant. These results are in line with Elite-Led Mobilization Theory and contrary to predictions of Mass Opinion Backlash.

As the substantive impact of interaction effects can be difficult to interpret, figure 7.3 plots the relationship between the evangelical population and roll-off for each year based on the estimates from the two right-hand columns in table 7.1.

The graphs in figure 7.3 show similar patterns for justices Ternus and Streit. Perhaps most striking are the dramatic decrease in roll-off and the shift in the impact of the white evangelical population between 2002 and 2010. Increased evangelical population is associated with somewhat increased roll-off when the justices first ran in 2002, as evangelicals were more likely to abstain from voting in these races. By 2010 they were significantly less likely to abstain.

Next we examine the change in support for retention of each justice between 2002 and 2010 by using pooled county-level election returns from 2002 and 2010. As with the roll-off analysis, we create interactions between the 2010 variable and *Turnout* % to assess the effect of backlash and create an interaction between the 2010 variable and *Evangelical* % population variable to test elite-led mobilization.

While changes in voter turnout and the white evangelical population allow us to assess the competing theories, other factors might influence support for the judges as well. One possibility is that increased opposition to the judges reflects increased conservative dissatisfaction with President Obama. To account for this possibility, we include county-level Obama vote share in 2008.[14] As the vote share data is normally distributed, we employ ordinary least squares (OLS) regression to estimate the results, which are seen in table 7.2.

Next we examine the change in Streit and Ternus support between 2002 and 2010. The significant and negative intercept reflects the large decrease in support for the justices between 2002 and 2010. Perhaps most striking, we see that *Evangelical* % is associated with decreased (change in) support for retaining the justices. In contrast, we do not observe a significant result for *Turnout* %. The models do a surprisingly good job of explaining change in support given the noisiness of the data.

The results presented in the right-most two columns are estimated on data pooled across 2002 and 2010 and allow us to assess the influence of

TABLE 7.2. Comparison of influences on retention votes in 2002 vs. 2010

	Streit Retention Difference	Ternus Retention Difference	Pooled Streit	Pooled Ternus
Constant	−.645***	−.643***	.51***	.46***
	(.072)	(.051)	(.07)	(.07)
Turnout	−.067	.054		
	(.162)	(.115)		
Turnout %			−.16	−.07
			(.14)	(.12)
Evangelical %	−.304**	−.190**	.50***	.38***
	(.132)	(.094)	(.10)	(.08)
2010 Dummy			−.24*	−.20*
			(.11)	(.09)
Obama %	.664***	.628***	.50***	.52***
	(.119)	(.085)	(.07)	(.06)
Turnout % x 2010			−.035	−.14
			(.20)	(.16)
Evangelical % x 2010			−.69***	−.56***
			(.13)	(.10)
N	99	99	198	198
Adj. R2	.43	.53	.90	.93

Standard errors in parentheses. *p < .10, **p < .05, ***p < .001

Note: Turnout variables are for 2010 and 2002 as appropriate; evangelical% is for 2010 and 2000.

evangelical percentage and turnout above and beyond the effect that dissatisfaction with Obama might have. In this case the key variables are the interaction terms that identify the effect of evangelical percentage in 2010 as compared to 2002 and voter turnout in 2010 as compared to 2002. These results are enlightening. It appears that opposition to Obama was highly (negatively) associated with support for the judges—thus, increased support for Obama in 2008 is a large and statistically significant predictor of support for retention. Equally striking, the interaction terms for the evangelical variable are also very large, negative, and statistically significant, just as Elite-Led Mobilization Theory predicts. Conversely, the interactions between turnout and the 2010 election are not significant, contrary to the expectations of Mass Opinion Backlash.

The effects of differences in white evangelical support across elections are more clearly depicted graphically. Building on the results in the two right-most columns in table 7.2 (i.e., controlling for Obama support), we plot the predicted level of support for retention for each justice as the size of the evangelical population increases across counties. Figure 7.4 presents these results.

Two results from figure 7.4 are particularly striking and emphasize the role that elite-led mobilization played. First, we see that vote share for both candidates dropped dramatically between 2002 and 2010. While the candidates won with just over 75 percent of the vote in 2002, they experienced 20- and 24-point drops in county-level support in 2010. Second, and most importantly, we see that the slope shifts directions across years. Whereas in 2002 we see an increase in support for retention as the evangelical population increases, in 2010 increased evangelical population is associated with decreased support for retention. The switch in support is difficult to explain absent elite-led mobilization.

Taken together, the data on voter participation are consistent with ELM in that voters in counties with larger evangelical populations were less likely to roll off and more likely to oppose retention of the justices. Moreover, we see no evidence that increased participation among the broader public is associated with reduced roll-off or support for retention.

Campaign Spending in Judicial Retention Elections:
2010–2014

While both elites and masses participate directly in elections, they differ with respect to how they financially contribute. As it is characterized by a

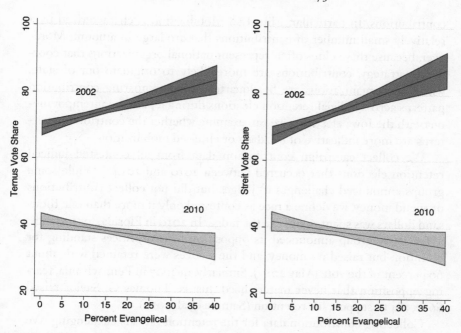

Figure 7.4. Vote to retain justices Ternus and Streit by evangelical population

widespread bottom-up reaction, Mass Opinion Backlash implies that the source of financial contributions should be relatively diffuse, reflecting broad-based opposition to changing the status quo. As a result, we should see contributions from a large number of people. Further, reflecting the financial resources of the average citizen, we also expect the amount of these contributions to be small. Finally, because backlash results from policy that threatens (or changes) the status quo, contributions should be largest among those who most directly experience this threat. As the Iowa judges' ruling on gay marriage applied only to Iowa, contributions to remove the justices should disproportionately come from individuals and organizations within Iowa, since citizens there were most directly affected by the policy change.

Elite-Led Mobilization, conversely, is predicated on the idea that individuals in positions of power, many of whom are opinion or organizational leaders, use salient events to push for policy and to gain credibility and resources. Because these individuals are fewer in number but disproportionately well resourced, patterns of financial contributions should reflect an outsize role for elites in terms of the size, number, and source of the contributions. In particular, Elite-Led Mobilization is characterized by a relatively small number of contributions that are large in amount. Moreover, because these elites often represent national organizations that coordinate strategy, contributions are more likely to originate out of state, where the organizations are headquartered. By comparing contribution patterns across judicial retention elections during a period contemporaneous with the Iowa elections, we can examine whether the contribution patterns are more indicative of backlash or elite-led mobilization.

We collect campaign contribution data from all contested judicial retention elections that occurred between 2010 and 2014.[15] While some groups announced challenges to judges but did not collect contributions or spend money, we define a race as contested only if more than one thousand dollars was spent to oppose the judge. In 2010 in Florida, for instance, a Tea Party group announced its opposition to two justices standing for retention but raised no money, and the justices were retained with about 60 percent of the vote (May 2013). Similarly, in 2007 in Pennsylvania, fearing opposition that never materialized, Justice Thomas G. Saylor raised $627,564 to support his retention (Sample et al. 2010).

Collecting contribution data for the retention races is challenging. We began by downloading data from the National Institute on Money in State Politics website FollowtheMoney.org, where we identified the races and then searched for contributions to groups opposing the judges.[16] In some cases, data were ambiguous or no contributions were found.[17] A summary of the races is seen in table 7.3.

Table 7.3 summarizes the contribution patterns from 2010 to 2014. While nonpartisan retention elections were held in sixteen states, relatively few (18 of 107) judges were opposed, and even among those targeted, the campaigns against them were not typically very well funded. In 2008, for instance, there were no well-funded races.[18] Moreover, justices were seldom defeated, as only the three Iowa justices lost during this period (Krietzer et al. 2014).

In retention elections, individuals who oppose retention typically contribute to a group that coordinates strategy, while organizations that oppose retention collect money and spend on their own. In practice, this simplifies the data collection process, as we can look for contributions to these independent opposition groups. An important complication is that in several states one or more groups coordinated a campaign against more than one judge. How do we compare, for example, the twenty-seven contributions totaling $636,210 to defeat Illinois justice Thomas Kilbride in 2010 to the six contributions totaling $990,851 given jointly to defeat Iowa

TABLE 7.3. Judicial retention races with funded opposition in 2010–2014

Year	State	Name	Vote	Issue	Money Against	In–State Money %
2010	Alaska	Dana Fabe	54.4	Abortion	67,749.00	4.1
2010	Colorado	Alex Martinez	59.5	Activism	13,026.43	98.3
2010	Colorado	Michael Bender	60.4	Activism	13,026.43	98.3
2010	Colorado	Nancy Rice	61.9	Activism	13,026.43	98.3
2010	Illinois	Thomas Kilbride	65.9	Tort Reform	636,210.00	71.7
2010	*Iowa*	*David Baker*	*45.9*	*Gay marriage*	*330,283.66*	*1.0*
2010	*Iowa*	*Marsha Ternus*	*45.1*	*Gay marriage*	*330,283.66*	*1.0*
2010	*Iowa*	*Michael Streit*	*45.7*	*Gay marriage*	*330,283.66*	*1.0*
2012	Florida	Barbara Pariente	68.0	Activism	76,877.33	32.7
2012	Florida	Peggy Quince	67.5	Activism	76,877.33	32.7
2012	Florida	R. Fred Lewis	67.5	Activism	76,877.33	32.7
2012	*Iowa*	*David Wiggins*	*54.5*	*Gay marriage*	*466,127.00*	*68.2*
2014	Illinois	Lloyd Karmeier	60.8	Partisan	3,030,566.00	30.3
2014	Kansas	Eric Rosen	52.7	Partisan	191,000.00	.
2014	Kansas	Lee Johnson	52.6	Partisan	191,000.00	.
2014	Tennessee	Cornelia Clark	55.3	Partisan	293,344.00	76.5
2014	Tennessee	Gary R. Wade	56.6	Partisan	293,344.00	76.5
2014	Tennessee	Sharon Lee	56.0	Partisan	293,344.00	76.5

Note: Races meeting the criteria for backlash are listed in italics.

justices Ternus, Streit, and Baker? In order to conduct conservative tests that should be more likely to find backlash than mobilization, we assume that the total money raised was divided equally to oppose each candidate.[19]

In order to test our hypotheses, we collect data on the number, amount, and geographic origin for all of the contributions given to the opposition group(s). We then calculate the per-candidate contribution average for the thirteen races in the non-backlash group and compare those results to the results from Iowa. The results are seen in figure 7.5.

The difference in donation patterns in Iowa, seen in figure 7.5, is striking. The left panel shows that Iowa saw far less money come from within state—only about 18 percent (i.e., about 82 percent came from out of state). In contrast, almost 62 percent of the money raised in other states came from in-state donations (i.e., about 38 percent came from out of state). The middle panel shows that while irrespective of state type the average number of donors is fairly small, it is dramatically smaller in Iowa than in the other states. The right panel depicts the average amount contributed. While the average contribution is large across all states but at almost $100,000 in Iowa, compared to $42,557 in other states, it is substantially larger in Iowa.

The pattern of contributions to judicial retention elections in Iowa

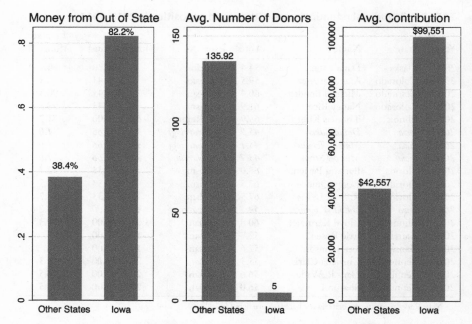

Figure 7.5. Percentage of out-of-state donations, average numbers of donors, and amount of donation in Iowa vs. other states, 2010–2014

appears more heavily elite-driven compared to other states. One concern with this analysis is that contribution patterns in a low-salience, nonpartisan judicial retention race in which the justices themselves do not mount campaigns may not accurately reflect the public's preferences. Alternatively, perhaps these results are less about elite-led mobilization than Iowans being less willing to financially contribute than are voters from other states. If that is true, a similar pattern should be evident across other major statewide races in Iowa.

Perhaps the ideal race in which to examine this possibility is the 2010 Iowa Senate race, in which popular incumbent Chuck Grassley trounced Democrat Roxanne Conlin, as it provides the most difficult test for the Elite-Led Mobilization Theory. The benefits of winning a senate seat accrue to the candidate's supporters both within and out of state. In particular, a senator's ability to affect policy for groups outside the state combined with the noncompetitiveness of the race make the contest seem especially likely to see money come from out of state.

If the contribution patterns seen in the judicial retention election are unique to Iowa elections, we should see few differences between the judi-

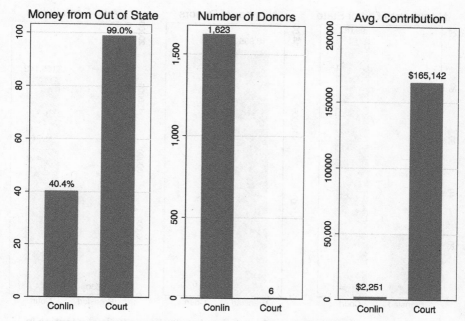

Figure 7.6. Contributions to Democratic senate challenger Roxanne Conlin and opposition to judicial retention in 2010

cial retention and senate elections. To examine this hypothesis, we obtain the number, amounts, and source of contributions to the challenger Roxanne Conlin, whose campaign is most similar to the campaign against the justices' retention. The results are depicted in figure 7.6.

The results in figure 7.6 depict large differences between contributions in the senate and judicial retention races. Despite conditions that seem likely to portend relatively low levels of participation, the percentage of money contributed from out of state (40.4 percent) was less than half of the amount seen in the judicial retention election, the number of donors was substantially larger (1,623 vs. 6), and at $2,251.35, the average contribution was less than 2 percent of the average contribution in the judicial race. The fact that Roxanne Conlin, a senate challenger with little popular support, shows much broader support within Iowa than did the victorious campaign to oppose retention is inconsistent with the claim that Iowans are less likely to contribute money to political campaigns. This finding is reinforced by examining the governor's race. The contribution data for Terry Branstad, the challenger to the incumbent governor, is seen in figure 7.7.

In figure 7.7 the public's desire to remove the unpopular incumbent

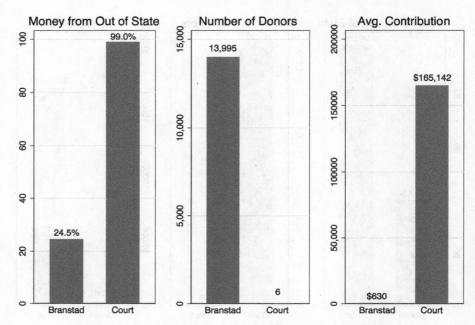

Figure 7.7. Contributions to Terry Branstad and opposition to judicial retention in 2010

governor is reflected in the fact that the vast majority of the money came from within the state (75.5 percent), the large number of donors (13,995), and the smaller average donation ($630.46). If mass backlash in response to the judicial ruling was occurring, we would expect a pattern of contributions that looks substantially more like those received by the Branstad campaign. These results suggest that the lack of citizen participation in funding the judicial retention race is not likely due to Iowans' unwillingness to participate financially in politics. With respect to contributions, we find very little evidence of mass-driven involvement in judicial retention elections for the state supreme court.

Conclusion

Elite-Led Mobilization Theory provides an alternative to backlash-based accounts of why advances in gay rights are frequently met with opposition and antipathy. This chapter tests our argument that opposition to gay rights is often the result of strategic action taken by anti-gay interest groups and the elites that represent them. Elites opposing gay rights take visible and forceful public positions in order to activate and mobilize their like-minded supporters.

Building on the research of the preceding chapters, we test the theories of Mass Opinion Backlash and Elite-Led Mobilization in the context of a campaign often described as the classic case of backlash: the 2010 Iowa judicial retention election. To do so, we develop and test the key implications of MOB and ELM by examining the origins of the campaign to oust the judges, public opinion both before and after the ruling, voter participation and behavior via roll-off and vote choice, and patterns of campaign contributions.

News reports describing the campaign to oust the justices show that it was not a bottom-up reaction consistent with backlash. Anti-gay elites led by Bob Vander Plaats coordinated a multifaceted campaign that used common themes to mobilize sympathetic voters. This was done by appealing to religious conservatives, especially white evangelicals, both directly, by appealing to religious leaders to use their positions to mobilize their congregants, and indirectly, through advertising campaigns targeting them.

We also examine public opinion on gay marriage immediately before and after the ruling. Contrary to the predictions of Mass Opinion Backlash, we find no change in opinion before versus after the court ruling. Moreover, we find that white evangelicals are more supportive of action to outlaw gay marriage in response to the ruling and are more likely to view gay marriage as the most important issue.

Next we examine voter participation and behavior using measures of roll-off and support for retaining the justices. Notably, examining roll-off allows us to assess not just interest but also receptivity to elite cues, since anti-retention advertising funded by national white evangelical groups emphasized the importance of both voting out the justices and of turning the ballot over in order to vote in the retention election. In contrast, pro-retention forces made limited direct appeals, relatively late in the campaign, and the need to turn over the ballot was not made using television ads. We find decreased roll-off only among like-minded (white evangelical) voters in Iowa in 2010, which represents a sharp change from 2002. These changes cannot be attributed to changes in ideological or partisan factors, as the results hold even after controlling for support of President Obama. Moreover, they are consistent with polling data, which depict no negative shift in attitudes toward gay marriage following the ruling despite high levels of exposure to the news about it. Similarly, we find increased opposition to retention in counties with larger evangelical populations.

Finally, we examine patterns of campaign contributions across all competitive state judicial retention elections between 2010 and 2014. Donation patterns are inconsistent with the predictions of Mass Opinion Backlash. The pattern of contributions in Iowa was small in number, large in amount, and disproportionately originated from out of state; it also differs significantly from both the senate and gubernatorial races. The campaign to oppose the justices' retention was funded by national anti-gay organizations.

While the results consistently support the predictions of Elite-led Mobilization and are inconsistent with Backlash, the analyses are subject to several potential limitations. First, these analyses speak to only one case––that of the 2010 Iowa Judicial Retention Election. While it was selected to be a difficult test for Elite-Led Mobilization Theory, to the extent that the Iowa election is not representative of other attempts to oppose gay rights, we may overstate the generalizability of the theory. Second, we employ county-level data to draw inferences about individual voting behavior. Conclusions drawn using such data must be viewed cautiously, as unobserved factors may correlate with the outcome. While we have attempted to account for the most plausible alternative explanations, such as race, education, income, and party, unrecognized factors pose a potential threat to the inferences we draw. Finally, while the campaign contribution data overcome some of these issues, nonpartisan judicial retention elections are rare and of low salience, and conclusions based on them may be susceptible to idiosyncratic factors.

Taken in combination, however, the results from a wide range of tests across a variety of data sources all point in the same direction: opposition to gay rights in the form of the judicial retention election appears to be a product of anti-gay elites mobilizing like-minded individuals. This finding is countenanced by the historical analysis of the preceding chapter, which avoids the statistical and methodological issues that limit particular aspects of the analysis conducted here. Assessing the implications of these results is the topic we turn to next.

EIGHT

Organize, Mobilize, Legislate, and Litigate

The events in Iowa help answer the questions that motivate this book: What best explains the politics of opposition to gay rights? To what extent does anti-gay backlash occur? Have attempts to advance gay rights led to public opinion backlash, or does some other phenomenon like elite-led mobilization better explain the opposition to gay rights that we see? We began by describing the puzzle posed by the effort to remove three justices from the Iowa Supreme Court election in November 2010. Recall that in 2010 three of the justices on the unanimous Iowa Supreme Court that legalized same-sex marriage were up for retention. Each of the three was voted out of office. News outlets ranging from Fox to PBS described the judges' removal as a classic case of backlash. Those in the public sphere and the academy who believed, accepted, or strategically promoted the backlash narrative—the idea that a group simply seeking rights can cause public opinion to turn away from support for the group and put the group in an even more precarious position—saw the Iowa election results as a confirmation of their claims of backlash.

Perhaps most problematic, the judges' removal appeared to confirm gay rights activists' worst fears. The idea that pursuing marriage equality could imperil the gains made by the gay rights movement by provoking public opinion backlash now had anecdotal support in the form of a compelling, easy-to-interpret, and straightforward story. Pundits, the press, and scholars quickly settled on a narrative that the judges who supported marriage equality in Iowa were punished by an angry public that had turned against gays and lesbians as a result of the overreach on the issue of marriage.

After all, an angry public had risen up to repudiate the activist court. The removal of the justices was just the latest backlash to follow a string of defeats dating back to *Bowers v. Hardwick*, Bill Clinton's support of DOMA, and the reaction to the Massachusetts Supreme Court's order to legalize gay marriage.

Or was it? As we showed in chapter 7, and contrary to the news coverage of the time, the public did not in fact mobilize en masse to oppose the justices. Close examination shows that marriage equality became *more* popular with the public both during and after the campaign to oust the justices. Nor was the antipathy toward the judges long lasting. When Justice David Wiggins, who also ruled in favor of marriage equality, stood for retention just two years later, in 2012, he was retained. In 2016, when the remaining pro-equality judges were on the ballot, all were retained. The anti-gay groups who had orchestrated the 2010 campaign now failed to even mount a meaningful campaign against them. The most important difference between the three retention elections was that the anti-gay elites only mobilized in 2010.

One might also reasonably expect mass backlash to result, at a minimum, in the reversal of the policy that incited it. Despite the massive campaign to punish the judges for legalizing gay marriage, however, no meaningful attempt to overturn the ruling occurred, and gay marriage—the policy said to drive this massive public backlash—remained legal in Iowa. Since Iowa law allows for passage of a constitutional amendment, the inability of gay-marriage opponents to rally support for such an amendment raises further questions about the extent to which backlash occurred.

How, then, can we explain the removal of the three justices? We argue that these events better reflect elite-led mobilization than a story of backlash. The campaign against Marsha Ternus, Michael Streit, and David Baker was incited by a politically ambitious religious zealot, Bob Vander Plaats, after his failed run for the 2010 GOP gubernatorial nomination. The campaign was organized and funded by conservative Christian anti-gay elites who funneled money into Iowa and mobilized local religious leaders and like-minded supporters, especially white evangelicals, to oppose the justices' retention. There is no evidence to support the fundamental premise of backlash—that pursuing marriage equality caused a shift in attitudes—because these voters disapproved of gay rights and marriage equality long before the Iowa court ruled. The campaign against the judges was overwhelmingly funded by a small number of groups from outside of Iowa that made very large donations. Taken by surprise by the challenge, the campaign was opposed not by the justices themselves—as they refused to campaign—but by a national and somewhat ham-handed group advocating judicial independence. Simply put, the Iowa Supreme Court election provides compelling support for elite-led mobilization and rather aggressively undercuts the argument that public opinion backlash resulted from the pro-equality ruling.

The case of the Iowa judicial retention elections is, in the end, an iconic example of how ambiguity regarding the concept of backlash led to mis-characterizations of what actually occurred. What was termed "backlash" by anti-gay activists, the media, and the academy was simply a continuation of a long-running campaign against the acceptance of LGBT people orchestrated by elites. Moreover, close examination shows that the events that occurred in Iowa are not unique. As we saw in chapter 6, examples of anti-gay mass opinion backlash are extraordinarily rare throughout American history. Instead, both historical and contemporary opposition to gay and trans rights are better explained by elite-led mobilization.

Our central mission in this book has been to explain how and why opposition to gay rights in contemporary American politics manifests. The conventional wisdom is that opposition to gay rights is characterized by backlash—the sharply negative and enduring change in opinion that occurs in response to challenges to the status quo. In this book we showed that this received wisdom is wrong. We began by showing that the term "backlash" is characterized by ambiguity and inconsistency in its logic and application. To address this, we defined and developed the theory of mass opinion backlash, or MOB. Doing so highlighted inconsistencies between the concept of backlash as well as recent events in American politics and current research in political science.

An important trend in American politics over the last two decades has been the increased acceptance of gays and lesbians. As one example, the percentage of voters who would find a lesbian or gay candidate for president acceptable shifted from 43 percent in 2006 to 68 percent in 2019 (Dann 2019). This trend is at odds with the prediction of backlash and offers something of a paradox. Similarly, research on opinion formation shows that, once formed, opinions are difficult to change, contrary to the implications of backlash. These observations highlight the need for alternative explanations to understand the politics of opposition to gay rights.

Our theory of elite-led mobilization explains at least three important aspects of opposition to gay rights. First, it explains events like the successful campaign to unseat the Iowa justices, which actually had no policy consequence, as it did not lead to the repeal of gay marriage in Iowa or the ouster of other pro-equality justices in future retention elections. And Iowa is just one case where close examination shows that mass opinion backlash did not occur. Rather, to the extent policy changed, it was preceded by elites organizing and acting to precipitate it. Second, elite-led mobilization is not subject to the opinion paradox that underlies backlash. Despite numerous high-profile conflicts over gay rights and attempts to advance gay rights, including precisely the type of challenges to the status quo that backlash advocates argue should incite public rebuke, the last two decades have delivered exponential growth in gay rights and in public acceptance of gays and lesbians. Both policy and public opinion have moved in favor of gay rights on virtually every dimension. Not only did the oft-predicted public opinion backlash not occur, but public support for gay rights and gay-friendly policies actually advanced whenever the gay rights movement made a concerted effort to prevail. Most striking, beginning in 2012, advances in gay rights increasingly occurred because of popular support as referenda advancing gay rights started passing across the country. Third, in contrast to mass opinion backlash, because Elite-led Mobilization Theory posits only that opposition to gay rights is led by anti-gay elites, it makes no prediction about attitude change among the general public. Elite-led Mobilization Theory is consistent with the research on the robustness of attitudes and attitude formation. This research simultaneously shows that, once formed, attitudes are resistant to change and that informed citizens develop their attitudes by taking cues from elites with whom they identify, particularly co-partisans (e.g., Zaller 1992).

We began in chapter 2 by describing the ambiguity that has been an endemic characteristic of the concept of backlash. Backlash has been used as a convenient explanation for virtually any negative reaction to a marginalized group's efforts to challenge the oppressive status quo. Often backlash has been used to describe preexisting animus—that is, hostile feelings that exist before any challenge to the status quo. In short, backlash has been ill-defined, under-theorized, and poorly operationalized. Despite the ambiguity underlying the idea of backlash, the press, the academy, popular discourse, and even gay rights advocates have collectively embraced the call for caution and making only incremental efforts when seeking rights in order to avoid or reduce the inevitable punishment from the public that awaits those who challenge the status quo. While revisiting the history of claims of backlash and refining the operationalization of backlash, we demonstrated that public opinion increasingly supports LGBT rights even as the contests over those rights have taken center stage in political and social discourse.

The ambiguity that has plagued the backlash conversation has also inhibited consideration of alternative explanations for opposition to gay rights. Our alternative theoretical framework, Elite-Led Mobilization Theory (ELM) posits that campaigns against gay rights are orchestrated by highly motivated, well-organized, and resource-rich elites. These elites are primarily white evangelical Christians who view gays and lesbians as inherently amoral, oppose LGBT rights, and work to contest the inclusion of gays and lesbians as legitimate members of society. While groups affiliated with other religions—like the Catholic Church and the Latter Day Saints—share much of the LGBT animus, white evangelical groups are larger, more unified, more focused, better resourced, and are the leaders on this issue. Moreover, they work together with these other anti-gay groups to oppose gay rights, as we saw with repeal of the nondiscrimination ordinance in Miami–Dade County, the organization of the Arlington Group, and the campaign to pass Proposition 8, to name just a few examples.

In Part II of the book we turned to answering the following questions: To what extent does anti-gay backlash occur? What kinds of events or policies trigger backlash? What form does backlash take? And which groups are most likely to lash back? In chapter 3 we attempted to induce backlash in an experimental setting. We examined whether different types of salient events altered opinions about gay marriage or attitudes toward gays and lesbians. The results of the experiments demonstrated that backlash did not occur. That the subjects were just as likely to become more positive toward gays as they were to become more negative toward gays aligns more directly with the political science understanding of changes in opinion than with the journalistic view of backlash. The findings we presented in chapter 3 suggest backlash either does not exist or occurs so infrequently that it cannot be detected and hence is not widespread.

In chapter 4 we examined the extent to which backlash has occurred following attempts to advance gay rights. In particular, we began examining whether public opinion changed after actual changes in policy were made or in response to challenges to the status quo. That is, we examined whether opinion backlash actually occurred. Our most powerful test occurred in the days following the seminal rulings in *Obergefell v. Hodges* and *United States v. Windsor*.

In June 2015 the U.S. Supreme Court ruled same-sex marriage legal throughout the country and thereby nullified the many state laws and constitutional amendments that banned it. Our examination of public opinion about gay rights before and after *Obergefell* and *Windsor* confirms the findings from our experiments in chapter 3. Even a pair of simultaneous Supreme Court rulings advancing gay rights did not induce backlash.

Rather, support for gay marriage continued to increase. By 2018 public support for marriage equality reached a record high of 67 percent.

The Supreme Court rulings failed to trigger any negative reaction by the public despite their breadth and broad impact. This led us to examine in chapter 5 whether different governmental institutions have a different impact on public opinion toward gay rights and gays and lesbians. Is it possible that the public is less willing to lash back against a court ruling than they are against the actions taken by other institutions? To examine this we conducted a series of experiments in which we varied the institution making the policy. Our experiments and observational studies demonstrated virtually no support for backlash regardless of the mechanism or institution responsible for the policy. Even when opinion change occurred, it was tiny and short-lived. Accordingly, as with the evidence presented in the earlier chapters, the information offered in chapter 5 also undermines the backlash narrative.

Having found no evidence of mass opinion backlash, in Part III we turned to test our alternative, Elite-Led Mobilization Theory in order to evaluate which theory best explains the politics of opposition to gay rights. In chapter 6 we more directly assessed Elite-Led Mobilization Theory. We began to do so by taking a historical lens to the question of whether Mass Opinion Backlash or Elite-Led Mobilization Theory best explains opposition to gay rights over time. Each theory offers differing predictions for what should occur depending on the extent to which attempts to expand gay and trans rights are contested. Before the "era of contestation," there was nothing for those opposing gay rights to lash back against or to mobilize in opposition to, as the status quo was one in which gay rights were almost universally circumscribed, and attempts to organize focused less on policy than on increasing social acceptance. Once contestation begins, Mass Opinion Backlash predicts that opposition is characterized by public uprising leading opposition to gay rights, while ELM argues that elites organize and then work to mobilize opponents of gay rights. In short, ELM requires citizens to be *told* that expanding gay rights is bad for them, while MOB requires the expansion itself to be the catalyst for opinion change.

Although gay rights activism is often traced to the Stonewall Inn riots in 1969, we find that gay rights did not become contested by religious conservatives until the passage of the nondiscrimination ordinance in Miami–Dade County in 1977. Tracing the history of gay rights from the early 1950s to the present, we described and considered a host of high-profile challenges to gay rights in the United States. From the Lavender Scare of the 1950s to the challenges to trans rights during the Trump administration, every decade saw some high-profile fight over LGBTQ rights. For each episode of rights contestation, we considered whether backlash or elite-led mobilization better explains the outcomes.

Despite the limitations of data—we cannot, after all, go back in time and survey citizens in real time as they react to gay rights advances—we found little evidence consistent with backlash. Given that public opinion has become much more supportive of gay rights over time, this finding is perhaps unsurprising. Instead, every major campaign against gay rights in the post-contestation era has been precipitated by elite behavior. Consequently, Elite-Led Mobilization Theory better explains opposition to gay rights than does Mass Opinion Backlash.

While historical analysis suggests Elite-Led Mobilization better explains the political conflict over gay rights, it provides relatively little leverage for evaluating each theory's mechanisms that drive the outcomes we observe. To examine these mechanisms, we employed a case study approach using perhaps the most famous example of backlash to test the theories. Specifically, in chapter 7 we studied the Iowa 2010 judicial retention election to directly test the two competing theories by examining public opinion before and after the same-sex marriage ruling and by exploiting the fact that anti-gay elites funded advertisements that were both disseminated to pastors and aired on TV reminding their followers about the importance of turning over their ballots to vote against retention. We then examined voter participation using measures of roll-off and support for retention of the judges to assess the impact that MOB and ELM had on those targeted by these appeals (white evangelicals) and the public as a whole. We found that elites coordinated the recall effort through a direct appeal to religious conservatives, most of whom already opposed gay rights. We also examined patterns of campaign finance as a surrogate for grassroots versus elite participation in the recall effort. Campaign contributions were small in number, large in amount, and came overwhelmingly from out of state. Contrary to Mass Opinion Backlash, we found that the public became more rather than less supportive of gay marriage after this campaign. In each dimension the evidence supports elite-led mobilization.

Why "Backlash"? The Role of the Media

One of our central arguments is that the concept of backlash so commonly used is sufficiently ambiguous to impede its evaluation. A central contribution of this book is to define and evaluate the concept of backlash in politics. To this point, however, we have yet to examine why the media, pundits, and scholars fall back on the term "backlash" to explain such a wide variety of concepts. While a full investigation into the reasons for the use of the term are beyond the scope of this study, significant research in media and politics offers one possible explanation why the media may refer to any reaction to attempts to advance gay rights as "backlash."

A basic journalistic standard holds that balance (and objectivity) in reporting—the idea that journalists are ethically obligated to report all sides of a story—is fundamental to the presentation of news (e.g., Reuters 2016). Journalists commonly strive to dispassionately present all sides of a story, including those that are among the most extreme, in order to forestall protests by extremists (Gans 1979). The media are especially likely to provide competing viewpoints when public opinion is split on an issue (Bennett 1990). In practice, when presenting stories describing advances in gay rights, journalists often interview representatives of organizations that are staunchly opposed to gay rights.

Research shows that journalists often rely on organizations run by elites for information that serves as the basis for news stories (Gans 1979). Even in coverage of unpitched or spontaneous news, journalists recruit representatives of these organizations to provide balance in the presentation of news (e.g., Lewis et al. 2008). Because journalists are themselves elites and often travel in the same social circles with other prominent people (e.g., interest group leaders), their interaction with the leaders of organizations can help shape how journalists themselves view an issue (Gans 1979).

The journalistic norms of balance and objectivity have two important implications for the politics of gay rights. First, the process by which the media covers news introduces the possibility that the *perception* of negative reactions, whether in response to challenges to the status quo or to policy changes, are a result of how the media chooses to cover gay rights. By embracing balance, journalists publicize anti-gay views at precisely the same time that advances in gay rights are being made, making it appear that opposition to the advances is a product of them rather than of the manner by which the media have chosen to cover them. By embracing objectivity, media often present the views in an unvarnished way, thus conveying a degree of equivalence, importance, and legitimacy to all views no matter how extreme or widely supported.

The Implications of Elite-Led Mobilization:
The Status of Gay Rights

Opposition to gay rights remains common and manifests in a variety of ways across settings. We have focused on change in public opinion because it is the foundation for claims of backlash. Public opinion change, however, does not tell the whole story of the contest over gay rights. Twenty years after the brutal and sadistic murder of Matthew Shepard, only eighteen states have hate crime statutes that address sexual orientation and gender identity, while another twelve have hate crime laws based on sexual orientation that are silent as to gender identity. The rest of the states have no specific statutes that address these types of hate crimes. Similarly, employment nondiscrimination protections for members of the LGBT community only recently became law, through the Supreme Court ruling in *Bostock*.

Assaults on gay and especially trans rights increased dramatically under President Trump. The *Bostock* ruling, for example, was opposed by the Justice Department, which under President Trump argued that employers could fire those who identify or are perceived as trans simply based on that status. Executive agencies under the Trump administration also issued orders banning trans people from serving in the military, repealed rulings protecting trans people from discrimination in homeless shelters, and sought to ban trans students from participating in sports (National Center for Transgender Equality 2020). In 2020 the Department of Health and Human Services announced it would not enforce antidiscrimination regulations based on gender identity, sexual orientation, and religion in all grant programs. These examples reflect just a few recent attempts to roll back or impede LGBT equality (National Center for Transgender Equality 2020).

Clearly, despite unprecedented advances in gay rights and public acceptance of gays and lesbians, the motivated anti-gay forces did not disappear simply because rights battles did not go their way. Andrew R. Lewis has presented a powerful explanation of the strategic shift of the religious right regarding cultural contestations (2017). As he explains, the religious right's original roster of arguments against the rights of members of the LGBT community were grounded in morality. The desires and acts of gay people were antithetical to moral propriety and an affront to God's word and will. Supporting these immoral desires would corrode decent ("Christian") society. As that version of the anti-gay argument lost favor in the courts over time, white evangelical Christians increasingly borrowed from Catholics and altered their strategic approach such that the objections of the religious right became grounded in a competing rights framework. By doing so, the right to hold deeply hostile opinions and attitudes toward gay people was elevated to be comparable to the fundamental rights of gay people. Hence, a baker has a rights-based claim to decline to make a cake for a gay couple. The First Amendment freedoms of religion and of association, among others, are the new foundation for rights deprivation of the

LGBT community. The fact that the elites of the anti-gay movement have deemed it prudent to shift their strategies from an overtly anti-gay argument (gays are immoral) to one grounded in free speech and free association (Christians have a constitutional right to believe gays are wicked and cannot be forced to mingle with them) suggests that not only does backlash not manifest but also that elites drive the shifting rationale for the anti-gay side of the debate.

It is not surprising that the religious right has moved from the position that gays are not entitled to any rights to the position that if gays are entitled to their rights, it infringes on the rights of those with anti-gay views. From Pope Innocent III's 1199 exploitation of his spiritual leadership to foster opposition to political enemies to modern white evangelicals changing positions on abortion to gain and expand political power, religious leaders have long used their office to achieve political objectives (Kennan 1971; A. Lewis 2017). Other social movements have employed a similar strategy. The civil rights movement faced a comparable strategic evolution in both voting rights (see, e.g., Weeks 1948) and public accommodation cases (e.g., Cortner 2001). Although the civil rights era effort in this regard was unsuccessful, there are reasons to be concerned that the judiciary may not be as gay-friendly in the future as it has been in the past. In particular, the effectiveness of the socially conservative interest group, the Federalist Society, in controlling the selection of Republican-appointed or -approved judges in concert with the Trump administration's aggressive judicial appointment strategy means that the federal bench has become a more hostile environment for gays and lesbians than in the recent past.

The Obama administration left more than one hundred federal judicial vacancies for the Trump administration to fill. This is a larger number than typical and was due in large part to an obstructionist Senate that refused to advance any of Obama's nominees during his last year in office (see *Heritage Judicial Tracker*). Moreover, President Trump appointed more than one-fourth of all federal judges. At this writing he had appointed 234 of the 852 federal court positions (27.4 percent) (*Heritage Judicial Tracker*). Obviously, the judicial selection and confirmation process poses an immense procedural task. To facilitate this, Senate Majority Leader Mitch McConnell recently moved to eliminate procedural restrictions that typically slow the confirmation process for lower-level federal judges, and the Trump administration relied heavily on the Federalist Society for candidate selection.

Of course, judges often evolve on the bench, and there is a body of scholarship suggesting that even the Supreme Court attempts to adhere to incremental changes when faced with contentious social policies (e.g.,

Smirnov and Smith 2013). And equality advocates can occasionally employ strategies designed to appeal to conservative jurists, such as when they made a textualist argument that laws banning discrimination on the basis of sex must protect transgender people. Still, this conservative shift in the judiciary underscores the importance of demonstrating the myth of backlash. Activists must embrace a multipronged elite-driven approach to complement their grassroots efforts. Just as importantly, the idea that any given strategy will potentially alienate the voting public because of mass opinion backlash should become a relic that activists remember as a tool of oppression and obstruction.

Advice to Activists: Organize, Mobilize, Legislate, and Litigate

Taken on its face, the dramatic increase in the number of conservative jurists populating the federal courts and the use of new rights-based strategies to leverage individual liberty-based arguments on behalf of religious conservatives pose serious challenges to the gay rights movement. The question facing activists, then, is how to overcome what seems likely to be an increasing number of hurdles that policy making through the judicial branch may pose. Setting aside the possibility of attempting to get the courts to weigh the relative merits of competing rights claims, and making appeals to conservative principles like textualism, the history of the gay rights movement and the theory of elite-led mobilization suggest another strategy: activists should broaden the institutions through which they pursue policy and, in particular, pursue legislation to obtain rights. Specifically, activists should look to leverage the recent massive gains in public support for gay rights by expanding the playing field both in terms of the policies pursued and the institutional venues used to obtain those policies. While policy advances are not guaranteed, this book has shown that the costs to pursuing such policy are far lower than previously thought. Consequently, by pushing for a broader range of policies at the local, state, and federal levels, both through the legislature and, where possible, through referendum, activists can best leverage the power of the people to advance gay rights.

One challenge is that despite massive increases in public support, very little pro-gay policy has passed through the U.S. Congress (e.g., Bishin, Freebourn, and Teten 2020). Most federal advances in gay rights have been the product of executive orders and court rulings. The primary obstacle has been the threat of filibuster in the U.S. Senate. The Biden administration, with narrow Democratic Senate control, and the repeal or relaxation of the filibuster, may offer a politically valuable opportunity to advance and protect gay and trans rights. Until federal laws pass, however, LGBT rights will at best remain uncertain and at risk of future courts rescinding existing protections, presidents issuing adverse executive orders, and states passing laws that further restrict LGBT rights, particularly in places where such rights remain less popular.

In a sense, pursuing a broad-based strategy across geographies, levels of government, and institutions entails a return to the roots of the gay rights movement. After all, many of the earliest victories for gay rights occurred in small cities and counties where the public was, if not supportive, at least not opposed to providing basic protections to gays and lesbians (e.g., Clendinen and Nagourney 1999). Recall that despite facing a hostile, if latent, public, the nondiscrimination ordinance that passed in Miami–Dade County in 1978 came about because a group of activists organized to endorse and promote candidates who supported gay rights (e.g., Fejes 2008). Executing a broad-based strategy that pursues numerous policies across multiple levels and venues, especially at the federal level, would allow for a broader assault against efforts by anti-gay elites to oppose the public acceptance of gays and lesbians. And to the extent that the courts, especially those populated by conservative jurists, prefer to defer to state and local law, such policies may have a greater chance of remaining intact. Moreover, from Harvey Milk and ACT UP through Proposition 8 and marriage equality, the history of the gay rights movement demonstrates that success follows effort, especially when that effort is made on multiple fronts. Activists should aggressively name and shame those anti-gay elites who drive anti-gay mobilization. The pro-gay efforts should be multi-scalar—that is, rights should be contested at every level of government and in every venue possible. The struggle for equality should not be shaped by fear of public opinion backlash. The only position certain to fail to advance gay rights is one that accepts the status quo. As Wayne Gretzky famously said, "You miss 100% of the shots you don't take."

Beyond Gay Rights: Elite-Led Mobilization on Other Issues

While media, politicians, and general society often lump gays, lesbians, and the trans community together, the roster of rights demands and discrimination faced by the groups do not align perfectly. Indeed, the specifics of the dimensions of transgender rights claims are mostly distinct from those of gays and lesbians. In *The Remarkable Rise of Transgender Rights* (2018), Jami K. Taylor and her coauthors demonstrate the path and strategies of a rights-based social movement that achieved public acceptance and policy successes for the trans community at a stunning pace. Even when elites tried to demonize the trans community as threats to children and public safety, for instance, through the myriad of public bathroom bills that were introduced across the South, the public largely rejected these elite-led efforts (Taylor et al. 2018, 3–6). The history and progress of the trans rights movement is distinct from, if intertwined with, the gay rights movement, yet it shows similar dynamics of Elite-Led Mobilization undertaken through a claim of threatened public opinion backlash.

There are a host of other sexual minorities who have rights concerns that are different from those of the gay and lesbian community or the trans community. Those who identify as polyamorous—that is, whose relationships involve more than two consenting adults—have no legal protections and often lose their jobs, get evicted from rentals, or lose custody of children when their polyamory is discovered. People in the BDSM community— that is, bondage, domination, and sadomasochism—face all the same rights challenges of the polyamory community, with the added difficulty that domestic violence and battery laws make no exception for consent, so many avenues of intimacy are felonies in every state. The lesson for these and other sexual minorities is that they need not fear backlash. These groups should pursue their rights in every available avenue—administration, legislation, and litigation should be pursued as a multipronged strategy, and elites should mobilize the masses in support of the effort to obtain the desired outcomes.

Critically, the concept that policies that impact rights should be pursued without fear of public opinion backlash is not just limited to discernible minority groups. Broad social issues often have the hallmarks of elite-led mobilization masquerading as fear of or actual popular opinion backlash on gay rights. While we found no evidence of backlash here, it is worth keeping in mind that while evidence of backlash may vary across issue areas, there is a normative imperative to work toward advancing equality and other fundamental democratic values even when doing so is unpopular.

Elite-led mobilization may also occur on the issue of climate change. Because the science of climate is grounded in highly technical ideas and sophisticated statistical methods, elites who have an interest in perpetuating factually incorrect positions use the approaches we have identified as part and parcel of Elite-Led Mobilization Theory. Since the 1980s the Republican Party has partnered with economic elites and their advocates to roll back environmental regulations and cast doubt on the settled science of climate change (Collomb 2014). Economic elites, including the fossil fuel industry and corporate lobbying groups like the U.S. Chamber of Commerce and the National Manufacturers Association, coupled with general conservative think tanks and foundations like those run by the Koch brothers, publicize false and misleading information through environmentally specific conservative foundations constructed to create skepticism about climate science (Dunlap and McCright 2011). These conservative environmental-policy think tanks then run their disinformation campaigns through friendly media echo chambers like Fox News and conservative talk radio bolstered by so-called astro-turf (or artificial) activism (Dunlap and McCright 2011, 174). This elite-led effort to discredit climate science has been successful with Republican voters as well as with Republican policy makers despite widespread acceptance of climate change among the population in general (Xifra 2016).

The contestation over gun rights in the United States is demonstrative. Attempts to construct gun control policy—defined in a variety of ways from background checks to enhanced sentencing for using a gun when committing a crime—began in earnest in the 1970s. There has been a predictable and persistent pattern of activity related to this topic. Generally, politicians and the public react to some horrific event like a mass shooting, such as those at Columbine; Sandy Hook; the Aurora, Colorado theater; or Las Vegas, or some high-profile use of a gun, such as the assassination attempts on Ronald Reagan and Gabrielle Giffords or the murder of Trayvon Martin (Spitzer 2015, xiii-xix). Initial outrage, salience, and public concern then subsides, and in the event any regulation actually does get implemented, the law has been watered down by those policy makers who are beholden or sympathetic to the National Rifle Association (NRA) (Goss 2006, 28–32). The reason that gun control efforts fail despite broad support among the voters is that there is an absence of powerful or resource-rich elites who consistently support the control side of the debate, while the NRA and those politicians who are supported by it are institutionalized (Wilson 2015). To achieve a sustained and successful effort on gun control, more elites need to lead more voter mobilization driven by the gun control issue in particular.

In our view, the answer to elite-led science skepticism, whether about gun control or the existential threat of climate change, is similar to the answer to opposition to rights. Elites matter and elite-led mobilization drives these debates. Political and policy leaders must step up and mobilize or risk losing the debate by choosing to not engage for fear of backlash. Perhaps the take-home point for those in social movements and those activists who hope to launch a social movement to change the status quo is that the public is unlikely to turn against you simply because you ask for your rights. Legislation, litigation, and executive administration all hold more promise for advancing policy than they do risk, as mass opinion backlash is not likely to occur. On balance, the only strategy certain to lose is to accept the status quo and hope one day in the future the circumstances and environment will be ideal in order to ask for your rights or try to change policy.

Appendices

Appendices

Chapter 3 Appendix

Experimental Vignettes

Respondents were assigned to 1 of 5 conditions randomly.

Court Condition: Court Overturns Gay Marriage Ban

In a highly anticipated decision in Salem today, the Oregon State Supreme Court voted to legalize gay marriage. The 6–3 decision, which goes into effect immediately, takes a major step toward legalizing gay marriage by overturning a long-standing prohibition banning it. Unless overturned by the United States Supreme Court, the ruling promises to grant gays and lesbians all of the protections and benefits extended to heterosexual couples.

Legislature Condition: Legislature Overturns Gay Marriage Ban

In a highly anticipated decision in Salem today, the Oregon State House of Representatives and Senate voted to legalize gay marriage by overturning a long-standing prohibition banning it. The vote passed both chambers by a 60–30 margin and the governor has promised to sign it immediately. Unless overturned by the United States Supreme Court, the ruling promises to grant gays and lesbians all of the protections and benefits extended to heterosexual couples.

Gun Control Condition: Court Overturns Conceal Carry Policy

In a highly anticipated decision in Salem today, the Oregon State Supreme Court voted to ban the carrying of concealed weapons on college campuses. The 6–3 decision, which goes into effect immediately, overturns a long-standing University of Oregon policy allowing "concealed carry" for permit holders. Unless overturned by the United States Supreme Court, the ruling would prevent Oregonians with a concealed weapons permit to carry a gun on any of the state college campuses.

Parade Condition: Thousands Attend Gay Pride Parade

Thousands of people filled the streets on Saturday for Salem's 41st annual Gay Pride Parade. The festivities began at 10:30 a.m. on Saturday and were still going on well into the evening. If there ever was a day in Oregon where just about anything goes, this is it. Whether a person is clothed, on a float, on a bike, on the sidewalk dancing or just plain watching, the 41st annual Gay Pride Parade kicked off in all its feathered and rainbow glory. While Oregon politicians were out in full force on Saturday, it was the parade's celebrity grand marshal, Chaz Bono, who won over the crowd. Police say it's been nothing but a calm and festive event.

Referendum Condition: Referendum Overturns Gay Marriage Ban

In a highly anticipated special election today, the citizens of Oregon voted to legalize gay marriage. The 60–40 result, which goes into effect immediately, takes a major step toward legalizing gay marriage by overturning a long-standing prohibition banning it. Unless overturned by the United States Supreme Court, the referendum promises to grant gays and lesbians all of the protections and benefits extended to heterosexual couples.

Experimental Vignette used in Panel Survey, wave 1 (May 2015)

Question Wording for SDO and ITT Groups

Social Dominance Orientation

Please indicate how strongly you agree or disagree with the following statements:

1. Some groups of people are simply not the equals of others.
2. Some people are just more worthy than others.

3. Some people are just more deserving than others.
4. It is not a problem if some people have more of a chance in life than others.
5. Some people are just inferior to others.
6. To get ahead in life, it is sometimes necessary to step on others.

Integrated Threat Theory

Symbolic

Please indicate how strongly you agree or disagree with the following statements:

1. American identity is being threatened by gays and lesbians.
2. Gays and lesbians are a threat to American culture.
3. American norms and values are being threatened by gays and lesbians.
4. The American way of life is being threatened by gays and lesbians.
5. The values and beliefs of gays and lesbians are similar to Americans.

Anxiety

Please indicate how strongly you agree or disagree with the following statements:

1. I would feel uncomfortable when interacting with a gay person.
2. When interacting with a gay person, I would feel relaxed.

Group Conflict

Please indicate how strongly you agree or disagree with the following statements:

1. Because of the presence of gays, Americans have more difficulty finding a job.
2. Because of the presence of gays, Americans have more difficulty finding a place to live.
3. Because of the presence of gays, unemployment in the U.S. will increase.
4. Because of the presence of gays, crime in the U.S. has increased.
5. Because of gays, the American people are less safe.

Stereotype

On a scale from 0 to 10 where 0 means not well at all and 10 means extremely well, how well do the following characteristics describe gays?

1. Well-dressed
2. Promiscuous
3. Mentally ill
4. Effeminate
5. Pedophiles
6. Industrious
7. Immoral
8. Burden on society
9. Hardworking

Questions Used to Measure Political Sophistication

1. Do you happen to know what job or political office is now held by Joe Biden? _____
2. Whose responsibility is it to determine if a law is constitutional or not? Is it the president, the Congress, or the Supreme Court? _____
3. How much of a majority is required for the U.S. Senate and House to override a presidential veto? _____
4. Do you happen to know which party currently has the most members in the House of Representatives in Washington, DC? _____
5. Which one of our two major, national political parties is more conservative? _____
6. How often do you watch news on TV?
   a. Every day
   b. A few times a week
   c. Once a week
   d. A few times a month
   e. Never

Approximate Power Calculations
(Statistics refer to the control condition)

TABLE A3.1 Favorability toward gay marriage (assuming effect size of 1 point)

Group	N	Mean	SD	Statistical Power
High SDO	114	2.22	1.10	>99.9%
High ITT	113	1.24	1.14	>99.9%
Evangelicals	45	1.09	1.31	95.2%
Unsophisticated	83	2.06	1.17	>99.9%
Independents	69	2.45	0.99	>99.9%
General Public	360	2.29	1.09	>99.9%

TABLE A3.2 Attitudes toward gays and lesbians (assuming effect size of 10 points)

Group	N	Mean	SD	Statistical Power
High SDO	123	64.35	29.95	74.5%
High ITT	127	44.57	24.21	90.8%
Evangelicals	50	50.4	29.08	40.5%
Unsophisticated	93	67.88	28.08	68.0%
Independents	69	71.58	20.62	81.3%
General Public	380	67.19	27.56	>99.9%

TABLE A3.3 Importance of gay marriage opinion (assuming effect size of 2 points)

Group	N	Mean	SD	Statistical Power
High SDO	122	6.42	2.93	>99.9%
High ITT	125	5.58	3.03	99.9%
Evangelicals	50	6.82	3.16	88.6%
Unsophisticated	92	5.75	3.40	97.9%
Independents	69	6.83	2.49	99.7%
General Public	378	6.61	2.85	>99.9%

These are approximate power calculations. These calculations are based on the assumption that the number of observations in each treatment condition is equal to the number of observations in the control condition (this is true in expectation) and that the standard deviation is the same across all treatment and control conditions.

Reanalysis Using Only Those Respondents Who Correctly Recall the Content of the Treatments They Read

TABLE A3.4 Main effects on those who correctly recall treatment

Attitudes toward Gays and Lesbians	Difference in Means	95% Confidence Interval
Legislature	.81	(–2.4, 4.1)
Parade	–.91	(–4.2, 2.4)
Court	–1.1	(–4.4, 2.11)
Referenda	1.98	(–1.28, 5.25)
Post–SCOTUS	–2.4	(–6.07, 1.25)

Support for Gay Marriage	Difference in Means	95% Confidence Interval
Legislature	.152	(.02, .28)
Parade	–.05	(–.18, .08)
Court	.03	(–.09, 1.6)
Referenda	.12	(–.0003, .258)
Post–SCOTUS	–.01	(–.16, .132)

Intensity of Feelings	Difference in Means	95% Confidence Interval
Legislature	–.07	(–.41, .27)
Parade	–.106	(–.46, .24)
Court	–.14	(–.49, .209)
Referenda	.096	(–.25, .44)
Post–SCOTUS	–.186	(–.573, .199)

Note: Differences in means refer to the differences relative to the gun control condition.

These results are entirely consistent with our main experimental results. We find absolutely no evidence of backlash. The only significant change in opinion we observe is a significant *increase* in support for gay marriage after learning (and accepting) information about the Oregon state legislature overturning a ban on same-sex marriage. Another possibility is that the AMT sample was substantially more favorably disposed toward gay marriage than the nation as a whole. This does not appear to be the case, however; as we discuss earlier in this chapter, our thermometer scores for evangelicals are comparable to those seen in a national sample.

Chapter 4 Appendix

TABLE A4.1 Ordered logit of FMA support before and after Bush announcement and court rulings

	Massachusetts Ruling				Bush Announcement				California Ruling			
	All	Born–Again	Independents	Low Info	All	Born–Again	Independents	Low Info	All	Born–Again	Independents	Low Info
Ruling	0.11	-0.02	0.11	0.22	-0.11	-0.18	-0.10	0.11	0.15	0.23	-0.00	-0.07
	(0.083)	(0.158)	(0.162)	(0.177)	(0.081)	(0.156)	(0.154)	(0.176)	(0.089)	(0.171)	(0.164)	(0.192)
GOP	0.34***	0.27		0.21	0.31***	0.34		0.06	0.39***	0.34		0.11
	(0.104)	(0.189)		(0.223)	(0.106)	(0.185)		(0.234)	(0.113)	(0.209)		(0.246)
Democrat	-0.10	0.05		-0.13	-0.30***	0.15		-0.15	-0.23**	0.09		-0.02
	(0.106)	(0.218)		(0.212)	(0.099)	(0.211)		(0.204)	(0.109)	(0.229)		(0.230)
Mormon	0.26	-0.07	0.07	0.12	0.40	-0.64	0.48	-0.63	1.11***	-0.35	1.44**	-1.99
	(0.317)	(0.774)	(0.506)	(0.594)	(0.282)	(0.586)	(0.603)	(0.593)	(0.406)	(0.873)	(0.674)	(1.240)
Catholic	-0.08	-0.38	-0.28	-0.50**	0.08	-0.15	0.56***	-0.06	0.05	-0.51	0.17	0.12
	(0.099)	(0.251)	(0.190)	(0.216)	(0.101)	(0.262)	(0.193)	(0.229)	(0.108)	(0.274)	(0.199)	(0.245)
Born–Again	0.79***		0.56***	0.32	0.83***		0.88***	0.69***	0.72***		0.70***	0.76***
	(0.106)		(0.202)	(0.214)	(0.104)		(0.200)	(0.224)	(0.113)		(0.216)	(0.236)
Attend	0.29***	0.39***	0.35***	0.23***	0.20***	0.37***	0.24***	0.12	0.23***	0.29***	0.12	0.22***
	(0.035)	(0.068)	(0.067)	(0.074)	(0.034)	(0.065)	(0.067)	(0.076)	(0.037)	(0.074)	(0.069)	(0.079)
White	-0.66***		-0.57**	-0.69	-0.20		-0.47	-0.01	-0.27		0.02	-0.49
	(0.185)		(0.319)	(0.364)	(0.177)		(0.304)	(0.352)	(0.197)		(0.318)	(0.375)
Black	-0.51**		-0.56	-0.53	0.26		0.01	-0.15	0.04		0.42	-0.71
	(0.248)		(0.486)	(0.455)	(0.223)		(0.429)	(0.423)	(0.251)		(0.461)	(0.471)
Hispanic	0.09	-0.37	0.08	0.17	0.57***	0.16	0.65**	0.82**	0.32	0.88	0.16	0.03
	(0.177)	(0.418)	(0.330)	(0.333)	(0.176)	(0.381)	(0.331)	(0.334)	(0.184)	(0.486)	(0.323)	(0.343)
Female	-0.23***	-0.25	-0.36**	-0.40**	-0.34***	-0.45***	-0.03	-0.32	-0.14	0.01	-0.08	-0.25
	(0.085)	(0.164)	(0.159)	(0.187)	(0.082)	(0.160)	(0.157)	(0.185)	(0.089)	(0.170)	(0.164)	(0.210)
Age	-0.00	-0.01	-0.00	-0.00	0.00	0.01	-0.00	0.01	0.00	0.01	0.01	0.01**
	(0.003)	(0.005)	(0.005)	(0.005)	(0.003)	(0.005)	(0.005)	(0.006)	(0.003)	(0.005)	(0.005)	(0.006)
Liberalism	-0.46***	-0.55***	-0.40***	-0.21**	-0.44***	-0.29***	-0.61***	-0.29***	-0.53***	-0.52***	-0.64***	-0.26**
	(0.050)	(0.097)	(0.095)	(0.098)	(0.049)	(0.093)	(0.098)	(0.101)	(0.055)	(0.104)	(0.101)	(0.109)
Obs.	2,242	688	601	468	2,405	705	665	483	2,077	646	587	425

Standard errors in parentheses. * $p < .10$, ** $p < .05$, *** $p < .01$.

Question Wordings from the 2004 Annenberg Opinion Questions

cAE06: "On a scale of zero to 10, how would you rate gay and lesbian organizations? Zero means very unfavorable, and 10 means very favorable. Five means you do not feel favorable or unfavorable. Of course you can use any number between zero and 10."

cCE17: "The federal government adopting a constitutional amendment banning gay marriage—do you favor or oppose the federal government doing this?" (recoded 1–5 such that higher scores indicate greater opposition to gay marriage).

cCE21: "Would you favor or oppose an amendment to the U.S. Constitution saying that no state can allow two men to marry each other or two women to marry each other?"

cCE24: "Would you favor or oppose a law in your state that would allow gays and lesbians to marry a partner of the same sex?"

TABLE A4.2. Differences in sample characteristics in periods before and after 2003 and 2004 court rulings and marriage announcement

	CA	FMA	MA
GOP	0.02	.03	0.06
Democrat	0.02	.00	−0.02
Mormon	0.00	−.01	0.00
Catholic	0.00	.01	0.01
Evangelical	0.00	−.01	−0.03
How often	0.10	.03	0.03
Massachusetts	0.00	−.01	0.00
White	0.00	.01	−0.01
Black	−0.01	.00	0.01
Hispanic	−0.02	−.01	−0.02
Female	0.00	.01	−0.01
Age (in years)	1.47	−1.09	0.34
Liberalism	−0.06	.01	−0.06

Note: These are calculated by subtracting the population means in the eight days preceding the ruling from the mean from the eight days following the rulings.

TABLE A4.3. OLS regression of gay group favorability before and after rulings and announcement

	Massachusetts Ruling				Bush Announcement				California Ruling			
	All	Born-Again	Independents	Low Info	All	Born-Again	Independents	Low Info	All	Born-Again	Independents	Low Info
Ruling	0.00	-0.09	-0.07	-0.08	-0.19	-0.18	-0.60**	0.02	0.11	0.34	-0.06	0.54
	(0.131)	(0.228)	(0.252)	(0.319)	(0.127)	(0.218)	(0.246)	(0.309)	(0.142)	(0.235)	(0.267)	(0.323)
GOP	-0.57***	-0.59**		-1.15***	-0.40**	-0.60**		-0.07	-0.18	-0.25		-0.29
	(0.165)	(0.275)		(0.408)	(0.166)	(0.255)		(0.403)	(0.182)	(0.297)		(0.403)
Democrat	0.19	0.08		0.43	0.15	-0.53		0.35	0.59***	0.19		0.07
	(0.166)	(0.324)		(0.384)	(0.158)	(0.312)		(0.366)	(0.174)	(0.333)		(0.384)
Mormon	-0.70	-0.55	-0.54	-0.49	-0.55	-0.36	-0.87	-0.40	-0.88	-1.59	-4.12***	-0.28
	(0.485)	(1.035)	(0.827)	(0.962)	(0.427)	(0.871)	(0.954)	(0.949)	(0.598)	(1.720)	(1.560)	(1.979)
Catholic	0.39**	0.93**	0.37	1.25***	0.25	0.59	0.41	0.76	0.41**	1.08**	0.66**	1.04**
	(0.157)	(0.380)	(0.294)	(0.394)	(0.162)	(0.387)	(0.318)	(0.408)	(0.176)	(0.423)	(0.324)	(0.414)
Born-Again	-1.00***		-0.73**	-0.25	-1.42***		-0.99***	-1.17***	-1.32***		-1.32***	-1.05***
	(0.166)		(0.315)	(0.387)	(0.166)		(0.323)	(0.395)	(0.185)		(0.348)	(0.406)
Attend	-0.27***	-0.56***	-0.29***	-0.41***	-0.24***	-0.43***	-0.36***	-0.25	-0.24***	-0.30***	-0.19	-0.41***
	(0.054)	(0.096)	(0.101)	(0.129)	(0.053)	(0.092)	(0.110)	(0.132)	(0.060)	(0.103)	(0.111)	(0.131)
White	0.54		0.78	0.67	0.34		0.63	0.13	0.80**		0.82	0.12
	(0.292)		(0.490)	(0.626)	(0.286)		(0.503)	(0.703)	(0.316)		(0.529)	(0.598)
Black	-0.22		1.30	0.41	-0.92**		-0.19	-0.34	-0.64		-0.82	-0.45
	(0.392)		(0.741)	(0.805)	(0.360)		(0.707)	(0.826)	(0.401)		(0.721)	(0.767)
Hispanic	-0.37	-0.56	-0.60	-0.39	-0.51	0.31	0.37	-1.03	-0.53	-1.01	-1.25**	-0.52
	(0.277)	(0.550)	(0.536)	(0.561)	(0.281)	(0.562)	(0.497)	(0.625)	(0.287)	(0.629)	(0.511)	(0.535)
Female	0.53***	0.46	0.85***	1.26***	0.47***	0.45**	-0.00	1.01***	0.48***	0.39	0.67**	1.00***
	(0.133)	(0.235)	(0.247)	(0.344)	(0.129)	(0.220)	(0.249)	(0.325)	(0.142)	(0.235)	(0.262)	(0.344)
Age	-0.02***	-0.02***	-0.02***	-0.02*	-0.03***	-0.03***	-0.02**	-0.04***	-0.03***	-0.03***	-0.03***	-0.03***
	(0.004)	(0.007)	(0.008)	(0.010)	(0.004)	(0.007)	(0.008)	(0.010)	(0.004)	(0.007)	(0.009)	(0.010)
Liberalism	0.87***	0.75***	0.93***	0.58***	0.93***	0.74***	0.91***	0.49***	0.82***	0.71***	0.94***	0.66***
	(0.078)	(0.137)	(0.144)	(0.177)	(0.075)	(0.125)	(0.151)	(0.172)	(0.085)	(0.149)	(0.155)	(0.186)
Constant	3.09***	3.95***	2.60***	3.18***	3.34***	3.54***	3.35***	4.09***	2.57***	2.61***	2.05**	3.41***
	(0.432)	(0.649)	(0.743)	(0.953)	(0.445)	(0.637)	(0.827)	(1.069)	(0.490)	(0.727)	(0.873)	(1.016)
Observations	1,597	500	437	348	1,726	504	474	353	1,460	446	415	313
R-squared	0.263	0.249	0.229	0.214	0.284	0.199	0.246	0.184	0.263	0.171	0.227	0.259

Standard errors in parentheses. * $p < .10$, ** $p < .05$, *** $p < .01$.

Chapter 5 Appendix

Experimental Vignettes

Respondents were assigned to 1 of 5 conditions randomly.

Court Condition: Court Overturns Gay Marriage Ban

In a highly anticipated decision in Salem today, the Oregon State Supreme Court voted to legalize gay marriage. The 6–3 decision, which goes into effect immediately, takes a major step toward legalizing gay marriage by overturning a long-standing prohibition banning it. Unless overturned by the United States Supreme Court, the ruling promises to grant gays and lesbians all of the protections and benefits extended to heterosexual couples.

Legislature Condition: Legislature Overturns Gay Marriage Ban

In a highly anticipated decision in Salem today, the Oregon State House of Representatives and Senate voted to legalize gay marriage by overturning a long-standing prohibition banning it. The vote passed both chambers by a 60–30 margin and the governor has promised to sign it immediately. Unless overturned by the United States Supreme Court, the ruling promises to grant gays and lesbians all of the protections and benefits extended to heterosexual couples.

Gun Control Condition: Court Overturns Conceal Carry Policy

In a highly anticipated decision in Salem today, the Oregon State Supreme Court voted to ban the carrying of concealed weapons on college campuses. The 6–3 decision, which goes into effect immediately, overturns a long-standing University of Oregon policy allowing "concealed carry" for permit holders. Unless overturned by the United States Supreme Court, the ruling would prevent Oregonians with a concealed weapons permit to carry a gun on any of the state college campuses.

Parade Condition: Thousands Attend Gay Pride Parade

Thousands of people filled the streets on Saturday for Salem's 41st annual Gay Pride Parade. The festivities began at 10:30 a.m. on Saturday and were still going on well into the evening. If there ever was a day in Oregon where just about anything goes, this is it. Whether a person is clothed, on a float, on a bike, on the sidewalk dancing, or just plain watching, the 41st annual Gay Pride Parade kicked off in all its feathered and rainbow glory. While Oregon politicians were out in full force on Saturday, it was the parade's celebrity grand marshal, Chaz Bono, who won over the crowd.

Police say it's been nothing but a calm and festive event.

Referendum Condition: Referendum Overturns Gay Marriage Ban

In a highly anticipated special election today, the citizens of Oregon voted to legalize gay marriage. The 60–40 result, which goes into effect immediately, takes a major step toward legalizing gay marriage by overturning a long-standing prohibition banning it. Unless overturned by the United States Supreme Court, the referendum promises to grant gays and lesbians all of the protections and benefits extended to heterosexual couples.

Experimental Vignette used in Panel Survey, wave 1 (May 2015)

Thousands Attend Charity Race

The Oregon Road Runners Club held its annual charity 5K yesterday in downtown Salem. The race netted around $25,000 for educational charities, about the same about as in years past. "About 20 percent of our runners were first-timers, so we were definitely excited to see so many new faces out there," said Samantha Holcombe, one of the event coordinators. "It's a great way to get outside and be active, and there are kids who have a real need for new textbooks and school supplies," she said. The post-race festivities featured food from local restaurants, and several former Olympians were among the runners. The event was hailed as a great success by all involved.

TABLE A5.1. Panel regression for respondent support of gay rights, with individual fixed effects (CCES 2010–2014) for general public

	Constitutional Amendment Banning SSM	End Don't Ask, Don't Tell
Age	.0100	−.00375
	(.00754)	(.00784)
Party	.00886**	−.00851**
	(.00353)	(.00371)
Ideology	.0170***	−.00549
	(.00483)	(.00509)
White	−.00109	.0189
	(.0161)	(.0169)
Hispanic	.0292	.0523*
	(.0285)	(.0300)
Unemployed	−.00737	−.00135
	(.0108)	(.0113)
Religiosity	.00375	.000879
	(.00474)	(.00497)
Born–again	.0153	−.0231*
	(.0113)	(.0119)
Church attendance	.00267	.000967
	(.00330)	(.00346)
Catholic	.0105	.00422
	(.0161)	(.0170)
Mormon	−.0226	.0333
	(.0524)	(.0546)
2012	−.0253	.0406**
	(.0155)	(.0162)
2014	−.0753**	.0470
	(.0304)	(.0316)
Constant	−.282	.840*
	(.422)	(.439)
R^2	.008	.006
Observations	27226	27080

Standard errors in parentheses. * $p < .10$, ** $p < .05$, *** $p < .01$.

TABLE A5.2. Panel regression for respondent support of gay rights, with individual fixed effects (CCES 2010–2014) for strong Democrats

	Constitutional Amendment Banning SSM	End Don't Ask, Don't Tell
Age	.0157**	−.00182
	(.00777)	(.00818)
Party	.00357	−.0151***
	(.00428)	(.00455)
Ideology	.0115**	−.00461
	(.00512)	(.00547)
White	−.00498	.0157
	(.0180)	(.0191)
Hispanic	.0422	.0540*
	(.0306)	(.0326)
Unemployed	.00497	−.00150
	(.0114)	(.0121)
Religiosity	.0120**	.00155
	(.00486)	(.00517)
Born–again	.00587	−.00816
	(.0125)	(.0133)
Church attendance	.00105	−.000629
	(.00354)	(.00376)
Catholic	−.00290	.00401
	(.0167)	(.0178)
Mormon	.0224	−.00717
	(.0558)	(.0592)
2012	−.0355**	.0315*
	(.0160)	(.0169)
2014	−.0827***	.0267
	(.0313)	(.0329)
Constant	−.651	.846*
	(.431)	(.453)
Observations	21563	21453
R^2	.004	.004

Standard errors in parentheses. * $p < .10$, ** $p < .05$, *** $p < .01$.

TABLE A5.3. Panel regression for respondent support of gay rights, with individual fixed effects (CCES 2010–2014) for strong Republicans

	Constitutional Amendment Banning SSM	End Don't Ask, Don't Tell
Age	−.00715	.00674
	(.0179)	(.0185)
Party	−.0142	.00897
	(.0184)	(.0191)
Ideology	.0226**	−.00289
	(.0114)	(.0118)
White	.00372	.0475
	(.0360)	(.0370)
Hispanic	.0241	.100
	(.0662)	(.0687)
Unemployed	−.0474*	.0136
	(.0259)	(.0268)
Religiosity	−.0128	−.0161
	(.0125)	(.0130)
Born–again	.0239	−.0378
	(.0237)	(.0245)
Church attendance	.00961	.00466
	(.00750)	(.00771)
Catholic	.0545	.0281
	(.0407)	(.0423)
Mormon	−.334**	.122
	(.144)	(.148)
2012	.0160	.0344
	(.0367)	(.0380)
2014	−.0477	.0484
	(.0722)	(.0747)
Constant	1.091	−.166
	(1.033)	(1.069)
Observations	8249	8193
R^2	.025	.016

Standard errors in parentheses. * $p < .10$, ** $p < .05$, *** $p < .01$

Chapter 7 Appendix

Sources and Coding for Issue and Spending Data for Contested Judicial Retention Elections by Year and State

Identifying contributions is challenging for several reasons. First, different states have different disclosure rules. While some states do not require disclosure for spending to defeat Supreme Court justices (i.e., Kansas), others only require disclosure for certain types of activities. In 2014, for instance, the Koch brothers' political action committees, or PACs, avoided disclosure in Florida by producing ads that were run on the Internet. Further complicating matters, the best national database, the National Institute on Money in State Politics, does not always match the data from individual state websites. And the quality and ease of finding information from these websites varies dramatically, even in states where disclosure is required.

The campaign contribution data presented in this chapter are based on the best available estimates of the amount, source, and number of unique contributions. The source for these estimates varies. Where possible, data on contributions are obtained from the National Institute on Money in State Politics website. In some cases, those data are incomplete or do not report spending for a race. This is especially true in races where opponents sought to depose multiple justices through one campaign. Where these data are unavailable or appear to be inconsistent, data were obtained from the state elections websites and from opensecrets.gov, a website run by the Center for Responsive Politics. Despite this multitude of sources, there are still several races where spending to oppose justices occurred but that do not show up in the databases. Often this is because of state disclosure requirements or because the money is being raised by groups that under federal law do not have to disclose their donors. In these cases, amounts are estimated by referring to the Buying Time reports from the Brennan Center for Justice. These reports typically state the amount spent by campaigns for and against the judges. In cases where they cannot obtain this data from existing databases, they obtain estimates of spending from a media consulting firm on the amount of advertising dollars spent to air the ads. When other data are not available, we impute the amount spent on television advertising to defeat the justices. Advertising-based expenditures always name the organization that funded them, and they can be identified as in or out of state. However, estimated contributions for these states may understate the proportion of money raised in state versus out of state, as well as the total amount raised. Importantly, in all of the cases we study, these "dark spending" ads always are funded by national organizations.

It is important to recognize that, at least theoretically, spending on advertising could exceed contributions, though this appears rare in the states for which records are available. Also, while television advertising is the most expensive expenditure purchased by these campaigns, substantial spending often occurs on other items, such as radio advertising and postage as well as political consulting. Consequently, the estimates we present should be viewed as conservative.

2008

There were no competitive retention elections.

2010

Alaska

A search of Alaska Public Offices records shows that Citizen Link, a Colorado-based interest group, contributed $50,000. An additional $10,000 came from the Family Research Council in Washington, D.C., and $5,000 came from the American Family Action Association in Tupelo, Mississippi. The remainder of the $67,749 came from small contributions by people whose addresses were in Alaska.

Abortion was the key issue motivating the campaign, although other social conservatives support the campaign. Coding comes from several sources, but issues in the race are well summarized in an article titled

"Allies Defend Fabe as Justice Fights Campaign to Oust Her." *Alaska Dispatch News*, October 28, 2010.

The ads can be found here:

http://www.adn.com/alaska-news/article/allies-defend-fabe-justice
-fights-campaign-oust-her/2010/10/29/ also https://www.bren
nancenter.org/sites/default/files/legacy/Buying%20Time%20
2010/STSUPCT_AK_AKJR_SHRED_THE_WILL.mov and
http://www.ncsc.org/conferences-and-events/nov-2-judicial-ele
ctions-roundup.aspx

Colorado

A search of the database National Institute on Money in State Politics finds a total of $40,552 donated to Clear the Bench Colorado. These are overwhelmingly from small ($100 or less) in-state donors. Following the methods described above, we report $13,740.37 as the amount contributed to each race. There were 439 unique donors. Only $669.10 came from out-of-state donors. (A small amount was spent on legal fees, as there was a challenge to the campaign finance laws restricting individual giving, though it is not reflected in our data.)

These races were coded as non-backlash races. Clear the Bench is a partisan Tea Party–driven campaign against judicial activism. A summary of the issues in this race can be found in Cardona 2010.

Illinois

Illinois had three judges up for retention but only one, Thomas Kilbride, was opposed as twenty-seven donors raised $636,210 against him. These donations were made by business interests upset with his ruling rejecting tort reform. These data were taken from the National Institute on Money in State Politics website Follow the Money.

The election was coded as a non-backlash race. A summary of the campaign issues can be found in C. Johnson 2010.

Iowa

Data here are from the Follow the Money database. They identify six contributors, five (Citizens United Political Victory Fund, Family Research Council, Campaign for Working Families, AFA Action, and National

Organization for Marriage) from out of state and one (Iowa Family Policy Center Action Network [$10,178]) from in state. Source: http://classic.fol lowthemoney.org/database/StateGlance/ierace.phtml?s=IA&y=2010&spe cial=1

In this election all three races were coded as backlash races. The election was focused on gay marriage. The issues surrounding the campaign are well described in Sulzberger 2010a.

2012

Florida

This race had mixed reporting, as web-based advertising is not required to be reported in Florida. Consequently, the largest expenditure on advertising was $155,000 by Americans for Prosperity, a Washington, D.C.–based group (an arm of the Koch brothers). This amount was estimated by CMG and reported by the Brennan Center in the report linked to above. Other amounts are reported, however. These include:

$70,876 from the OpenSecrets database ($0 from out of state; 2 contributors but several too small to be recorded)
$4,756 from the Florida Campaign Finance Database ($100 from out of state; 59 different contributors)

These estimates assume that the small contributions in the OpenSecrets database that are below the threshold to be recorded by name (amount is given) are from among those who are listed in the state files. Consequently, if false, our estimates may slightly understate the number of contributors.

This was a partisan challenge and is not coded as a case of backlash. A description of the politics of the 2012 race can be found here: http://www .orlandosentinel.com/news/politics/os-judges-merit-retention-20161006 -story.html last accessed 10 February 2017

Iowa

A total of $466,127 was raised to defeat David Wiggins. Of this, $317,795 was spent by the Family Leader, an Iowa-based PAC. It disclosed it received two contributions—one from the Family Leader (itself) and the other from the Faith, Family, Freedom Fund (a D.C. PAC). Also $148,332 was from the National Organization for Marriage, a D.C.–based PAC. These were the only contributors.

A summary of contributions is seen here: https://www.followthemon
ey.org/show-me?dt=2&is-y=2012&f-fc=2&is-t-eid=13009832#[{1 | gro=is
-f-eid,is-t-toff.

This election was coded as a backlash race. Once again the race centered
on gay marriage, as the only judge targeted for removal was David Wiggins, who was the only one of the four up for retention who had ruled to
strike the marriage ban. The other three judges were all recent appointees
who joined the court after the ruling. A summary of the race and results is
found in Dalby 2012.

2014

Illinois

In total, $3,030,566 was raised to defeat Lloyd A. Karmeier. Of this, about
$1,809,653.42 was from out of state. There were eighty-seven contribu-
tions, of which only eighteen were from in state. (This excludes money
from the Illinois State Rifle Association Political Victory Fund (ISRAPVF),
since it is untraceable.) According to the Follow the Money database, there
were four groups that targeted Karmeier in 2014.

Eagle State Forum raised $2,362 with thirteen contributors, all of which
were from in state. A group called Campaign for 2016 spent $2,062,513
and had seven contributors, of which four were from out of state (they
raised $960,000). The Republican State Leadership Committee (RSLC)
is a national PAC that spent $963,626 on this race to defeat Karmeier.
However, they raise lots of money for lots of different groups (over $4
million in 2014), so we identified all contributors in 2016 and then calculated the percentage of money raised from out of state (98.55 percent) and
then multiplied that by the amount they spent to defeat Karmeier, which is
$949,653.42. Sixty-five of sixty-seven contributions were from out of state.

The ISRAPVF spent $2,065. All of their contributions in 2014 were
below the threshold required to disclose donor information, so we assume
that all were in state. Also, only $810 was raised in 2014 (presumably they
had money from previous years).

A link to these results is seen here: http://followthemoney.org/show
-me?dt=2&is-t-eid=3169525#[{1 | gro=is-f-eid

This race is coded as a non-backlash case. The race was focused on business interests and Karmeier's rulings against plaintiffs and his pro-business
bent. He was supported by national Republican groups. A description of
the politics in the race can be found in Sachdev 2014.

Kansas

Kansas campaign finance law excludes from disclosure those who donate to races for the state supreme court (it's a loophole). Searches of campaign finance databases have no records for this race, since contributions and spending were not publicly disclosed. However, the Brennan Center had analysis done to estimate the advertising spending in this race. It does not allow us to identify their donors, so we cannot determine the proportion of money or how many of the contributors come from out of state.

Kansans for Justice spent $382,000 on ads but there is no estimate of the amount spent by other groups (at least one of which also ran ads). So the groups in total spent $191,000 against each and $135,500 for each. A pro-retention group (Kansans for Fair Courts) spent at least $271,000 to retain them. The details of the spending are reported here: https://www.br ennancenter.org/press-release/bill-gates-and-obama-join-fray-record-out side-spending-judicial-races-takes-crucial

This election was coded as a non-backlash race. The race was seen by some as an opportunity to pack the court with Republican jurists by letting Governor Samuel Brownback select the replacements. According to news accounts, several conservative groups have raised and spent money to defeat the justices. The two most prominent are Kansans for Conservative Values (which pursues conservative causes generally) and Kansans for Justice. The former seems to have general conservative interests; the latter is organized around support for the death penalty. The following links describe the politics involved.

http://www.kansas.com/news/politics-government/article3327699
    .html
http://www.hutchnews.com/news/elections/current-former-staffers
    -of-kobach-start-pac-to-promote-conservative/article_f32e970e
    -fd2d-572c-9c78-d48aa1e2a796.html

Tennessee

Two groups spent money to oppose justices Cornelia Clark, Gary Wade, and Sharon Lee: the Tennessee Forum ($224,562 against each) and the Republican State Leadership Committee ($68,782 against each). These data were obtained from the National Institute on Money in State Politics. The data for Lee are seen here: http://followthemoney.org/show-me?dt=2 &is-t-eid=6564653#[{1 | gro=is-f-eid

These elections are coded as non-backlash races. The challenge to these justices was partisan, as the Republican lieutenant governor led a campaign to defeat the three justices, who were appointed by a Democratic governor. A summary describing the politics around the race is seen here: http://www .slate.com/articles/news_and_politics/jurisprudence/2014/06/tennessee _supreme_court_justices_gary_wade_cornelia_clark_and_sharon_lee.html

Background information was also found here: http://www
.brennan
center.org/sites/default/files/publications/The_New_Politics_of
_Judicial_Election_2013_2014.pdf

Mullin, Jeff. 2010. Iowa Pastors. https://www.youtube.com/watch
?v=1Dn4Y3ED6VUb

TABLE A7.1. Alternative specifications of roll-off

	Streit Roll-off	Ternus Roll-off	Streit 2010 Roll-off	Streit 2002 Roll-off	Ternus 2010 Roll-off	Ternus 2002 Roll-off	Streit 2010 Roll-off	Streit 2010 Roll-off
Turnout %	.332 (.259)	.239 (.244)						
Evangelical % 2010	-.476** (.212)	-.56*** (.2)	-0.128* (0.0713)		-0.126* (0.0707)		-0.098 (0.085)	-0.096 (0.084)
Obama %	.247 (.208)	.251 (.196)					0.05 (0.074)	0.05 (0.074)
Turnout%			-0.127 (0.105)	-0.138 (0.272)	-0.109 (0.104)	-0.229 (0.250)	-0.122 (0.105)	-0.104 (0.104)
Income	-1.16 (2.4)	-3.71 (22.6)						
Education	-.000 (.005)	-.002 (.004)						
Black %	.008 (.009)	.011 (.008)						
Evangelical 2002				0.544*** (0.167)		0.624*** (0.15)		
Intercept	-.258 (.379)	-.166 (.357)	0.209*** (0.0560)	0.407*** (0.152)	0.199*** (0.056)	0.445*** (0.14)	0.177*** (0.074)	0.166** (0.073)
N	99	99	99	99	99	99	99	99
adj. R^2	.119	.165	0.031	0.083	0.026	0.135	0.025	0.021

Standard errors in parentheses. $*p < 0.10$, $**p < 0.05$, $***p < 0.01$

TABLE A.7.2. Alternative specifications of retention support

	Streit Change	Ternus Change	Streit Change	Ternus Change	Streit 2010	Streit 2002	Ternus 2010	Ternus 2002	Streit 2010	Ternus 2010
Turnout %	-0.320*	-0.185	-.049	.065						
	(0.178)	(0.138)	(.162)	(.112)						
Evangelical % 2010	-0.709***	-0.573***	-.305**	-.187*	-0.497***		-0.500***		-0.0071	-0.0082
	(0.126)	(0.098)	(.133)	(.095)	(0.101)		(0.101)		(0.074)	(0.072)
Turnout % 2010 or 2002					-0.244	-0.016	-0.272*	0.073	-0.157*	-0.185**
					(0.148)	(0.162)	(0.148)	(0.118)	(0.093)	(0.091)
Evangelical % 2002						0.178*		0.039		
						(0.10)		(0.073)		
Obama %			.581***	.565***					0.808***	0.812***
			(.131)	(.093)					(0.065)	(0.064)
Education			.003	.003						
			(.003)	(.002)						
Income			-7.32	-1.97						
			(15.0)	(107.0)						
Black %			.009	.006						
			(.006)	(.004)						
Intercept	-0.256***	-0.275***	-.926***	-.886***	0.590***	0.725***	0.601***	0.693***	0.0648	0.0736
	(0.020)	(0.016)	(.238)	(.169)	(0.079)	(0.090)	(0.079)	(0.066)	(0.065)	(0.064)
N	99	99	99	99	99	99	99	99	99	99
Adjusted R^2	0.252	0.259	.536	.536	0.213	0.012	0.222	-0.014	0.695	0.707

Standard errors in parentheses. * $p < 0.10$, ** $p < 0.05$, *** $p < 0.01$.

Notes

Chapter 1

1. Further, in 2016 anti-marriage groups opposed the retention of the remaining three justices, Mark Cady, Brent Appel, and Daryl Hecht, but declined to invest significant resources required to defeat them (Boshart 2016).

2. We use the term "anti-gay" to refer to acts, positions, and policies intended to sustain a culture in which gay, lesbian, bisexual, transgender, and queer persons are treated as illegitimate members of society not deserving of equal treatment. We recognize important differences between lesbian, gay, bisexual, transgender, and queer individuals. As opposition to each sector of that group tends to be shared, however, we employ the term "gay" and "gay and lesbian" in reference to this broad group for semantic ease. We further recognize that we have little data about bisexual, transgender, and queer individuals and that documenting differences is important (e.g., Worthern 2013). Nonetheless, those who oppose the policy preferences of gays and lesbians seem likely to oppose them as well (e.g., Norton and Herek 2013). We similarly use the term "gay rights" broadly to refer to policies that extend equality and freedom for members of the gay, lesbian, bisexual, and transgender community. We recognize that in some cases this leads us to include policies that are not typically thought of as rights (e.g., hospital visitation for same-sex couples or bathroom use).

3. We employ the ProQuest search engine, as it provides the most content during our period of interest. Data are only available for the period from February 1992 on.

4. Mass opinion backlash differs from pluralist accounts that typically assume groups' interests are already organized against a policy or competing faction. With mass opinion backlash, one or more events galvanize individuals to develop opinions shared by the group.

5. Similarly, Lambda Legal initially declined to represent the plaintiffs in the *Baehr v. Lewin* case in Hawaii (Pinello 2006).

6. Democratic theory suggests that public opinion should play little or no role in determining whether fundamental rights—those that speak to questions of liberty and equality—are extended.

7. The Iowa Supreme Court ruling was issued on April 3, 2009. The October 2008 Big 10 Battleground Poll found that 28 percent of Iowans supported same-sex marriage (Redlawsk and Tolbert 2008), while the 2010 Iowa Exit Poll found that 38 percent of voters supported same-sex marriage (CNN Politics 2010).

8. We use the acronyms ELM to refer to elite-led mobilization theory for semantic ease. We vary our use when we desire to emphasize different aspects of the theory.

9. Backlash may also appear to occur when opinion against gays and lesbians shifts briefly in response to challenges to the status quo that are characterized by asymmetric information flows. This may occur when some cue-giving elites who might normally advocate one side of an issue do not take a visible public position. One example may be the sodomy cases (e.g., *Bowers v. Hardwick*).

Chapter 2

1. Longitudinal studies confirm these findings, although the negative opinion shifts are short-lived and appear likely to arise from a confluence of factors (Egan, Persily, and Wallsten 2006).

2. Another reason not to expect backlash is because among those who already hold well-formed opinions, some portion of them hold such extreme attitudes against the policy or group such that further negative movement may no longer be possible.

3. Follow-up work by Garretson (2018) suggests that at least some of these findings may be an artifact of changes in question ordering in the study in which the data were derived.

4. Elite-Led Mobilization differs from frontlash in several respects, perhaps most importantly in that a central aspect of frontlash is that losers in a policy debate come to accept and support the policy they once opposed. Consequently, the theory seems less applicable to moral issues.

5. Anschutz is owner of the Coachella and Stagecoach music festivals, as well as the sports and entertainment company AEG Worldwide, and the Los Angeles Kings. He denies supporting anti-LGBTQ organizations, though campaign finance records show that his contributions continued after he made such claims (Dukoff 2018).

6. While the modern gay rights movement began after the 1969 Stonewall riots, it became a national political movement with the March on Washington in 1979 (Fetner 2008).

7. Another important implication is implicit in the theory: in the absence of a visible challenge, we should not see the large negative reactions by the public.

Chapter 3

1. We also test whether the institution that extends gay rights matters for backlash in chapter 5.

2. We deliberately left out a "neutral" option.

3. On our original survey experiment, we embed this feeling thermometer inside a battery of other feeling thermometers, presented in a randomized order.

4. We are careful to differentiate between fear of contact with disliked out-group members, a latent trait that could be activated by exposure to out-group members, and contact theory, which identifies conditions under which intergroup contact can reduce prejudice and increase tolerance (Allport 1954). We do not expect our experimental stimuli to meet the conditions specified in contact theory, but it is plausible that they could activate intergroup anxiety.

5. We also conduct all of our statistical tests using each of the four ITT measures separately and reach identical conclusions. All of the results we present in this chapter use the combined, integrated measure of threat.

6. We also replaced the gun control baseline condition with a news excerpt about a charity road race in Oregon and found no differences when we used this apolitical story. It is therefore unlikely that any effects we observe are due to a broad reaction by conservatives to the baseline condition but instead are reactions to our experimental vignettes.

7. This group accounts for 28 percent of the survey population. Our results are robust to alternative specifications, in which we include only those identifying as independent and exclude leaners.

8. In statistical terminology, a factor analysis of the threat items yields a single dimension with an eigenvalue over 9. No other component had an eigenvalue greater than 1.

Chapter 4

1. Specifically, panel data in which the same individuals are asked their opinions on the same questions at multiple points in time allow an examination of potential opinion change unmasked by group averages.

2. Research suggests that backlash is induced by threats as well as changes to the status quo. While the California court ruling affirmed the ban and Bush expressed support for the FMA, the fact that the ruling was required reflected a threat to existing power arrangements.

3. Question wording and item numbers can be found in the appendix to this chapter.

4. One possibility for this result is that the Massachusetts Supreme Court ruling produced backlash only among Massachusetts residents. We find no evidence of backlash even when restricting our results to residents of the commonwealth.

5. As our results may be driven by changes in response rates, we compare demographics (see appendix) before and after each event and find no significant differences.

6. An earlier and smaller experiment shows that the gay groups question corresponds to our thermometer scores, at r = .88. Unfortunately, the NAES did not include instruments that allow us to assess SDO or ITT.

7. We use paired t-tests to examine opinion change. An advantage of the paired approach is that it would enable us to identify small changes in opinion as statistically significant.

8. Our measure of respondents' willingness to contribute to a political cause or campaign does not specify a political slant or purpose.

Chapter 5

1. We note that while the majority of our analyses examine the effects of court rulings, several of our tests reach the same results while examining other institutions as well.

2. Importantly, Tesler (2015) also notes that subgroup opinions may change while aggregate opinion remains unchanged.

3. President Obama signed the bill ending DADT in December 2010; however the law took effect the next year, on September 20, 2011. Importantly for our analyses, the first wave of respondents from the CCES panel study came before the 2010 midterm elections.

4. Additionally, it is possible that the samples we studied using online polls differed in some important way from the American public, either overall or among key groups we expected to be most likely to lash back. Individuals who might have more libertarian leanings than the general population of Republican voters could make up a disproportionate share of AMT samples. As the CCES is a nationally representative survey, however, we can be more confident that such is not the case for this data. Another potential limitation we encountered using our online survey experiments is that the factors that were meant to stimulate backlash (a policy change in Oregon) did not trigger a challenger to the status quo for many people. A policy change in Oregon might not matter to most people, as the state is far away and may matter little. The case of the president's shifting stance on gay marriage, however, is a nationally salient event and thus likely to elicit reactions from most Americans. Finally, one might argue that opinions are in fact shifting in response to extensions of gay rights (elicited through experimental methods or otherwise); however, changes are concealed by taking averages of opinions and intensity across groups. Such averages might conceal substantial intergroup variation. Once again, the advantage of a panel study is that the same individuals' preferences are measured repeatedly over time. Thus, by shifting the unit of analysis from group averages to individual preferences over time, the CCES panel data allow us to examine whether any intergroup variation occurs.

5. While the Republican schoolmaster and power to the people perspectives each make the same prediction in this instance, our data do not allow us to examine differences in this case.

6. In order to test whether backlash occurred, we also ran the results on other groups, such as independents and white evangelicals. The results are consistent with those presented here in that most differences are not statistically significant, but when significantly different from zero, differences are small and in the opposite direction as predicted by backlash.

7. We examine reactions across institutions to ensure they are not the source of observed changes.

8. Adam J. Berinsky and his colleagues (2012) find AMT to be more representative than in-person convenience or student samples. Further, experimental work demonstrates this procedure is both internally and externally valid. Employing weights on age, race, gender, income, education, and party identification does not alter our results. Respondents recruited through AMT were given a pretest that asked basic demographic and psychological questions, randomly assigned to one

of five possible stimuli (see appendix to this chapter), and a posttest, which asked a variety of questions about political knowledge, equality, and attitudes toward gays and lesbians. Overall, we recruited 2,402 respondents (who completed surveys) over twelve days.

9. The correlation between support for gay marriage and the importance of the issue is .15.

10. There is no evidence that strong partisans shift their preferences, once again depicting no support for opinion convergence.

Chapter 6

1. We use as a guide to help identify these events the adapted timeline from GSAFE, "A Timeline of Lesbian, Gay, Bisexual, and Transgender History in the United States," https://www.gsafewi.org/wp-content/uploads/US-LGBT-Time-line-UPDATED.pdf last accessed 1/11/2019.

2. For example, Julius and Ethel Rosenberg were convicted of espionage in 1951 and executed in 1953.

3. Although the press suggested McCarthy recused himself so as not to judge the validity of his claims, Johnson points out that McCarthy was a single middle-age man whose sex life had long been the subject of gossip and rumors (D. Johnson 2004, 3). Moreover, his chief assistant was Roy Cohn.

4. This assimilationist strategy would dramatically change in the wake of the Stonewall Inn riots (see later in this chapter).

5. Personal interview on February 22, 2019, with Michael I. Abrams, chair of the Miami-Dade Democratic Party at the time.

6. Ironically, *Bowers* was prosecuted by Michael Bowers, the attorney general for the State of Georgia, as he was planning a run for governor and hoped to establish his anti-gay bona fides with the Republican Party and the Christian Right before he switched parties. His campaign was derailed when his long-term girlfriend came forward and publicized his fondness for sodomy with proof of their relationship, which ended both his marriage and his campaign (Sack 1997).

7. See, for example, Lemieux 2013. "Rosenberg's argument that using litigation to advance same-sex marriage was foolish and counterproductive has been disproved as thoroughly as such a counterfactual can be."

Chapter 7

1. The Hawkeye Poll, April 2009 (see Kreitzer et al. 2014).

2. Owing to Iowa's racial homogeneity, for sematic ease we use the terms "white evangelical" and "evangelical" interchangeably. We recognize important differences between these groups.

3. The frequency statistics are derived from the data Buller provided the authors.

4. These results differ slightly if averages of each sample are compared such that 15.7 percent of evangelicals support gay marriage before but only 12.9 percent support it after the ruling. These differences are small and not statistically significant and, most importantly, do not allow for examination of how individual attitudes change as do the results for those who participated in both waves.

5. Unfortunately, these questions were asked only in the post-ruling wave. Differences in the importance of instrument preclude examining changes in importance before and after the ruling.

6. Nation for Marriage, "NOM: Iowans for Freedom against Radical Judges: David A. Baker, Michael J. Streit, Marsha Ternus," October 19, 2010, YouTube, https://www.youtube.com/watch?v=MIFnBBLX_OE last accessed 8/28/2020.

7. All of the television ads we found emphasized the importance of turning the ballot over, but we cannot be certain ads were not run that did not mention this.

8. See, for instance, Mullen 2010.

9. Text of this ad can be found in Belin 2010b.

10. Roll-off totals are comparable across candidates.

11. This provides a test favorable to MOB, since decreased roll-off could result from people mobilizing to *support* the judges.

12. Analyses examining results for David Baker in 2010 are virtually identical, as the justices' vote share correlates at over .99. Comparison to 2002 is not possible, as Baker was not yet appointed.

13. As we examine aggregate county-level data to draw individual level inferences, our results are somewhat more uncertain and are especially susceptible to omitted variable bias. Roll-off robustness tests are presented in the appendix to this chapter. Similar results are obtained if roll-off for each year is substituted as the dependent variable. The pooled results are robust to the inclusion of 2008 Obama vote, which is not included because it is not clear why Obama support should be associated with abstention in the judicial retention races. Models in the appendix also include controls for race, median family income, and education (percent earning high school diploma or equivalent) measured using data from the 2010 census.

14. Robustness tests for voting presented in the appendix to this chapter show that similar results are obtained if retention votes for 2010 and 2002 are examined separately and if Obama support is omitted. Similar results obtain when Democratic Party registration is used in place of Obama support. These variables correlate at about .74. We also account for race, income, and education. Results are substantively similar across models.

15. We considered examining 2016, but donors and spending could be identified in only one state.

16. Coding of issues and spending data and competition are presented in the appendix to this chapter. Owing to a quirk in the disclosure laws, out-of-state donors and contributions for the Kansas Supreme Court are not kept.

17. In such cases we first combed through individual disclosure files on state elections websites and, if data were still missing, imputed contribution data based on estimates of amounts spent to produce and air ads as reported by the Brennan Center. To ensure we did not overlook possible contributions for races for which no disclosure forms existed, we cross-checked these ad spending figures and augmented them with data from opensecrets.gov and the respective state election commission websites.

18. The 2010 challenge to Justice Dana Fabe in Alaska arguably meets the backlash criteria. When we re-estimate our analyses counting this race as a case of backlash, our results are unchanged.

19. Specifically, we divide the gross dollar amount of contributions by the num-

ber of candidates the committee opposed in a state. Similarly, we assume that each group divided their money across candidates. For states in which joint campaigns occur, this process minimizes the average amount spent per race and maximizes the number of contributions, both of which bias the results in favor of MOB (since it predicts a large number of smaller contributions). Alternative methods of analysis that either assume the total spent by each group was used to oppose each judge or that analyze each opposition campaign as the unit of analysis produce similar results.

References

Abraham, Henry J. 1977. *Freedom and the Court.* 3rd ed. New York: Oxford University Press.

Abrajano, Marisa. 2010. "Are Blacks and Latinos Responsible for the Passage of Proposition 8? Analyzing Voter Attitudes on California's Proposal to Ban Same-Sex Marriage in 2008." *Political Research Quarterly* 63 (4): 922–32.

Abrajano, Marisa, and Zoltan Hajnal. 2017. *White Backlash.* Princeton, NJ: Princeton University Press.

Adam, Barry D. 2003. "The Defense of Marriage Act and American Exceptionalism: The 'Gay Marriage' Panic in the United States." *Journal of the History of Sexuality* 12 (2): 259–76.

Adam, Erin. 2017. "Intersectional Coalitions: The Paradoxes of Rights-Based Movement Building in LGBTQ and Immigrant Communities." *Law & Society Review* 51 (1): 132–67.

Adamany, David. 1973. "Legitimacy, Realigning Elections, and the Supreme Court." *Wisconsin Law Review* 3: 790–846.

Allport, Gordon W. 1954. *The Nature of Prejudice.* Cambridge, MA: Addison-Wesley.

Andreas, Peter. 2014. *Smuggler Nation: How Illicit Trade Made America.* Oxford: Oxford University Press.

ANES 2008. https://electionstudies.org/data-center/2008-time-series-study/

Ansolabehere, Stephen, and Brian Schaffner. 2015. *Cooperative Congressional Election Study: 2010–2014 Panel Study* (version [Computer File] Release 1: June 10, 2015). Amherst: University of Massachusetts, Amherst [producer].

Armstrong, Elizabeth A., and Suzanna M. Crage. 2006. "Movements and Memories: The Making of the Stonewall Myth." *American Sociological Review* 17 (October): 724–51.

Arthur Lupia, Jon A. Krosnick, Pat Luevano, Matthew DeBell, and Darrell Donakowski. 2009. *User's Guide to the ANES 2008 Time Series Study*. Ann Arbor, MI and Palo Alto, CA: University of Michigan and Stanford University.

Asmeleash, Leah. 2020. "How Black Lives Matter Went from a Hashtag to a Global Rallying Cry." CNN. July 26, 2020. https://www.cnn.com/2020/07/26/us/black -lives-matter-explainer-trnd/index.html

Associated Press. 2006. "Minuteman Project Gains Mainstream Appeal." MSNBC. com. April 26, 2006. http://www.nbcnews.com/id/12500049/ns/us_news-securi ty/t/minuteman-project-gains-mainstream-appeal/

Associated Press. 2010. "Iowa Justice Supporters Launch Radio Ads." October 15, 2010. *The Gazette*. Accessed April 2, 2019. https://www.thegazette.com/2010 /10/15/iowa-justice-supporters-launch-radio-ads

The Association of Religion Data Archives. 2000. "Religious Congregations and Membership Study, 2000 (Counties File) | Data Archive |." 2000. http://www .thearda.com/Archive/Files/Descriptions/RCMSCY.asp

Association of Statisticians of American Religious Bodies (ASARB). 2002. http:// www.thearda

Baehr v. Lewin 74 Haw. 530, 852 P.2d 44 (Haw. 1993)

Baker v Nelson 191 N.W.2d 185 (1971)

Ball, Carlos A. 2006. "The Backlash Thesis and Same-Sex Marriage: Learning from *Brown v. Board of Education* and Its Aftermath." *William & Mary Bill of Rights Journal* 14. http://scholarship.law.wm.edu/wmborj/vol14/iss4/8

Barclay, Scott, and Andrew Flores. 2014. "Backlash, Consensus, or Naturalization: The Impact of Policy Shift on Subsequent Public Opinion Levels." *Law & Society Review* 69(1): 43–56.

Baunach, Dawn Michelle. 2012. "Changing Same-Sex Marriage Attitudes in America from 1988 through 2010." *Public Opinion Quarterly* 76: 364–78. https://www .uow.edu.au/~sharonb/antienvironmentalism.html

Belin, Laura. 2010a. "Case against Iowa Supreme Court Justices Hits TV Screens." *Bleeding Heartland* (blog). September 14, 2010. https://www.bleedingheartland .com/2010/09/14/case-against-iowa-supreme-court-justices-hits-tv-screens/

Belin, Laura. 2010b. "Moderate Republicans Co-Chair New Group for Retaining Supreme Court Justices (Updated)." *Bleeding Heartland* (blog). October 14, 2010. https://www.bleedingheartland.com/2010/10/14/moderate-republicans -co-chair-new-group-for-retaining-supreme-court-justices-updated/

Belin, Laura. 2010c. "Coalition against Iowa Supreme Court Justices Launches Second TV Ad." *Bleeding Heartland* (blog). October 20, 2010. https://www.bl eedingheartland.com/2010/10/20/coalition-against-iowa-supreme-court-justic es-launches-second-tv-ad/

Benford, Robert D., and David A. Snow, and. 2000. "Framing Processes and Social Movements: An Overview and Assessment." *Annual Review of Sociology* 26 (2000): 611–39.

Bennett, W. Lance. 1990. "Toward a Theory of Press-State Relations in the United States." *Journal of Communication* 40 (2): 103–25.

Berinsky, Adam J. 2015. "Rumors and Health Care Reform: Experiments in Political Misinformation." *British Journal of Political Science* 47 (2): 241–62. https://doi .org/10.1017/S0007123415000186

Berinsky, Adam J., Gregory A. Huber, and Gabriel S. Lenz. 2012. "Evaluating Online Labor Markets for Experimental Research: Amazon.com's Mechanical Turk." *Political Analysis* 20: 351–68.

Berlet, Chip. 1998. "Who Is Mediating the Storm? Right-Wing Alternative Information Networks." In *Media, Culture, and the Religious Right*, edited by Linda Kintz and Julia Lesage, 249–73. Minneapolis: University of Minnesota Press.

Bernstein, Mary, and Verta Taylor, eds. 2013. *The Marrying Kind? Debating Same-Sex Marriage within the Lesbian and Gay Movement*. Minneapolis: University of Minnesota Press.

Biggers, Daniel R. 2014. *Morality at the Ballot: Direct Democracy and Political Engagement in the United States*. New York: Cambridge University Press.

Bishin, Benjamin G. 2009. *Tyranny of the Minority: The Subconstituency Politics Theory of Representation*. Philadelphia: Temple University Press.

Bishin, Benjamin G., Justin Freebourn, and Paul Teten. 2020. "The Power of Equality? Polarization and Collective Mis-Representation on Gay Rights in Congress, 1989–2019." *Political Research Quarterly*. September 2, 2020. https:// doi.org/10.1177%2F1065912920953498

Bishin, Benjamin G., Thomas J. Hayes, Matthew B. Incantalupo, and Charles Anthony Smith. 2016. "Opinion Backlash and Public Attitudes: Are Institutional Advances in Gay Rights Counterproductive?" *American Journal of Political Science* 60: 625–48.

Bishin, Benjamin G., Thomas J. Hayes, Matthew B. Incantalupo, and Charles Anthony Smith. 2020. "Elite Mobilization: A Theory Explaining Opposition to Gay Rights." *Law & Society Review* 54 (1): 233–64. https://doi.org/10.1111 /lasr.12457

Bishin, Benjamin G., Karen M. Kaufmann, and Daniel Stevens. 2012. "Turf Wars: Local Context and Latino Political Development." *Urban Affairs Review* 48 (1): 111–37. https://doi.org/10.1177/1078087411418292

Bishin, Benjamin G., and Casey A. Klofstad. 2012. "The Political Incorporation of Cuban Americans: Why Won't Little Havana Turn Blue?" *Political Research Quarterly* 65 (3): 588–601.

Bishin, Benjamin G., and Charles Anthony Smith. 2013. "When Do Legislators Defy Popular Sovereignty? Testing Theories of Minority Representation Using DOMA." *Political Research Quarterly* 66 (4): 794–803.

Blair, Karen L. 2016. "A 'Basket of Deplorables'? A New Study Finds That Trump Supporters Are More Likely to Be Islamophobic, Racist, Transphobic, and Homophobic." *LSE US Centre* (blog). October 10, 2016. https://blogs.lse.ac .uk/usappblog/2016/10/10/a-basket-of-deplorables-a-new-study-finds-that-tr ump-supporters-are-more-likely-to-be-islamophobic-racist-transphobic-and -homophobic/

Blake, Judith. 1977. "The Supreme Court's Abortion Decisions and Public Opinion in the United States." *Population and Development Review* 3 (1/2): 45–62.

Boehmke, Frederick J. 2013. "Hawkeye Poll Fall 2009." *Harvard Dataverse* V5: 5 1 0. https://doi.org/10.7910/DVN/OCM08E

Boshart, Rod. 2016. "Some Looking to Oust Iowa Supreme Court Justices." *Waterloo Cedar Falls Courier.* October 17, 2016. https://wcfcourier.com/news/local/go vt-and-politics/some-looking-to-oust-iowa-supreme-court-justices/article_c2e 98004-1c2d-5b24-b91f-01d9b660ec9d.html

Bostock v Clayton County 590 U.S. 140 S. Ct. 1731 (2020)

Bowers v. Hardwick, 478 U.S. 186 (1986)

Bowers, Becky. 2012. *Tampa Bay Tribune.* May 11, 2012. https://www.tampabay.com /archive/2012/05/11/president-barack-obama-s-shifting-stance-on-gay-marri age/

Boy Scouts of America v Dale 530 U.S. 640 (2000)

Brandzel, Amy L. 2005. "Queering Citizenship? Same Sex Marriage and the State." *GLQ: A Journal of Gay and Lesbian Studies* 11 (2): 171–204.

Bratton, Kathleen A. 2002. "The Effect of Legislative Diversity on Agenda Setting: Evidence from Six State Legislatures." *American Politics Research* 30 (2): 115–42.

Brennan Center for Justice. 2011. "The New Politics of Judicial Elections 2009–10." Brennan Center for Justice. October 26, 2011. https://www.brennancenter .org/our-work/research-reports/new-politics-judicial-elections-2009-10

Brier, Jennifer. 2009. *Infectious Ideas: U.S. Political Responses to the AIDS Crisis.* Chapel Hill: University of North Carolina Press.

Brown v Board of Education 347 U.S. 483 (1954)

Bull, Chris, and John Gallagher. 1996. *Perfect Enemies: The Religious Right, the Gay Movement, and the Politics of the 1990s.* New York: Crown Publishers.

Buller, Tyler J. 2011. "Framing the Debate: Understanding Iowa's 2010 Judicial Retention Election through a Content Analysis of Letters to the Editor." SSRN. March 27, 2011. https://ssrn.com/abstract=1793313

Bullough, Vern. 2002. *Before Stonewall: Activists for Gay and Lesbian Rights in Historical Context.* New York: Harrington Park Press.

Bumiller, Elisabeth. 2011. "Obama Ends 'Don't Ask, Don't Tell' Policy." *New York Times.* July 22, 2011. https://www.nytimes.com/2011/07/23/us/23military.html

Burack, Cynthia. 2008. *Sin, Sex, and Democracy: Antigay Politics and the Christian Right.* New York: State University of New York Press.

Burge, Kathleen. 2003. "SJC: Gay Marriage Legal in Mass." *Boston.com.* November 18, 2003. http://archive.boston.com/news/local/massachusetts/articles/2003 /11/18/sjc_gay_marriage_legal_in_mass/

Burke, William Kevin. 1993. "The Wise Use Movement: Right-Wing Anti-Environmentalism." Political Research Associates. June 5, 1993. https://www .politicalresearch.org/1993/06/05/the-wise-use-movement-right-wing-anti-en vironmentalism/

Burris, Christopher T., and Lynne M. Jackson. 2010. "Social Identity and the True Believer: Responses to Threatened Self-Stereotypes among the Intrinsically

Religious." *British Journal of Social Psychology* 39 (2): 257–78. https://doi.org/10.1348/014466600164462

Burstein, Paul. 2014. *American Public Opinion, Advocacy, and Policy in Congress: What the Public Wants and What It Gets*. New York: Cambridge University Press.

Burwell v. Hobby Lobby Stores, 573 US 682 (2014)

Caldeira, Gregory A. 1986. "Neither the Purse nor the Sword: Dynamics of Public Confidence in the Supreme Court." *American Political Science Review* 80 (4): 1209–26.

Campbell, Angus, Philip E. Converse, Warren E. Miller, and Donald E. Stokes. 1960. *The American Voter*. Chicago: University of Chicago Press.

Campbell, David E., and J. Quin Monson. 2008. "The Religion Card: Gay Marriage and the 2004 Presidential Election." *Public Opinion* 72 (3): 399–419.

Canes-Wrone, Brandice. 2010. *Who Leads Whom?: Presidents, Policy, and the Public*. Chicago: University of Chicago Press.

Canon, Bradley C., and Charles A. Johnson. 1984. *Judicial Policies: Implementation and Impact*. Washington, DC: CQ Press.

Capehart, Jonathan. 2016. "Here They Are, the 'Enemies of Equality' for LGBT Americans." *Post Partisan Opinion*. July 7, 2016. https://www.washingtonpost.com/blogs/postpartisan/wp/2016/07/07/here-they-are-the-enemies-of-equality-for-lgbt-americans/?utm_term=.f58f3a112914

Cardona, Felesa. 2010. "Four Supreme Court Justices Face a Tough Vote in Elections." *Denver Post*. February 14, 2010. http://www.denverpost.com/2010/02/14/four-supreme-court-justices-face-a-tough-vote-in-elections/

Carmines, Edward G., and James A. Stimson. 1981. "Issue Evolution, Population Replacement, and Normal Partisan Change." *American Political Science Review* 75 (1): 107–18.

Carmines, Edward G., and James A. Stimson. 1989. *Issue Evolution: Race and the Transformation of American Politics*. Princeton, NJ: Princeton University Press.

Carter, David. 2004. *Stonewall: The Riots That Sparked the Gay Revolution*. New York: St. Martin's Press.

Casey, Logan. 2016. "The Politics of Disgust: Public Opinion toward LGBTQ People and Policies." PhD diss. University of Michigan.

Castle, Jeremiah. 2019. "New Fronts in the Culture Wars? Religion, Partisanship, and Polarization on Religious Liberty and Transgender Rights in the United States." *American Politics Research* 47 (3): 650–79. https://doi.org/10.1177/1532673X18818169

Caute, David. 1978. *The Great Fear: The Anti-Communist Purge under Truman and Eisenhower*. New York: Simon and Schuster.

Chambre, Susan M. 2006. *Fighting for Our Lives: New York's AIDS Community and the Politics of Disease*. New Brunswick, NJ: Rutgers University Press.

Claassen, Ryan L., and Andrew Povtak. 2010. "The Christian Right Thesis: Explaining Longitudinal Change in Participation among Evangelical Christians." *Journal of Politics* 72 (1): 2–15.

Clendinen, Dudley, and Adam Nagourney. 1999. *Out for Good: The Struggle to Build a Gay Rights Movement in America*. New York: Simon and Schuster.

Clopton, Andrew J., and C. Scott Peters. 2013. "Justices Denied: A County-Level Analysis of the 2010 Iowa Supreme Court Retention Election." *Justice System Journal* 34 (3): 321–44.

CNN. 2004. "Bush Calls for Ban on Same-Sex Marriages." February 25, 2004. https://www.cnn.com/2004/ALLPOLITICS/02/24/elec04.prez.bush.marri age/

CNN Politics. 2010. "Exit Poll of Iowa Voters." http://www.cnn.com/ELECTION /2010/results/polls/

Cohen, Jeffrey E. 1997. *Presidential Responsiveness and Public Policymaking*. Ann Arbor: University of Michigan Press.

Coleman, Korva. 2010. "Iowa Judges Ousted." *NPR*. November 3, 2010. http://www.npr.org/sections/itsallpolitics/2010/11/03/131032419/iowa-judges-ou sted

Collingwood, Loren, Nazita Lajevardi, and Kassra A. R. Oskooii. 2018. "A Change of Heart? Why Individual-Level Public Opinion Shifted against Trump's 'Muslim Ban.'" *Political Behavior* 40 (4): 1035–72. https://doi.org/10.1007/s11109 -017-9439-z

Collomb, Jean-Daniel. 2014. "'The Ideology of Climate Change Denial in the United States." *European Journal of American Studies* 9 (1). Spring 2014. https://doi.org/10.4000/ejas.10305

Converse, Philip E. 1964. "The Nature of Belief Systems in Mass Publics." *Critical Review* 18: 1–74. https://doi.org/10.1080/08913810608443650

Cortner, Richard C. 2001. *Civil Rights and Public Accommodation: The Heart of Atlanta Motel and McClurg Cases*. Lawrence: University Press of Kansas.

Cottrell, Catherine A., and Steven L. Neuberg. 2005. "Different Emotional Reactions to Different Groups: A Sociofunctional Threat-Based Approach to 'Prejudice.'" *Journal of Personality and Social Psychology* 88 (5): 770–89.

Dahl, Robert A. 1956. *A Preface to Democratic Theory*. Chicago: University of Chicago Press.

Dalbey, Beth. 2012. "Election 2012: Iowans Reverse Trend, Retain Supreme Court Justice Who Ruled on Same-Sex Marriage." *Patch.com*. November 6, 2012. http://patch.com/iowa/westdesmoines/election-2012-judicial-retention-vote

Dann, Carrie. 2019. "Most Americans Are A-OK with a Gay Presidential Candidate. That's a Big Shift in 15 Years." *NBC News* 4. January 2019. https://www.nb cnews.com/card/most-americans-are-ok-gay-presidential-candidate-s-big-shi ft-n989541

Davey, Monica. 2009. "Iowa Court Voids Gay Marriage Ban." *New York Times*. April 3, 2009. http://www.nytimes.com/2009/04/04/us/04iowa.html

D'Emilio, John. 1983. *Sexual Politics, Sexual Communities: The Making of a Homosexual Minority in the United States*. Chicago: University of Chicago Press.

D'Emilio, John. 1992. "Gay Politics, Gay Community: San Francisco's Experience." In *Making Trouble: Essays on Gay History, Politics, and the University*, edited by John D'Emilio. New York: Routledge. 74–95.

D'Emilio, John. 2006. "The Marriage Fight Is Setting Us Back." *Gay & Lesbian Review Worldwide*. November 1, 2006. 10–11.

DeVogue, Ariane. 2013. "*Roe v. Wade*: Opinion Backlash Persists 40 Years Later." ABC News. January 21, 2013. https://abcnews.go.com/Politics/OTUS/roe-wade-abortion-backlash-persists-40-years/story?id=18271433

Diamond, Dan. 2018. "Trump Administration Dismantles LGBT-Friendly Policies." *Politico*. February 19, 2018. https://www.politico.com/story/2018/02/19/trump-lgbt-rights-discrimination-353774

Dorf, Michael C., and Sidney Tarrow. 2014. "Strange Bedfellows: How an Anticipatory Countermovement Brought Same-Sex Marriage into the Public Arena." *Law & Social Inquiry* 39 (2): 449–73. https://doi.org/10.1111/lsi.12069

Dovere, Edward-Isaac. 2014. "Book: W.H. Scrambled after Biden Gay Marriage Comments." April 16, 2014. *Politico*. Accessed February 14, 2019. https://www.politico.com/story/2014/04/joe-biden-gay-marriage-white-house-response-105744

Druckman, James N., and Lawrence R. Jacobs. 2006. "Lumpers and Splitters: The Public Opinion Information That Politicians Collect and Use." *Public Opinion Quarterly* 70 (4): 453–76.

Druckman, James N., and Lawrence R. Jacobs. 2011. "'Segmented Representation: The Reagan White House and Disproportionate Responsiveness.'" In *Who Gets Represented?*, edited by Peter Enns and Christopher Wlezien, 166–88. New York: Russell Sage Foundation.

Dunlap, Mary C. 1989. "AIDS and Discrimination in the United States: Reflections on the Nature of Prejudice in a Virus." *Villanova Law Review* 34 (5): 909–932.

Dunlap, Richard E., and Aaron M. McCright. 2011. "Organized Climate Change Denial." In *The Oxford Handbook of Climate Change*, edited by John S. Dryzek, Richard B. Norguard, and David Schlosberg. Oxford: Oxford University Press. 144–160.

Dunne, Robert. 2002. *Antebellum Irish Immigration and Emerging Ideologies of "America."* New York: Edwin Mellen Press.

Duberman, Martin B. 1993. *Stonewall*. New York: Plume.

Eckholm, Erik. 2011. "An Iowa Stop in a Broad Effort to Revitalize the Religious Right." *New York Times*. April 2, 2011. https://www.nytimes.com/2011/04/03/us/politics/

Eckholm, Erik. 2013. "Hawaii Nears Approval of Gay Marriage." *New York Times*. November 9, 2013. https://www.nytimes.com/2013/11/10/us/hawaii-nears-approval-of-gay-marriage.html

Edwards, George C. 2003. *On Deaf Ears: The Limits of the Bully Pulpit*. New Haven: Yale University Press.

Egan, Patrick J., Nathaniel Persily, and Kevin Wallsten. 2008. "Gay Rights." In *Public Opinion and Constitutional Controversies*, edited by Jack Citrin, Nathaniel Persily, and Patrick J. Egan. New York: Oxford University Press. 234–266.

Egan, Patrick J., and Nathaniel Persily. 2009. "Court Decisions and Trends in Support for Same-Sex Marriage." *Polling Report.* August 17, 2009. http://www.polli ngreport.com/penp0908.htm

Egan, Patrick J, and Kenneth Sherrill. 2009. "California's Proposition 8: What Happened, and What Does the Future Hold?" January 5, 2009. Report commissioned for the Evelyn and Walter Hess Jr. Fund, San Francisco. National Gay and Lesbian Task Force Policy Institute.

"Eisenhower Cleans House." 1958. *Chicago Tribune.* March 10, 1958. http://arch ives.chicagotribune.com/1958/03/10/page/18/article/mr-eisenhower-cleans -house

Eldersveld, Samuel J. 1989. *Political Elites in Modern Societies: Empirical Research and Democratic Theory.* Ann Arbor: University of Michigan Press.

Eshbaugh-Soha, Matthew. 2006. *The President's Speeches: "Beyond Going Public."* Boulder, CO: Lynne Rienner Publishers.

Eskridge, William N., Jr. 2005. "Body Politics: *Lawrence v. Texas* and the Constitution of Disgust and Contagion." *Florida Law Review* 57: 1011.

Eskridge, William N., Jr. 2013. "Backlash Politics: How Constitutional Litigation Has Advanced Marriage Equality in the United States." *Boston University Law Review* 93 (2): 275–323.

Ewers, Justin. 2008. "California Same-Sex Marriage Initiative Campaigns Shatter Spending Records." *US News and World Report.* October 30, 2008.

Faderman, Lillian. 2015. *The Gay Revolution: The Story of the Struggle.* New York: Simon and Schuster.

Fadulu, Lola, and Annie Flanagan. 2019. "Trump's Rollback of Transgender Rights Extends Through Entire Government." *The New York Times,* December 6, 2019, sec. U.S.

Faludi, Susan. 1991. *Backlash: The Undeclared War against Women.* New York: Chatto and Windus.

Farrell, Megan E. 1995. "*Baehr v. Lewin:* Questionable Reasoning; Sound Judgment." *Journal of Contemporary Health Law and Policy* 11 (2): 589–618.

Fejes, Fred. 2008. *Gay Rights and Moral Panic: The Origin of America's Debate on Homosexuality.* New York: Palgrave Macmillan.

Festinger, Leon. 1954. "A Theory of Social Comparison Processes." *Human Relations* 7 (2): 117–40.

Fetner, Tina. 2001. "Working Anita Bryant: The Impact of Christian Anti-Gay Activism on Lesbian and Gay Movement Claims." *Social Problems* 48 (3): 411–28.

Fetner, Tina. 2008. *How the Religious Right Shaped Lesbian and Gay Activism.* Minneapolis: University of Minnesota Press.

Fitzgerald, Frances. 2017. *The Evangelicals: The Struggle to Shape America.* New York: Simon and Schuster.

Flagg, Barbara J. 1997. "Animus and Moral Disapproval: A Comment on *Romer v. Evans.*" *Minnesota Law Review* 82 (3): 833–54.

Fleischmann, Arnold, and Laura Moyer. 2009. "Competing Social Movements and Local Political Culture: Voting on Ballot Propositions to Ban Same-Sex Marriage in the U.S. States." *Social Science Quarterly* 90 (1): 134–49.

Flores, Andrew. 2015. "Examining Variation in Surveying Attitudes on Same-Sex Marriage: A Meta-Analysis." *Public Opinion Quarterly* 79 (2): 580–93.

Flores, Andrew R. 2014. "National Trends in Public Opinion on LGBT Rights in the United States." *The Williams Institute.* https://williamsinstitute.law.ucla.edu/wp-content/uploads/POP-natl-trends-nov-2014.pdf

Flores, René D. 2017. "Do Anti-Immigrant Laws Shape Public Sentiment? A Study of Arizona's SB 1070 Using Twitter Data." *American Journal of Sociology* 123 (2): 333–84.

Fogelson, Robert M. 1968. "From Resentment to Confrontation: The Police, The Negroes, and the Outbreak of the Nineteen-Sixties Riots." *Political Science Quarterly* 83 (2): 217–47.

Fontana, David, and Donald Braman. 2012. "Judicial Backlash or Just Backlash? Evidence from a National Experiment." *Columbia University Law Review* 112 (4): 731–99.

Frank, Larry. 2009. *Unfriendly Fire, How the Gay Ban Undermines the Military and Weakens America.* New York: St. Martin's Press.

Frankl, Razelle. 1998. "Transformation of Televangelism: Repackaging Christian Family Values." In *Media, Culture, and the Religious Right*, edited by Linda Kintz and Julia Lesage, 163–89. Minneapolis: University of Minnesota Press.

Franklin, Charles H., and Liane C. Kosaki. 1989. "Republican Schoolmaster: The U.S. Supreme Court, Public Opinion, and Abortion." *American Political Science Review* 83 (3): 751–71.

Freeland, Richard. 1971. *The Truman Doctrine and the Origins of McCarthyism: Foreign Policy, Domestic Politics, and Internal Security 1946–1948.* New York: Knopf.

Frymer, Paul. 1999. *Uneasy Alliances: Race and Party Competition in America.* Princeton, NJ: Princeton University Press.

Fuchs, Erin. 2013. "Gay Rights Groups Thought Going to the Supreme Court on Prop 8 Would Be a Huge Mistake." *Business Insider.* http://www.businessinsider.com/aclu-and-lambda-opposed-proposition-8-case-2013-6

Gadarian, Shana Kushner, and Eric van der Vort. 2018. *Political Behavior* 40 (2): 521–43.

Gailmard, Sean, and Jeffery Jenkins. 2007. "Negative Agenda Control in the Senate and House: Fingerprints of Majority Party Power." *Journal of Politics* 69 (3): 689–700. https://onlinelibrary.wiley.com/doi/abs/10.1111/j.1468-2508.2007.00568.x

Gaines, Brian J., and Wendy K. Tam Cho. 2004. "On California's 1920 Alien Land Law: The Psychology and Economics of Racial Discrimination on California's 1920 Alien Land Law: The Psychology and Economics of Racial Discrimination." *State Politics & Policy Quarterly* 4 (3): 271–93. https://doi.org/10.1177/153244000400400302

Gallup. 2020a. "Gays and Lesbians: Historical Trends." Accessed at https://news.ga llup.com/poll/1651/gay-lesbian-rights.aspx

Gallup. 2020b. "In-Depth Topics A-Z: Marriage." Gallup.com.2020. https://news .gallup.com/poll/117328/Marriage.aspx

Galvan v Press 347 U.S. 522 (1954)

Gans, Herbert J. 1979. *Deciding What's News: A Study of CBS Evening News, NBC Nightly News, Newsweek, and Time.* New York: Random House.

Garretson, Jeremiah J. 2014a. "Changing with the Times: The Spillover Effects of Same-Sex Marriage Ballot Measures on Presidential Elections." *Political Research Quarterly* 67 (2): 280–92.

Garretson, Jeremiah J. 2014b. "Exposure to the Lives of Lesbians and Gays and the Origin of Young People's Greater Support for Gay Rights." *International Journal of Public Opinion Research* 27 (2): 277–88.

Garretson, Jeremiah J. 2018. *The Path to Gay Rights: How Activism and Coming Out Changed Public Opinion.* New York: New York University Press.

Geer, John Gray. 1996. *From Tea Leaves to Opinion Polls: A Theory of Democratic Leadership.* Power, Conflict, and Democracy. New York: Columbia University Press.

Gerstman, Evan. 2017. *Same-Sex Marriage and the Constitution.* 3rd ed. Cambridge: Cambridge University Press.

Gilens, Martin, and Benjamin I. Page. 2014. "Testing Theories of American Politics: Elites, Interest Groups, and Average Citizens." *Perspectives on Politics* 12 (3): 564–81.

Girard, Françoise. 2017. "Implications of the Trump Administration for Sexual and Reproductive Rights Globally." *Reproductive Health Matters* 25 (49): 6–13.

Goldberg-Hiller, Jonathan. 2002. *The Limits to Union: Same-Sex Marriage and the Politics of Civil Rights.* Ann Arbor: University of Michigan Press.

Golway, Terry. 2014. *Machine Made: Tammany Hall and the Creation of Modern American Politics.* New York: W. W. Norton.

Goodridge v. Department of Public Health 798 N.E.2d 941 (Mass. 2003)

Goss, Kristin A. 2006. *Disarmed: The Missing Movement for Gun Control in America.* Princeton, NJ: Princeton University Press.

Gossett, Charles W. 2018. "Trumped up Data." *Equality, Diversity, and Inclusion: An International Journal* 37 (1): 88–95. https://doi.org/10.1108/EDI-09-2017-0179

Gould, Deborah B. 2009. *Moving Politics Emotion and ACT UP's Fight against AIDS.* Chicago: University of Chicago Press.

Gramlich, John. 2010. "Judges' Battles Signal a New Era for Retention Elections." *Washington Post.* December 5, 2010. http://www.washingtonpost.com/wp-dyn /content/article/2010/12/04/AR2010120400180.html

Grauerholz, Stephanie L. 1995. "Colorado's Amendment 2 Defeated: The Emergence of a Fundamental Right to Participate in the Political Process." *DePaul Law Review* 44 (3): 841.

Green, John C., and James L. Guth. 1988. "The Christian Right in the Republican Party: The Case of Pat Robertson's Supporters." *Journal of Politics* 50 (1): 150–65.

Greenhouse, Linda, and Reva B. Siegel. 2011. "Before (and After) *Roe v. Wade*: New Questions about Backlash." *Yale Law Journal* 120 (8): 2028–87.

Griffith, Robert. 1987. *The Politics of Fear: Joseph R. McCarthy and the Senate*. Amherst: University of Massachusetts Press.

"Group Forms to Support Iowa Supreme Court Justices." 2010. *Waterloo Cedar Falls Courier*. October 14, 2010. Accessed April 2, 2019. https://wcfcourier.com /news/local/govt-and-politics/group-forms-to-support-iowa-supreme-court -justices/article_ef54bedc-d7d5-11df-8d6b-001cc4c03286.html

Grzymała-Busse, Anna. 2015. *Nations under God: How Churches Use Moral Authority to Influence Policy*. Princeton: Princeton University Press.

Haider-Markel, Donald P. 2001. "Policy Diffusion as a Geographical Expansion of the Scope of Political Conflict: Same-Sex Marriage Bans in the 1990s." *State Politics & Policy Quarterly* 1 (1): 5–26.

Haider-Markel, Donald P. 2007. "Representation and Backlash: The Positive and Negative Influence of Descriptive Representation." *Legislative Studies Quarterly* 32 (1): 107–33.

Haider-Markel, Donald P. 2010. *Out and Running: Gay and Lesbian Candidates, Elections, and Policy Representation*. Washington, DC: Georgetown University Press.

Haider-Markel, Donald P., Mark R. Joslyn, and Chad J. Kniss. 2000. "Minority Group Interests and Political Representation: Gay Elected Officials in the Policy Process." *Journal of Politics* 62 (2): 568–77.

Haider-Markel, Donald P., and and Kenneth J. Meier. 1996. "The Politics of Gay and Lesbian Rights: Expanding the Scope of Conflict." *Journal of Politics* 58 (2): 332–49.

Haider-Markel, Donald P., and and Kenneth J. Meier. 2003. "Legislative Victory, Electoral Uncertainty: Explaining Outcomes in the Battles over Lesbian and Gay Civil Rights." *Review of Policy Research* 20 (4): 671–90.

Hall, Andrew B. 2015. "What Happens When Extremists Win Primaries?" *American Political Science Review* 109 (1): 18–42. https://doi.org/10.1017/S000305541 4000641

Hanley, John, Michael Salamone, and Matthew Wright. 2012. "Reviving the Schoolmaster: Reevaluating Public Opinion in the Wake of *Roe v. Wade*." *Political Research Quarterly* 65 (2): 408–421.

Harley, R. M. 1980. "The Evangelical Vote and the Presidency." *Christian Science Monitor*. June 25, 1980. https://www.csmonitor.com/1980/0625/062555.html

Harris, Allison P. 2019. "Voter Response to Salient Judicial Decisions in Retention Elections." *Law and Social Inquiry* 44 (1): 170–91.

Harris, Chris. 2008. "Barack Obama Answers Your Questions about Gay Marriage, Paying for College, More." *MTV News*. http://www.mtv.com/news/1598407/ba rack-obama-answers-your-questions-about-gay-marriage-paying-for-college -more/

Harrison, Brian F., and Melissa R. Michelson. 2017. *Listen, We Need to Talk: How to Change Attitudes about LGBT Rights*. Oxford: Oxford University Press.

Heritage Foundation. 2020. "Judicial Appointment Tracker." Heritage Judicial Tracker. https://www.heritage.org/judicialtracker

Hetherington, Marc J., and Jonathan D. Weiler. 2009. *Authoritarianism and Polarization in American Politics.* New York: Cambridge University Press.

Hillygus, D. Sunshine, and Todd G. Shields. 2005. "Moral Issues and Voter Decision Making in the 2004 Presidential Election." *PS: Political Science and Politics* 38 (2): 201–9.

Hirschman, Albert O. 1991. *The Rhetoric of Reaction.* Cambridge: Harvard University Press.

Hoekstra, Valerie J. 1995. "The Supreme Court and Opinion Change: An Experimental Study of the Court's Ability to Change Opinion." *American Politics Research* 23 (1): 109–29.

Howard, John. 2005. "Fifties, Fags, and Femmes." *GLQ: A Journal of Gay and Lesbian Studies* 11 (1): 162–64.

Hughey, Matthew W. 2014. "White Backlash in the 'Post-Racial' United States." *Ethnic and Racial Studies* 37 (5): 721–30. https://doi.org/10.1080/01419870.20 14.886710

Hui, Iris, and David O. Sears. 2018. "Reexamining the Effect of Racial Propositions on Latinos' Partisanship in California." *Political Behavior* 40: 149–74.

Hume, Robert J. 2013. *Courthouse Democracy and Minority Rights: Same-Sex Marriage in the States.* New York: Oxford University Press.

Jackson, Sharyn. 2014. "Iowa Gay Marriage Ruling a Turning Point for Justices." *USA Today.* April 2, 2014. https://www.usatoday.com/story/news/nation/2014 /04/02/iowa-gay-marriage-ruling-a-turning-point-for-justices/7237453/

Jacobs, Andrew. 2008. "For Gay Democrats, a Primary Where Rights Are Not an Issue, This Time." *New York Times.* January 28, 2008. https://www.nytimes.com /2008/01/28/us/politics/28gay.html

Jacobs, Lawrence R., and Robert Y. Shapiro. 1994. "Issues, Candidate Image, and Priming: The Use of Private Polls in Kennedy's 1960 Presidential Campaign." *American Political Science Review* 88 (3): 527–40. https://doi.org/10.2307/294 4793

Jacobs, Lawrence R., and Robert Y. Shapiro. 2000. *Politicians Don't Pander: Political Manipulation and the Loss of Democratic Responsiveness.* Studies in Communication, Media, and Public Opinion. Chicago, IL: University of Chicago Press.

Jaffe, Ina. 1996. "A State Judge in Honolulu Has Ordered the State of Hawaii to Grant Marriage Licenses to Three Gay Couples—the First Such Occasion in the Country." NPR. December 4, 1996. https://www.npr.org/templates/story /story.php?storyId=1030357

Jensen, Tom. 2011. "Dems Win NH Generic Leg. Ballot, NH Supports Gay Marriage." *Public Policy Polling.* April 11, 2011. https://www.publicpolicypolling.com /polls/dems-win-nh-generic-leg-ballot-nh-supports-gay-marriage/

Johnson, Carrie. 2010. "No Opponent but Big Money in Illinois Justice's Race." NPR. https://www.npr.org/templates/story/story.php?storyId=130810189

Johnson, David K. 2004. *The Lavender Scare: The Cold War Persecution of Gays and Lesbians in the Federal Government.* Chicago: University of Chicago Press.

Johnson, Timothy R., and Andrew D. Martin. 1998. "The Public's Conditional Response to Supreme Court Decisions." *American Political Science Review* 92 (2): 299–309.

Jones, P. E., and P. R. Brewer. 2018. "Elite Cues and Public Polarization on Transgender Rights." *Politics, Groups, and Identities* 8 (1): 1–15.

Jost, Kenneth. 1990. "Initiatives: True Democracy or Bad Lawmaking?" *Editorial Research Reports* CQ Researcher Report. August 17, 1990. 462–75.

Kahneman, Daniel, and Amos Tversky. 1973. "Availability: A Heuristic for Judging Frequency and Probability." *Cognitive Psychology* 5 (2): 207–32.

Kaiser, Charles. 1997. *The Gay Metropolis: The Landmark History of Gay Life in America.* New York: Houghton Mifflin.

Karol, David. 2009. *Party Position Change in American Politics: Coalition Management.* New York: Cambridge University Press.

Karol, David. 2012. "How Does Party Position Change Happen? The Case of Gay Rights in the U.S. Congress." Paper presented at the annual meeting of the Southern Political Science Association, New Orleans, January 2012.

Keck, Thomas M. 2009. "Beyond Backlash: Assessing the Impact of Judicial Decisions on LGBT Rights." *Law & Society Review* 43 (1): 151–85.

Keith, Bruce E., David B. Magleby, Candice J. Nelson, Elizabeth Orr, Mark C. Westyle, and Raymond E. Wolfinger. 1992. *The Myth of the Independent Voter.* Berkeley: University of California Press.

Kennan, Elizabeth. 1971. "Innocent III and the First Political Crusade: A Comment on the Limitations of Papal Power." *Traditio* 27: 231–49.

Kenney, Moira Rachel. 1998. "Remember Stonewall Was a Riot: Understanding Gay and Lesbian Experience in the City." In *Making the Invisible Visible, A Multicultural Planning History,* edited by Leonie Sandercock, 120–32. Berkeley: University of California Press.

Kernell, Samuel. 2006. *Going Public: New Strategies of Presidential Leadership.* Washington, DC: CQ Press.

Khalil, Ramy K. 2012. "Harvey Milk and California Proposition 6: How the Gay Liberation Movement Won Two Early Victories." *WWU Graduate School Collection* 208. https://cedar.wwu.edu/wwuet/208

Kinder, Donald R., and David O. Sears. 1981. "Prejudice and Politics: Symbolic Racism versus Racial Threats to the Good Life." *Journal of Personality and Social Psychology* 40 (3): 14–431.

Kingkade, Tyler. 2010. "Citizens United, Huckabee Target Iowans over Judicial Retention Vote." *Iowa State Daily,* October 31, 2010. http://www.iowastatedaily.com/news/article_27bfe720-e536-11df-9c40-001cc4c03286.html

Kirp, David L. 1989. "The AIDS Perplex." *Public Interest* 96 (Summer): 61–72.

Klarman, Michael J. 2005. "Brown and Lawrence (and Goodridge)." *Michigan Law Review* 104 (3): 431–90.

Klarman, Michael J. 2013. *From the Closet to the Altar: Courts, Backlash, and the Struggle for Same-Sex Marriage*. Oxford: Oxford University Press.

Klemp, Nathaniel, and Stephen Macedo. 2011. "The Christian Right, Public Reason, and American Democracy." In *Evangelicals and Democracy in America*, Vol. 2, edited by Steven Brint and Jean Reith Schroedel, 209–46. New York: Russell Sage Foundation.

Kneupper, Charles W. 1981. "No on Proposition 6: The San Francisco Campaign." *Free Speech Yearbook* 20 (1): 36–41. https://doi.org/DOI:10.1080/08997225.19 81.10556010

Koppelman, Andrew. 1997. "Dumb and DOMA: Why the Defense of Marriage Act Is Unconstitutional." *Iowa Law Review* 83 (1): 1–34.

Koppelman, Andrew, and Tobias Barrington Wolf. 2009. *A Right to Discriminate: How the Case of Boy Scouts of America v. James Dale Warped the Law of Free Association*. New York: Yale University Press.

Kreitzer, Rebecca J., Allison J. Hamilton, and Caroline J. Tolbert. 2014. "Does Policy Adoption Change Opinions on Minority Rights? The Effects of Legalizing Same-Sex Marriage." *Political Research Quarterly* 67 (4): 795–808.

Krieger, Linda Hamilton. 2010. *Backlash against the ADA: Reinterpreting Disability Rights*. Ann Arbor: University of Michigan Press.

Krim, Mathilde. 2011. "Elizabeth Taylor's Contribution to the Fight against AIDS: Personal Memories." *AIDS Patient Care STDS* 12: 703–5.

Kuhn, Betsy. 2011. *Gay Power! The Stonewall Riots and the Gay Rights Movement, 1969*. Minneapolis: Twenty-First-Century Books.

Lascher, Edward L., Michael G. Hagen, and Steven A. Rochlin. 1996. "Gun behind the Door? Ballot Initiatives, State Policies and Public Opinion." *Journal of Politics* 58 (3): 760–75.

Lattin, Don. 2000. "Mormon Church: The Powerful Force behind Proposition 22." *SFGate*. February 6, 2000. https://www.sfgate.com/news/article/Mormon -Church-The-Powerful-Force-Behind-2778116.php

Lawrence v. Texas. 539 U.S. 558 (2003)

Lax, Jeffrey R., and Justin H. Phillips. 2009a. "Gay Rights in the States: Public Opinion and Policy Responsiveness." *American Political Science Review* 103 (3): 367–86.

Lax, Jeffrey R., and Justin H. Phillips. 2009b. "How Should We Estimate Public Opinion in the States?" *American Journal of Political Science* 53 (1): 107–21.

Lebo, Matthew J., and Daniel Cassino. 2007. "The Aggregated Consequences of Motivated Reasoning and the Dynamics of Partisan Presidential Approval." *Political Psychology* 28 (6): 719–46.

Lee, Erika. 2017. "Essay 4: Immigration, Exclusion, and Resistance, 1800s–1940s." In *Asian American and Pacific Islander National Historic Landmarks Theme Study*, edited by Franklin Odo for the U.S. National Park Service. Washington, DC: U.S. Government Publishing Office, 2017. Accessed August 2, 2018. https:// www.nps.gov/articles/aapi-theme-study-essay-4-immigration.htm

Lemieux, Scott. 2013. "Why the Courts Matter for LGBT Rights." *American Prospect* July 25, 2013. http://prospect.org/article/why-courts-matter-lbgt-rights

Lerner, Ralph. 1967. "The Supreme Court as Republican Schoolmaster." *Supreme Court Review* 1967: 127–80.

Lesage, Julia. 1998. "Christian Coalition Leadership Training." In *Media, Culture, and the Religious Right,* edited by Linda Kintz and Julia Lesage, 295–325. Minneapolis: University of Minnesota Press.

Lewis, Andrew R. 2017. *The Rights Turn in Conservative Christian Politics: How Abortion Transformed the Culture Wars.* Cambridge: Cambridge University Press.

Lewis, Daniel C. 2011. "Bypassing the Representational Filter?: Minority Rights Policies under Direct Democracy Institutions in the U.S. States." *State Politics & Policy Quarterly* 11 (2): 198–222. https://doi.org/10.1177/1532440011406227

Lewis, Daniel C.. 2013. *Direct Democracy and Minority Rights: A Critical Assessment of the Tyranny of the Majority in the American States.* 1st ed. New York: Routledge.

Lewis, Gregory B. 1997. "Lifting the Ban on Gays in the Civil Service: Federal Policy on Gay and Lesbian Employees since the Cold War." *Public Administration Review* 57 (5): 387–95.

Lewis, Seth C., and Stephen D. Reese. 2009. "What Is the War on Terror? Framing through the Eyes of Journalists." *Journalism & Mass Communication Quarterly* 86: 85–102.

Lewkowicz, Michael A. 2006. "The Effectiveness of Elite Cues as Heuristics in Proposition Elections." *American Politics Research* 34 (1): 51–68.

Lienesch, Michael. 1982. "Right-Wing Religion: Christian Conservatism as a Political Movement." *Political Science Quarterly* 97 (3): 403–25.

Lipsett, Seymour M., and Earl Raab. 1970. *The Politics of Unreason: Right-Wing Extremism in America, 1790–1977.* Chicago: University of Chicago Press.

Liptak, Adam. 2015. "Supreme Court Ruling Makes Same-Sex Marriage a Right Nationwide." *New York Times.* June 26, 2015. https://www.nytimes.com/2015/06/27/us/supreme-court-same-sex-marriage.html

Lizzi, Maria C. 2008. "'My Heart Is as Black as Yours': White Backlash, Racial Identity, and Italian American Stereotypes in New York City's 1969 Mayoral Campaign." *Journal of American Ethnic History* 27 (3): 43–80.

Lugg, Catherine A. 1998. "The Religious Right and Public Education: The Paranoid Politics of Homophobia." *Educational Policy* 12 (3): 267–83.

Madison, James. 1787. "No. 10: The Same Subject Continued." In *The Federalist Papers,* edited by Alexander Hamilton, James Madison, and John Jay. New York: Penguin Books. 41–47.

Makarechi, Kia. n.d. "Republicans Break with Trump as Backlash over 'Muslim Ban' Grows." *The Hive.* Accessed January 22, 2019. https://www.vanityfair.com/news/2017/01/republicans-trump-muslim-ban

Mansbridge, Jane, and Shauna L. Shames. 2008. "Toward a Theory of Backlash: Dynamic Resistance and the Central Role of Power." *Politics and Gender* 4 (4): 623–34.

Marcus, Eric. 1992. *Making History: The Struggle for Gay and Lesbian Equal Rights, 1945–1990: An Oral History*. Harper Collins: New York.

Margolin, Emma. 2016. "Backlash Grows Over 'Religious Freedom' and 'Anti-Discrimination' Push." April 11, 2016. https://www.nbcnews.com/news/us-ne ws/backlash-grows-over-religious-freedom-anti-discrimination-push-n554016

Marshall, Thomas. 1987. "The Supreme Court as an Opinion Leader." *American Politics Quarterly* 15 (1): 147–68.

Mason, Liliana. 2018. *Uncivil Agreement: How Politics Became Our Identity*. Chicago: University of Chicago Press.

Mate, Manoj, and Matthew Wright. 2008. "The 2000 Presidential Election Controversy." In *Public Opinion and Constitutional Controversy*, edited by Nathaniel Persily, Jack Citrin, and Patrick J. Egan, 333–52. Oxford: Oxford University Press.

May, Melissa H. 2013. "Judicial Retention Elections after 2010." *Indiana Law Review* 46 (1): 59–86.

McCann, Michael W. 1994. *Rights at Work: Pay Equity Reform and the Politics of Legal Mobilization*. Chicago: University of Chicago Press.

McDonald, Michael P. 2004. "Up, Up and Away! Voter Participation in the 2004 Presidential Election." *The Forum* 2 (4): n.p.

McGann, Anthony J., Charles Anthony Smith, Michael Latner, and Alex Keena. 2016. *Gerrymandering in America: The House of Representatives, the Supreme Court, and the Future of Popular Sovereignty*. Cambridge: Cambridge University Press.

McGuire, William J. 1968. "Personality and Attitude Change: An Information-Processing Theory." In *Psychological Foundations of Attitudes*, edited by Anthony G. Greenwald, Timothy C. Brock, and Thomas M. Ostrom, 171–95. New York: Academic Press.

Meeker, Martin. 2001. "Behind the Mask of Respectability: Reconsidering the Mattachine Society and Male Homophile Practice, 1950s and 1960s." *Journal of the History of Sexuality* 10 (1): 78–116.

Mello, Joseph. 2015. "Rights Discourse and the Mobilization of Bias: Exploring the Institutional Dynamics of the Same-Sex Marriage Debates in America." In *Studies in Law, Politics, and Society*, Vol. 66, edited by Austin Sarat, 1–34. Emerald Group Publishing Limited. https://doi.org/10.1108/S1059-433720150000 066001

Milk, Harvey. 1978. *The Hope Speech*. http://terpconnect.umd.edu/~jklumpp/ARD /MilkSpeech.pdf

Miller, Zeke J. 2015. "Axelrod: Obama Misled Nation When He Opposed Gay Marriage in 2008." *Time*. February 10, 2015. http://time.com/3702584/gay-ma rriage-axelrod-obama/

Mishler, William, and Reginald S. Sheehan. 1993. "The Supreme Court as a Countermajoritarian Institution? The Impact of Public Opinion on Supreme Court Decisions." *American Political Science Review* 87 (1): 87–101.

Morales, Lymari. 2009. "Knowing Someone Gay/Lesbian Affects Views of Gay

Issues." Gallup.com. May 29, 2009. https://news.gallup.com/poll/118931/Kno wing-Someone-Gay-Lesbian-Affects-Views-Gay-Issues.aspx

Morris, Mike. 2014. "Council Extends Rights Protection for Gays, Transgendered." *Houston Chronicle*. May 28, 2014. https://www.houstonchronicle.com/news/hou ston-texas/houston/article/Council-extends-rights-protection-for-gays-55118 69.php

Movement Advancement Project. 2018. "The Power of State Preemption: Preventing Progress and Threatening Equality." Report from Movement Advancement Project. May 2018. https://www.lgbtmap.org/power-of-preemption-report

Mullen, Jeff. 2010. "Iowa Pastors." September 22, 2010. https://www.youtube.com /watch?v=1Dn4Y3ED6VU

Murib, Zein. 2017. "Rethinking GLBT as a Political Category." In *LGBTQ Politics: A Critical Reader* edited by Marla Brettschneider, Susan Burgess, and Christine Keating, 14–33. New York: New York University Press.

Murphy, Dean E. 2005. "Schwarzenegger to Veto Same-Sex Marriage Bill." *New York Times*. September 8, 2005. http://www.nytimes.com/2005/09/08/us/schwa rzenegger-to-veto-samesex-marriage-bill.html

Murray, Melissa. 2009. "Marriage Rights and Parental Rights: Parents, the State, and Proposition 8." *Stanford Journal of Civil Rights and Civil Liberties* 5: 357–408.

National Annenberg Election Surveys: 2000 and 2004 presidential elections. [machine-readable data file] / University of Pennsylvania. Annenberg Public Policy Center [principal investigator(s)] / Annenberg Public Policy Center, University of Pennsylvania.

National Center for Transgender Equality (NCTE). 2017. "The Discrimination Administration." National Center for Transgender Equality. April 20, 2017. https://transequality.org/the-discrimination-administration

National Gay Task Force v Board of Education 729 F.2d 1270 (1985)

NBC News. 2012. "Meet the Press." May 6, 2012. Transcript accessed at http:// www.nbcnews.com/id/47311900/ns/meet_the_press-transcripts/t/may-joe-bid en-kelly-ayotte-diane-swonk-tom-brokaw-chuck-todd/#.W9sA5npKjv0

Neff, Christopher L., and Luke R. Edgell. 2013. "The Rise of Repeal: Policy Entrepreneurship and Don't Ask, Don't Tell." *Journal of Homosexuality* 60 (2/3): 232–49.

Nelson, Thomas E., Rosalee A. Clawson, and Zoe M. Oxley. 1997. "Media Framing of a Civil Liberties Conflict and Its Effect on Tolerance." *American Political Science Review* 91 (3): 567–83.

Newman, Benjamin J., Sono Shah, and Loren Collingwood. 2018. "Race, Place, and Building a Base: Latino Population Growth and the Nascent Trump Campaign for President." *Public Opinion Quarterly* 82 (1): 122–34.

Norton, Aaron T., and Gregory M. Herek. 2013. "Heterosexuals' Attitudes toward Transgender People: Findings from a National Probability Sample of U.S. Adults." *Sex Roles* 68: 738–53. https://doi.org/10.1007/s11199-011-0110-6

Norton v Macy 417 F.2d 1161 (D.C. Cir. 1969)

NPR Morning Edition. 2010. http://www.npr.org/templates/story/story.php

Nussbaum, Martha C. 2010. *From Disgust to Humanity: Sexual Orientation and Constitutional Law*. Oxford: Oxford University Press.

Nyhan, Brendan, and Jason Reifler. 2010. "When Corrections Fail: The Persistence of Political Misperceptions." *Political Behavior* 32 (2): 303–30.

Obergefell v. Hodges, 135 S. Ct. 2071 (2015)

Oshiro, Sandra. 1996. "Hawaiian Judge Puts Same-Sex Marriage Ruling on Hold." *The Nation*. December 6, 1996. https://news.google.com/newspapers?id=4BYu
AAAAIBAJ&sjid=zjADAAAAIBAJ&pg=4305,2060755&

Ott, Brian L., and Eric Aoki. 2002. 'The Politics of Negotiating Public Tragedy: Media Framing of the Matthew Shepard Murder.'" *Rhetoric & Public Affairs* 5 (3): 483–505.

Pacheco, Julianna. 2012. "The Social Contagion Model: Exploring the Role of Public Opinion on the Diffusion of Antismoking Legislation across the American States." *Journal of Politics* 74 (1): 187–202.

Paul, Deanna. 2018. "Trump Promised to Remake the Courts. He's Installing Conservative Judges at a Record Pace." *Washington Post*. July 19, 2018. https://www
.washingtonpost.com/news/powerpost/wp/2018/07/19/trump-promised-to-re
make-the-courts-hes-installing-conservative-judges-at-a-record-pace/

Paulson, Michael. 2004. "Ruling on Gay Marriage Ignited a National Debate." *Boston Globe*. February 15, 2004. http://archive.boston.com/news/local/articles/20
04/02/15/ruling_on_

Perry v Hollingsworth (fka Perry v Schwarzennegger) 570 U.S. 693(2013)

Petersen, Jennifer. 2011. *Murder, the Media, and the Politics of Public Feelings: Remembering Matthew Shepard and James Byrd Jr*. Bloomington: Indiana University Press.

Petrocik, John R. 1974. "An Analysis of Intransitivities in the Index of Party Identification." *Political Methodology* 1 (3): 31–47.

Pettys, Todd E. 2011. "Letter from Iowa: Same-Sex Marriage and the Ouster of Three Justices." *Kansas Law Review* 59 (4): 715–45.

Pew Research Center. 2013. "A Survey of LGBT Americans." June 13, 2013. http://
www.pewsocialtrends.org/2013/06/13/a-survey-of-lgbt-americans/

Pew Research Center. 2016. "About Four-in-Ten Americans Often Get News Online." https://www.journalism.org/2016/07/07/the-modern-news-consumer
/pj_2016-07-07_modern-news-consumer_1-01/

Pew Research Center. 2018. "Changing Attitudes on Gay Marriage." http://www
.pewforum.org/fact-sheet/changing-attitudes-on-gay-marriage/

Pierceson, Jason. 2010. "Deconstructing the Backlash: Same-Sex Marriage Litigation and Social Change in the United States and Canada." In *Same-Sex Marriage in the Americas: Policy Innovation for Same-Sex Relationships*, edited by Jason Pierceson, Adriana Piatti-Crocker, and Shawn Schulenberg, 161–80. Lanham, MD: Lexington Books.

Pierceson, Jason. 2015. "From Kameny to Kennedy: The Road to the Positive Rights Protection of Marriage Equality in *Obergefell v. Hodges*." *Politics, Groups, and Identities* 3 (4): 703–10.

Pierceson, Jason. 2016. *Sexual Minorities and Politics: An Introduction.* Lanham, MD: Rowman and Littlefield.

Pinello, Daniel. 2006. *America's Struggle for Same-Sex Marriage.* New: York: Cambridge University Press.

Pinello, Daniel R. 2017. *America's War on Same-Sex Couples and Their Families and How the Courts Rescued Them.* Cambridge: Cambridge University Press.

Plant, E. A., and Patricia Devine. 2003. "The Antecedents and Implications of Interracial Anxiety." *Personality and Social Psychology Bulletin* 29 (6): 790–801.

Potter, Claire Bond. 2012. "Paths to Political Citizenship: Gay Rights, Feminism, and the Carter Presidency." *Journal of Policy History* 24 (1): 95–114.

Pratto, Felicia, James Sidanius, Lisa M. Stallworth, and Bertram F. Malle. 1994. "Social Dominance Orientation: A Personality Variable Predicting Social and Political Attitudes." *Journal of Personality and Social Psychology* 67 (4): 741–63.

Preuhs, Robert R. 2007. "Descriptive Representation as a Mechanism to Mitigate Policy Backlash: Latino Incorporation and Welfare Policy in the American States." *Political Research Quarterly* 60 (2): 277–92.

Queerty Staff. 2009. "Bad Litigation: Is Filing a Lawsuit against Prop 8 Actually the Worst Idea Ever?" https://www.queerty.com/is-filing-a-lawsuit-against-prop-8-actually-the-worst-idea-ever-20090527

Redlawsk, David P. 2002. "Hot Cognition or Cool Consideration? Testing the Effects of Motivated Reasoning on Political Decision Making." *Journal of Politics* 64 (4): 1021–44.

Redlawsk, David, and Caroline Tolbert. 2008. "Big Ten Battleground Poll: Iowans' Views on Gay Marriage and Civil Unions, Topline Results."

Reiner, Robert. 2016. "Conservatives and the Constabulary in Great Britain: Cross-Dressing Conundrums." In *The Politics of Policing: Between Force and Legitimacy. Sociology of Crime, Law, and Deviance* 21, edited by Mathieu Deflem, 79–96. Bingley, UK: Emerald Publishing.

Reumann, Miriam G. 2005. *American Sexual Character: Sex, Gender, and National Identity in the Kinsey Reports.* Berkeley: University of California Press.

Reuters. 2016. *Handbook of Journalism.* http://handbook.reuters.com/index.php?title=Main_Page

Rich, B. Ruby, and Lourdes Arguelles. 1985. "Homosexuality, Homophobia, and Revolution: Notes toward an Understanding of the Cuban Lesbian and Gay Male Experience, Part II." *Signs: Journal of Women in Culture and Society* 11 (1): 120–36.

Riek, Blake M., Eric W. Mania, and Samuel L. Gaertner. 2006. "Intergroup Threat and Outgroup Attitudes: A Meta-Analytic Review." *Personality and Social Psychology Review* 10 (4): 336–53.

Rimmerman, Craig A. 2008. *The Lesbian and Gay Movements: Assimilation or Liberation?* Boulder, CO: Westview Press.

Riverstone-Newell, Lori. 2017. "The Rise of State Preemption Laws in Response to Local Policy Innovation." *Publius: The Journal of Federalism* 47 (3): 403–25. https://doi.org/10.1093/publius/pjx037

Roe v Wade 410 U.S. 113 (1973)

Rogin, Michael. 1966. "Wallace and the Middle Class: The White Backlash in Wisconsin." *Public Opinion Quarterly* 30 (1): 98–108. https://doi.org/10.1086/26 7384

Roscoe, Will. 2013. "The Radicalism of Harry Hay." *Gay and Lesbian Review Worldwide* 20 (6): 11–14.

Rosenberg, Alyssa. 2018. "In Three Years, LGBT Americans Have Gone from Triumph to Backlash." *Washington Post* January 25, 2018. https://www.washingto npost.com/news/act-four/wp/2018/01/25/in-three-years-lgbt-americans-have -gone-from-triumph-to-backlash-blame-trump/

Rosenberg, Gerald N. 1991. *The Hollow Hope: Can Courts Bring About Social Change?* Chicago: University of Chicago Press.

Rosenberg, Gerald N. 2008. *The Hollow Hope: Can Courts Bring about Social Change?* 2nd ed. Chicago: University of Chicago Press.

Rottinghaus, Brandon. 2010. *The Provisional Pulpit: Modern Presidential Leadership of Public Opinion.* College Station: Texas A&M University Press.

Rubin, Lillian B. 1973. *Busing and Backlash: White against White in a California School District.* Berkeley: University of California Press.

Rubin, Ruth Bloch, and Gregory Elinson. 2017. "Anatomy of Judicial Backlash: Southern Leaders, Massive Resistance, and the Supreme Court, 1954–1958." *Law and Social Inquiry* 43 (3): 944–80.

Rudalevige, Andrew. 2005. *The New Imperial Presidency: Renewing Presidential Power after Watergate.* Ann Arbor: University of Michigan Press.

Saad, Lydia. 2017. "Gallup Vault: Issue of Gays in Military Split Americans in 1993." Gallup.com. July 28, 2017. https://news.gallup.com/vault/214745/gall up-vault-issue-gays-military-split-americans-1993.aspx

Sachdev, Ameet. 2014. "Outside Money Pouring into State Supreme Court Race." Accessed February 13, 2017. http://www.chicagotribune.com/business/ct-karm eier-supreme-court-1029-biz-20141027-story.html

Sack, Kevin. 1997. "Georgia Candidate for Governor Admits Adultery and Resigns Commission in Guard." *New York Times*, June 6, 1997. https://www.nytimes .com/1997/06/06/us/georgia-candidate-for-governor-admits-adultery-and-res igns-commission-in-guard.html

Sample, James, Adam Skaggs, Jonathan Blitzer, and Linda Casey. 2010. *The New Politics of Judicial Elections, 2000–2009: Decade of Change.* The Brennan Center at NYU. https://www.brennancenter.org/sites/default/files/legacy/JAS-NPJE-De cade-ONLINE.pdf

Sanbonmatsu, Kira. 2008. "Gender Backlash in American Politics?" *Politics & Gender* 4 (4): 634–42.

Schattschneider, E. E. 1960. *The Semisovereign People.* New York: Holt, Rinehart, and Winston.

Schulte, Grant. 2010. "Iowa Pastor: Churches Will Urge Voters to Remove 3 Justices." *Des Moines Register.* October 19, 2010.

Segal, David J. 2018. "Website Scores Churches on the Transparency of Their LGBTQ Policies." *Houston Chronicle*. January 6, 2018. https://www.houstonc hronicle.com/life/houston-belief/article/Website-scores-churches-on-the-tran sparency-of-12478780.php

Shapiro, Edward S., and John Higham. 1986. "American Anti-Semitism." *American Jewish History* 76 (2): 201–13.

Sheldon, Kennon M., and Tim Kassèr. 2008. "Psychological Threat and Extrinsic Goal Striving." *Motivation and Emotion* 32 (1): 37–45. https://doi.org/10.1007 /s11031-008-9081-5

Sherif, Muzafer, O. J. Harvey, B. Jack White, William R. Hood, and Carolyn W. Sherif. 1961. *The Robbers Cave Experiment: Intergroup Conflict and Cooperation*. Norman, OK: University Book Exchange.

Sherrill, Kenneth S. 1996. "The Political Power of Lesbians, Gays, and Bisexuals." *PS: Political Science and Politics* 29 (3): 469–73.

Shilts, Randy. 1982. *The Mayor of Castro Street: The Life and Times of Harvey Milk*. New York: St. Martin's Press.

Shilts, Randy. 1987. *And the Band Played On: Politics, People, and the AIDS Epidemic*. New York: St: Martin's Press.

Shin, Michael E. 2009. "Show Me the Money! The Geography of Contributions to California's Proposition 8." *California Journal of Politics and Policy* 1 (1).

Sidanius, Jim, and Felicia Pratto. 1999. *Social Dominance: An Intergroup Theory of Social Hierarchy and Oppression*. Cambridge: Cambridge University Press.

Simon, Mallory. 2010. "Iowa Voters Oust Justices Who Made Same-Sex Marriage Legal." November 3, 2010. CNN Politics http://www.cnn.com/2010/POLITI CS/11/03/iowa.judges/index.html

Sinclair, G. Dean. 2009. "Homosexuality and the Military: A Review of the Literature." *Journal of Homosexuality* 56 (6): 701–18.

Siniscalco, Gary R. 1976. "Homosexual Discrimination in Employment." *Santa Clara Law Review* 16 (3): 495–512.

Siplon, Patricia D. 1999. "A Brief History of the Political Science of AIDS Activism." *PS: Political Science & Politics* 32 (3): 578–79.

Siplon, Patricia D. 2002. *AIDS and the Policy Struggle in the United States*. Washington, DC: Georgetown University Press.

Skocpol, Theda. 2003. *Diminished Democracy: From Membership to Management in American Civic Life*. Norman: University of Oklahoma Press.

Smirnov, Oleg, and Charles A. Smith. 2013. "Drift, Draft, or Drag: How U.S. Supreme Court Justices React to New Members." *Justice System Journal* 34 (2): 228–45.

Smith, Charles A. 2007. "The Electoral Capture of Gay and Lesbian Americans: Evidence and Implications from the 2004 Election." In *Studies in Law, Politics, and Society* 40, edited by A. Sarat, 103–21. Bingley, UK: Emerald Group Publishing Limited.

Smith, Charles A. 2011. "Gay, Straight, or Questioning? Sexuality and Political Science." *PS: Political Science & Politics* 44 (1): 35–38.

Smith, Daniel A., Matthew DeSantis, and Jason Kassel. 2006. "Same-Sex Marriage Ballot Measures and the 2004 Presidential Election." *State and Local Government Review* 38 (2): 78–91.

Smith, Miriam. 2008. *Political Institutions and Lesbian and Gay Rights in the United States and Canada*. New York: Routledge.

Socarides, Richard. 2013. "Why Bill Clinton Signed the Defense of Marriage Act." *New Yorker*. March 8, 2013. https://www.newyorker.com/news/news-desk/why -bill-clinton-signed-the-defense-of-marriage-act

Socarides, Richard. 2014. "Forcing Obama's Hand on Gay Marriage." *New Yorker*. April 15, 2014. https://www.newyorker.com/news/news-desk/forcing-obamas -hand-on-gay-marriage

Spitzer, Robert J. 2015. *Guns across America: Reconciling Gun Rules and Rights*. Oxford: Oxford University Press.

Steinmetz, Katy. 2010. "See Obama's 20-Year Evolution on LGBT Rights." *Time*. April 10, 2015. Accessed February 14, 2019. https://time.com/3816952/obama -gay-lesbian-transgender-lgbt-rights/

Stenner, Karen. 2005. *The Authoritarian Dynamic*. New York: Cambridge University Press.

Stern, Mark Joseph. 2014. "An Unexpected Triumph for Justice." *Slate*. November 7, 2014. https://slate.com/news-and-politics/2014/11/state-judicial-elections -2014-conservatives-failed-to-stack-supreme-courts-with-republican-justices .html

Stone, Amy. 2012. *Gay Rights at the Ballot Box*. Minneapolis: University of Minnesota Press.

Stone, Amy. 2013. "Winning for LGBT Rights Laws, Losing for Same-Sex Marriage: The LGBT Movement and Campaign Tactics." In *The Marrying Kind? Debating Same-Sex Marriage within the Lesbian and Gay Movement*, edited by Mary Bernstein and Verta Taylor. Minneapolis: University of Minnesota Press. 135–66.

Stout, David. 2007. "House Votes to Expand Hate-Crime Protection." *New York Times*. May 4, 2007. http://www.nytimes.com/2007/05/04/washington/04hate .html

Stoutenborough, James W., Donald P. Haider-Markel, and Mahalley D. Allen. 2006. "Reassessing the Impact of Supreme Court Decisions on Public Opinion: Gay Civil Rights Cases." *Political Research Quarterly* 59 (3): 419–33.

Strode, Tom. 2014. "Tilt toward Gay Marriage Hits Hiccup." *Biblical Recorder*. August 21, 2014. https://www.brnow.org/news/Tilt-toward-gay-marriage-hits -hiccup/

Sulzberger, A. G. 2010a. "In Iowa, Voters Oust Judges over Marriage Issue." *New York Times*. November 3, 2010. http://www.nytimes.com/2010/11/03/us/politi cs/03judges.html

Sulzberger, A. G. 2010b. "Ouster of Iowa Judges Sends Signal to the Bench." *New York Times*. November 4, 2010. http://www.nytimes.com/2010/11/04/us/politi cs/04judges.html

Sunstein, Cass R. 2007. "Backlash's Travels." University of Chicago Public Law & Legal Theory Working Paper No. 157.

Taber, Charles S., and Milton Lodge. 2006. "Motivated Skepticism in the Evaluation of Political Beliefs." *American Journal of Political Science* 50 (3): 755–69.

Tajfel, Henri, and John Turner. 1979. "An Integrative Theory of Inter-group Conflict." In *The Social Psychology of Inter-Group Relations*, edited by William G. Austin and Stephen Worchel, 33–47. Pacific Grove, CA: Brooks/Cole Publishing.

Tankard, Margaret E., and Elizabeth Levy Paluck. 2017. "The Effect of a Supreme Court Decision Regarding Gay Marriage on Social Norms and Personal Attitudes." *Psychological Science* 28 (9): 1334–44.

Taylor, Jami K., Daniel C. Lewis, and Donald Haider-Markel. 2018. *The Remarkable Rise of Transgender Rights*. Ann Arbor: University of Michigan Press.

Terry, Jennifer. 1999. *An American Obsession: Science, Medicine, and Homosexuality in Modern Society*. Chicago: University of Chicago Press.

Tesler, Michael. 2015. "Priming Predispositions and Changing Policy Positions: An Account of When Mass Opinion Is Primed or Changed." *American Journal of Political Science* 59 (4): 806–824.

Theoharis, Athan. 1971. *Seeds of Repression: Harry S. Truman and the Origins of McCarthyism*. Chicago: Quadrangle Press.

Trout, Matthew. 2015. "Hate: Constitutional and Practical Limitations to the Matthew Shepard and James Byrd, Jr. Hate Crimes Prevention Act of 2009." *American Criminal Law Review* 52 (1): 131–54.

Truman, David B. 1951. *The Governmental Process: Political Interests and Public Opinion*. New York: Alfred A. Knopf.

Tuch, Steven A. 2006. *Race and Policing in America*. New York: Cambridge University Press.

US v Windsor 570 U.S. 744 (2013)

U.S. Religion Census: Religious Congregations and Membership Study, 2010 (County File. 2012. http://www.thearda.com/Archive/Files/Descriptions/

Uslaner, Eric M., and Ronald E. Weber. 1979. "Public Support for Pro-Choice Abortion Policies in the Nation and the States: Changes and Stability after the *Roe* and *Doe* Decisions." *Michigan Law Review* 77: 1772–88.

Vaid, Urvashi. 1985. *Virtual Equality: The Mainstreaming of Gay and Lesbian Liberation*. New York: Doubleday.

Varnum v. Brien, 763 N.W. 2d 862 (2009)

Wald, Kenneth D., James W. Button, and Barbara A. Rienzo. 1996. "The Politics of Gay Rights in American Communities: Explaining Antidiscrimination Ordinances and Policies." *American Journal of Political Science* 40 (4): 1152–78.

Wang, Timothy, Sophia Geffen, and Sean Cahill. 2016. "The Current Wave of Anti-LGBT Legislation." Fenway Institute. http://fenwayhealth.org/wp-content/uploads/The-Fenway-Institute-Religious-Exemption-Brief-June-2016.pdf

Wasow, Omar. 2020. "Agenda Seeding: How 1960s Black Protests Moved Elites, Public Opinion, and Voting." *American Political Science Review* 114 (3): 638–59.

Weaver, Vesla M. 2007. "Frontlash: Race and the Development of Punitive Crime Policy." *Studies in American Political Development* 21 (2): 230–65.

Weeks, O. Douglas. 1948. "The White Primary: 1944–1948." *American Political Science Review* 42 (3): 500–510.

Wilcox-Archuleta, Bryan. 2018. "The Treatment Works: Revisiting a Key Link in Contextual Theories of Political Behavior." *Research & Politics* 5 (2). doi:10.11 77/2053168018768672

Wilson, Harry L. 2015. *The Triumph of the Gun-Rights Argument: Why the Gun Control Debate Is Over*. Santa Barbara, CA: Praeger Press.

Witosky, Tom, and Marc Hansen. 2015. *Equal before the Law: How Iowa Led Americans to Marriage Equality*. Iowa City: University of Iowa Press.

WMUR/UNH Survey Center, University of New Hampshire. 2011. "Granite State Poll: NH Opposed to Repeal of Gay Marriage 10/13/2011." https://scho lars.unh.edu/survey_center_polls/259

Wolf, Richard. 2015. "Timeline: Same-Sex Marriage through the Years." *USA Today*. https://www.usatoday.com/story/news/politics/2015/06/24/same-sex -marriage-timeline/29173703/

Wood, Thomas, and Ethan Porter. 2019. "The Elusive Backfire Effect: Mass Attitudes' Steadfast Factual Adherence." *Political Behavior* 41 (2): 135–63.

Worthen, Meredith G. F. 2013. "An Argument for Separate Analyses of Attitudes toward Lesbian, Gay, Bisexual Men, Bisexual Women, MtF and FtM Transgender Individuals." *Sex Roles* 68 (11/12): 703–23. https://doi.org/10.1007/s11199 -012-0155-1

Xifra, Jordi. 2016. "Climate Change Deniers and Advocacy: A Situational Theory of Publics Approach." *American Behavioral Scientist* 60 (3): 276–87.

Yoder, Janice D. 1991. "Rethinking Tokenism: Looking beyond Numbers." *Gender & Society* 5 (2): 178–92.

Young, Perry Dean. 1982. *God's Bullies: Native Reflections on Preachers and Politics*. New York: Holt, Rinehart, and Winston.

Ysseldyk, Renate, Kimberly Matheson, and Hymie Anisman. 2010. "Religiosity as Identity: Toward an Understanding of Religion from a Social Identity Perspective." *Personality and Social Psychology Review* 14 (1): 60–71. https://doi.org/10.11 77/1088868309349693

Zaller, John. 1990. "Political Awareness, Elite Opinion Leadership, and the Mass Survey Response." *Social Cognition* 8 (1): 125–53.

Zaller, John R. 1992. *The Nature and Origins of Mass Opinion*. Cambridge: Cambridge University.

Index

257